Practice,

KT-443-447

Nigel Edley and Margaret Wetherell

SH>   Heult

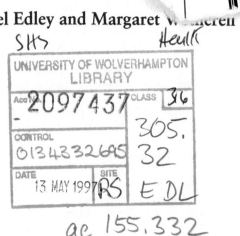
PRENTICE HALL
HARVESTER WHEATSHEAF

London   New York   Toronto   Sydney   Tokyo   Singapore
Madrid   Mexico City   Munich

First published 1995 by
Prentice Hall/Harvester Wheatsheaf
Campus 400, Maylands Avenue
Hemel Hempstead
Hertfordshire, HP2 7EZ
A division of
Simon & Schuster International Group

Typeset in 10/12pt Sabon
by Create Publishing Services Limited, Bath, Avon

Printed and bound in Great Britain by
T. J. Press Ltd, Padstow, Cornwall

Library of Congress Cataloging-in-Publication Data

Edley, Nigel
    Men in perspective: practice, power, and
identity/Nigel Edley and Margaret Wetherell.
    p.   cm.
    Includes bibliographical reference and index.
    ISBN 0-13-433269-5
    1. Men—Psychology.
    2. Masculinity (Psychology)
    3. Sex role.
    I. Wetherell, Margaret, 1954–   . II. Title.
HQ1090.E32   1995
155.3'32—dc20   94-45226
                                                CIP

British Library Cataloguing in Publication Data

A catalogue record for this book is available from
the British Library

ISBN 0-13-433269-5

---

2   3   4   5   99   98   97   96   95

Contents

Acknowledgements

We would like to acknowledge support received from the Economic and Social Research Council (Grant No. R000233129), the Open University Research Committee and from the Psychology Discipline, Faculty of Social Sciences, Open University. A number of people read earlier drafts of chapters or considered our arguments and we are particularly grateful to Norma Sherratt, Marilyn Ricci, Stephen Frosh and Lynne Segal for their helpful comments. We owe a particular debt to Rose Croghan for drawing our attention to the literature on fathering and mothering described in Chapter 4, and for allowing us to work from a review of this material prepared for the Open University D311 Family Life and Social Policy Course Team. At various points, especially in Chapter 6, our argument is founded on joint work conducted by Margaret Wetherell and Christine Griffin for the journal *Feminism and Psychology*. This collaboration was an important resource and invaluable preparation for this text. Farrell Burnett, our editor at Harvester Wheatsheaf during the main stages of the book's preparation, was, as ever, supportive and efficient. Caz Kershaw deserves thanks for her impeccable secretarial support during the later stages of the project. Finally, we owe an enormous debt on a number of levels – intellectual, material and emotional – to Helen Haines, Laurie Haines, Jonathan Potter and Sam Wetherell.

Introduction
Putting men in perspective

SOREN: We're puzzling to you, aren't we?

RIKER: On the whole... it's hard to grasp the idea of no gender.

SOREN: It is just as hard for us to understand the... strange division in your species... males and females. You are male?

RIKER: Hmm.

SOREN: Tell me about males. What is it that makes you different from females?

RIKER: [*Exhales forcibly*] Snips and snails and puppy-dog tails.

SOREN: You have a dog's tail?

RIKER: [*Shakes head*] It's an old nursery rhyme. Girls are made of sugar and spice and boys are made from snips and... snails. [*Waves hand dismissively*]

SOREN: That makes it sound better to be female.

RIKER: It's an old-fashioned way of looking at the sexes. Not to say that there's no real difference between them. Physically men are bigger, stronger in the upper body. We have different sexual organs. Men can't bear young.

SOREN: Well, what about feelings or emotional attitudes? Are they different?

RIKER: [*Laughs*] Most people think so. But that's the kind of question that would take a lifetime to answer. Let me ask you... what's it like on a planet where the people have no gender?

SOREN: I'm afraid I don't understand.

RIKER: Well... who leads when you dance... if you dance?

SOREN: We do... and whoever's taller leads.

Star Trek: The Next Generation

Conversations like this are surely the stuff of (science) fiction, for it is difficult to imagine a real-life situation in which someone would genuinely need to ask what it means to be male or masculine. It is little wonder that Commander Riker of the *Starship Enterprise* is somewhat taken aback when 'Soren', a

1

member of an alien and androgynous race of people, poses these very questions. Yet it is interesting, and significant, that Riker does not find it all that easy to come up with satisfactory answers. He does not really know where to start, and when he does he merely 'trots out' an age-old and fairly unhelpful cliché.

Like Commander Riker, most men probably have not spent much time thinking about their status as men. Masculinity tends to be something men take for granted, something which is not easy to articulate. One reason for this may be that identity tends to come into focus most clearly when it is seen as problematic in some way. People often find it easiest to define both themselves and others in terms of their difference from various norms (*see* the box below), but, to a much greater extent than femininity, masculinity has been regarded as the standard case, the usual pattern, synonymous with humanity in general. This relative invisibility and lack of articulation tell us something about masculinity and men's surplus of power. It is generally only the most powerful groups in society who can legislate normality; deciding what should be seen as natural, inevitable and unquestionable and what should be seen as deficient and different.

The invisible man

'The American sociologist Michael Kimmel tells a revealing anecdote about one of his first graduate classes in Women's Studies in which he heard a dispute going on between a white and a black woman. The white woman was arguing that the universal oppression of women by men bound black and white women together in a common plight. The black woman disagreed and asked, "When you wake up in the morning and look in the mirror, what do you see?" "I see a woman", the white woman replied. "That's precisely the problem", said the black woman, "When I wake up in the morning and look in the mirror, I see a *black* woman. My race is visible to me every day because I am not privileged in this culture. Because you *are* privileged, your race is invisible to you". Kimmel was very much struck by this exchange because he realised that when he looked in the mirror he saw neither his whiteness nor his masculinity. All he saw was a simple human being.'

(Kimmel, cited in Wetherell and Griffin, 1991, pp.377–8)

Inside and outside the academy, it has been women who largely have been seen as mysterious, enigmatic and 'difficult' to understand. Femininity has been regarded as a puzzle which must be subject to further investigation. While men's interests undoubtedly have been well served by this tendency to hold up masculine modes of being as most normal and most healthy, it has meant a remarkable imbalance in the social scientific treatment of men and women. If you go into any town or university library and look carefully at the social science and gender studies sections, you will find an impressive body of writing on women, but much less pertaining to male experience and the activities of men *as men*. Certainly there is little which predates the 'second wave' of the feminist movement.

During the late 1960s and early 1970s, feminists began to develop a radical view of society and the relations between men and women. They began to talk in a new voice about 'sexual politics', 'patriarchy' and the 'oppressiveness' of the male gender class. The concept of sexual politics was particularly important insofar as it lent a certain gravity or seriousness to matters previously considered trivial. It enabled feminists to make their argument that relationships in the home and in the bedroom were just as important, just as political, as all the stuff that went on in the traditionally male preserve of the public sphere. 'If there is a problem with women,' feminists seemed to be saying, 'it is the menfolk they live with.'

One consequence of this challenge was to provoke a new interest in men and masculinity and some new thinking about gender relations in the 1970s. Men responded in a range of different ways. Some authors, such as Stephen Goldberg (1973) hit back at feminists, arguing that patriarchal societies were natural, biologically ordained and, thus, inevitable. Others took on board feminist criticisms and accepted the need for a radical shake-up (e.g. Snodgrass, 1977; Tolson, 1979). A third group of writers appropriated feminist forms of analysis in order to argue that masculinity was just as damaging for *men* as it was for women (e.g. Farrell, 1974; Nichols, 1975; H Goldberg, 1976). Men, they pointed out, die earlier than women, are the principal victims of violence (as well as, of course, its main instigators) and are more likely to fall foul of drug and alcohol abuse. As such, they seemed equally in need of liberation.

The 1980s and early 1990s witnessed another minor explosion of academic writing upon men and masculinity, spread across a number of different disciplines. Within sociology there have been attempts to construct a social theory of masculinity drawing upon, for example, developments in Marxist theory (Hearn, 1987) and role theory (Pleck, 1981; Pleck and Sawyer, 1980). There has also been a move towards institutionalising 'Men's Studies' as an equivalent discipline to Women's Studies (Brod, 1987). Within cultural studies researchers have begun investigating the images of men in the popular media (e.g. Chapman and Rutherford, 1988), while a more established tradition of work on sex differences and the biological bases of sexual behaviour can be found in experimental psychology. There have also been a number of studies which focus upon specific aspects of men's lives, such as fatherhood (e.g. Lewis and O'Brien, 1987) and sexuality (e.g. Hite, 1981) as well as the emergence of a small collection of semi-autobiographical accounts of male experience (e.g. Cohen, 1990; Jackson, 1990; Seidler, 1991b).

At the same time there has been a small flurry of activity around masculinity within popular culture. In the UK, for example, there have been a number of television series (such as *Wimps to Warriors*, *Men Talk* and *Men Only* – all on Channel 4), *The Locker Room* series on Radio Four, as well as a whole host of newspaper and magazine articles dedicated to investigating the masculine condition, all in the early part of the 1990s. The situation in North America seems little different with, if anything, even more activity among men with the development of various men's movements such as Robert Bly's 'Iron John' based on 'mytho-poetic' concepts. Michael Kimmel points out that the idea of American men being confused about what it means to be a 'real man' has become 'a cultural commonplace, staring down at us from every magazine rack and television talk show in the country'. Men, it seems, are in a position where it is increasingly difficult for them to ignore the issue of their gendered status, for they are faced with a growing barrage of advice on how to become better fathers, more sensitive lovers, and more compassionate friends (Kimmel, 1987a).

This new interest in masculinity, along with feminism itself, has been fuelled by much broader social and cultural changes in Western societies such as the shifts from manufacturing-based economies to those organised more around service industries and computer-based technologies, and from full-time employment to part-time employment. These developments have contributed significantly to a change in the profile of the workforce. As a columnist in a British newspaper noted in the mid 1990s, it will not be long before more women are in employment than men (albeit mostly in part-time positions). In December 1993, the actual number of women with jobs was 10.53 million in the UK, compared with 10.83 million men (Victor Keegan in The *Guardian*, 1994, April 9, p. 25). The last General Household Survey in 1989 similarly noted that 40 per cent of British mothers with children under five now go out to work, as do 75 per cent who have children aged 10 or older. This means, of course, that the proportion of men who enjoy the status of sole breadwinner is in rapid decline.

The old ideal of the nuclear family is under threat in other ways too, with figures for recent population trends showing not only that fewer people are getting married in the 1990s, but also that the proportion of British marriages ending in divorce is fast approaching that of the United States (i.e. one in two or, 50 per cent). As a consequence, fewer and fewer men's lives fit neatly into the wife-and-two-kids stereotype that still dominates media representations of family life. Accompanying these changes, there have been new concerns about single parents, family maintenance, men's 'flight from fatherhood' and the break-up of relationships between men and their children.

It goes without saying that this book represents another instance of the rising tide of interest in men and masculinity. However, our aim is neither to advance nor develop a particular approach to the subject of men and their experiences. Like Soren, the alien from outer space, we want (for the moment) to take a detached and 'naïve' stance and ask: What is it about these people? Why are men like this? What is going on here? This book is a response to what we see as a real need to take stock of what has so far been achieved, reviewing the answers found in the social sciences to questions about men and their experiences. While we seek frequently to summarise, our text should in no way be thought of as a conclusion. It is a moment of reflection before, once again, setting out in a whole variety of different directions.

We write as social psychologists with a broad interest in the inter-relationship between public and private narratives of self and the role of discourse and ideologies in shaping identities (cf. Potter and Wetherell, 1987; Wetherell and Potter, 1992). More importantly, however, we write with the assumption that research on forms of masculinity must be conducted from an interdisciplinary standpoint. The psychology of men is incomprehensible without some analysis of their social and economic position. One cannot understand men without understanding modern feminism or, for that matter, developments in biology. Equally, any sociology of men will be incomplete without an account of male subjectivities.

There are two broad aims for the volume. First, we attempt to provide a clear and yet critical review of the main perspectives and theories (biological analyses, psychoanalysis, role theories, social theories, cultural studies and feminism) through which the topic of men and masculinity has been under-stood. One of the advantages of this kind of structure is that it allows us to consider not only the relative adequacy of different theoretical perspectives through a series of contrasts, but also encourages a view of these theories as alternative problematics which make different assumptions and give rise to different upshots or implications. Our second aim is to review the most important recent developments in the new and growing literature on men and masculinity, positioning these within our scheme of perspectives. Generally speaking, the book is aimed at a student audience, with an emphasis upon accessibility. The text is interspersed with boxes designed to open up, illustrate and enrich the main lines of argument.

Each chapter addresses a similar set of basic questions from a different theoretical perspective. The first question seeks to discover how the chosen approach defines the *substance* of masculinity. What binds men together as a distinctive group? What does each perspective consider men hold in common? The second question asks why masculinity takes the particular shape (or shapes) that it does. Why, in other words, do men behave in certain ways rather than others? A third question concerns the mechanisms by which males become masculine. Precisely how does masculinity 'get into' men? Finally, we look at how each broad perspective accounts for differences between men. How are idiosyncrasy and diversity explained, as well as patterns of continuity?

The book begins, like so many other social science textbooks on sex and gender, with a chapter on biology. Often this reflects a tendency to see biological explanations of human behaviour as more fundamental than social or cultural accounts. As a direct consequence, social scientists often feel it necessary first to assess the influences of biological factors so that they can then see what remains to be explained by other kinds of theory. This is not a view that we would endorse. Instead, the reason why we decided to start with the biological perspective stems from an organisational principle; namely, to work from the most individual through to the most social kinds of approach.

Chapter 1 begins by reviewing the evidence for the existence of a fundamental and irreducible physical difference between the sexes. This is an important starting point, because it is often assumed that any sex differences in the psychological and behavioural characteristics of men and women originate from the physical differences. The chapter goes on to examine the evidence for this link drawing upon work in anthropology, ethology and human physiology, as well as from a variety of different sub-branches of psychology – including studies by Corrine Hutt, Alice Eagly, and Eleanor Maccoby and Carol Jacklin. The chapter concludes with the arguments of those who suggest that the whole enterprise of searching for a biological basis of behaviour is fundamentally misguided.

Chapter 2 consists mainly of a review of the recent attempts to refine psychoanalytic analyses of male identity and experience. In particular, the chapter examines what has been called the 'object relations' explanation of masculine development, which moves away from the classic psychoanalytical accounts of Sigmund Freud insofar as it tends to focus upon the very earliest (i.e. pre-Oedipal) stages of psycho-sexual development, and foregrounds the boy's relations with his mother rather than his father. However, the chapter also describes some of the contrasting currents in psychoanalytic theorising of masculinity and outlines some of the key arguments within the psychoanalytic community. In reviewing the writings of a number of theorists, including Nancy Chodorow, Wendy Hollway, Klaus Theweleit, Robert Stoller and Stephen Frosh, the chapter pays particular attention to the issues of male sexuality and the production of an exaggerated form of masculinity described as the 'soldier male'.

In Chapter 3 we review the work of those who have sought to describe the activities of men in terms of a prescribed social role. Beginning with the attempts of researchers to describe the male sex-role, the chapter then moves on to look at a number of different theories of how the role is 'taken up' or internalised. In so doing, it considers the work of Talcott Parsons, Joseph Pleck, social learning theorists such as Walter Mischel, and the different cognitive approaches of Lawrence Kohlberg and Sandra Bem. The second half of the chapter consists of a detailed discussion of the very serious criticisms that have been lodged against the sex-role paradigm, focusing mainly upon the comments made by Arthur Brittan, Robert Connell and Michael Kimmel. In the final section of the chapter, we ask whether it is possible to reformulate sex-role theory in such a way as to satisfy its critics.

Although the first three chapters of the book offer very divergent explanations of masculinity, they share in common the assumption that if you want to find out about masculinity, you begin by looking at men themselves; at the characteristics of male individuals. More specifically, the perspectives considered in these first chapters begin with the question of how male individuals *acquire* their masculinity. In contrast to this, the perspectives reviewed in the second half of the book take a very different starting point. These views suggest that if you want to understand men, you should look first at the characteristics of the societies in which they live. The answer to the puzzles of masculinity will be found in the nature of social organisation.

Chapter 4 examines the arguments of those who claim that a man's identity or sense of self reflects his particular position within the economic framework of society. This perspective offers a view of masculinity as the sum of men's characteristic 'practices' at work, at home, and as members of different groups or institutions. Working through the literature on class, race, and then patriarchy, the chapter considers how these different social divisions interact to produce specific patterns of regularity and diversity across a range of different individuals from the black married miner to the gay white teacher. Within this structure, the chapter has a double focus. On the one hand, it examines the writing of people such as Andrew Tolson who develop socialist critiques of capitalism emphasising the way men are victimised both by their working conditions and by class divisions. On the other hand, it reviews authors such as Jeff Hearn and Robert Connell who see masculinity as an effect of men's privileges and advantages in relation to women. By combining these two strands of analysis, we come to see men as both 'victims' and oppressors.

In Chapter 5 we return to the notion of masculinity as a kind of social *script*, but this time from the perspective of those working within Cultural Studies. Drawing upon the work of, among others, Paul Hoch, David Gilmore, Clyde Franklin, Catherine Hall and Victor Seidler, this perspective makes the point that there is no single, unitary definition of masculinity. Rather, at any particular time, a culture will contain a multiplicity of different, even contradictory representations of what it means to be a man. In part, the chapter presents a limited social history of masculinity, illustrating the different ways in which the concept has been defined over the last 2000 years. It reveals this history to be a story, not of smooth transitions, but of struggle and bitter dispute. Most importantly, the chapter serves to illustrate how the history of the meaning of masculinity has been, and remains, inextricably bound up with the struggle for social, economic and political power between different groups of people. The chapter concludes by looking at the ways in which individual men are constituted through these different 'cultures', and asks to what extent they are able to intervene in this process.

Chapter 6 consists of an explicitly political perspective on men and masculinity, developing a feminist analysis. Men are examined from the standpoint of women and others oppressed by conventional forms of masculinity. The chapter begins by looking at the nature of male power, focusing

specifically upon the extent of male control of public life and men's objectification of women. From there it moves to examine feminist work on male
sexuality in order to indicate some of the cross-currents in feminist theorisations of masculinity, before considering men's responses to feminism and
the kind of politics which have emerged from various men's movements.
Time and again the chapter raises the issue of change: Can men change? In
what areas of their lives are men most open to and in need of reconstruction?
Have men changed already in response to feminism? To what extent can
individual men be expected to take responsiblity for their own and other
men's actions? How should feminists best work with men, if at all? In
pursuing these questions the chapter outlines the contributions of, among
others, Simone de Beauvoir, Catherine MacKinnon, Sylvia Walby, Elizabeth
Stanko, Lynne Segal, Deborah Cameron, Liz Fraser, and Susan Brownmiller.

Finally, in the conclusion, we try to sketch out some of the main tensions
and choices across these different perspectives, along with lines of possible
synthesis. We return to our initial questions – the what, why and how of
masculinity – and summarise the answers each perspective presents. Every
reader will have his or her own view of how to progress from this point, but
we also try to indicate how we see the basis for future research building on this
groundwork.

Chapter 1

The biological basis of masculinity

Every known culture in the world makes a distinction between males and females (Ortner and Whitehead, 1981). All see the two sexes or gender categories as in some way fundamentally different from each other. In Western cultures, of course, this is no less true. For us, the existence of two sexes, men and women, seems as obvious and concrete as the existence of trees and houses, and while we know very well that little boys are not really made out of slugs and snails and puppy-dogs' tails, there remains a widespread and deeply held feeling that males are substantially different from females.

From an early age we learn that the key to sexual difference lies in the make-up of men's and women's bodies. To say that men have a penis is not so much to describe something about men as to define them. In a very real sense, anatomical features such as penises and breasts come to signify or stand for the sexes themselves. A penis *means* masculinity or manhood, while breasts and vaginas denote femininity or womanhood. Common-sense ideas about sex differences also extend beyond the bounds of physical bodies to men's and women's psychological 'make-up' and patterns of behaviour. It is not unusual to hear people arguing that men are naturally the more aggressive sex, for example, or that women are much more emotional than men. As Sandra Bem (1974) demonstrated in her work on gender stereotypes, there is a whole range of different aptitudes and dispositions which people feel mark out men from women (*see* Table 1.1).

Yet stereotypes, almost by definition, can be very unreliable sources of information about the world. For example, the image of a well-spoken civil servant dressed in a pin-striped suit and a bowler hat might represent the stereotype of a British gentleman, but it accurately describes neither all nor even the average British gent. Similarly, the idea of men as competitive, forceful and independent need not necessarily correspond in any way to how men really are. Indeed, even the idea of men as the physically bigger, stronger and more athletic sex should be seen as a matter for empirical investigation rather than trust.

Table 1.1: Gender stereotypes

Feminine	Masculine
Affectionate	Acts as a leader
Cheerful	Aggressive
Childlike	Ambitious
Compassionate	Analytical
Does not use harsh talk	Assertive
Eager to soothe hurt feelings	Athletic
Feminine	Competitive
Flatterable	Defends own beliefs
Gentle	Dominant
Gullible	Forceful
Loves children	Independent
Loyal	Individualistic
Sensitive to others' needs	Leadership abilities
Shy	Makes decisions easily
Soft-spoken	Masculine
Sympathetic	Self-reliant
Tender	Self-sufficient
Understanding	Strong personality
Warm	Willing to take a stand
Yielding	Willing to take risks

Source: Archer and Lloyd, 1985

In this chapter we will be considering the extent to which masculinity can be seen as a reflection or product of fundamental biological forces. We will begin by reviewing the evidence for the existence of a fundamental, irreducible *physical* difference between men and women. This is an important starting point, because of the assumption that any differences in the psychological and behavioural characteristics of men and women originate, more or less directly, from such physical differences. The chapter will then go on to review the evidence for this link. In the process we will draw from work in anthropology, sociobiology, ethology as well as a variety of different sub-branches of psychology. In the final section, we take up the arguments of people such as Lynne Segal who suggest that the whole enterprise of searching for a biological basis of behaviour which exists outside or independent of society and culture is fundamentally misguided (Segal, 1990). However, before embarking upon any of this, we would like to look at one of the main reasons why work in this area is so hotly contested – politics.

The politics of sex difference research

In the 'Story of Science' politics has no place. Scientists are merely in the business of transforming hearsay and ignorance into knowledge. The desire to know is all that drives them. Like intrepid detectives, they are after the

Truth, whatever its colour. However, in reality it is very often impossible to separate politics from science. At its most innocent, political values and assumptions can inadvertently enter into and influence our perceptions of what constitutes an interesting and researchable topic. For instance, we might be interested in the causes of abnormal or 'anti-social' behaviour such as vandalism or hooliganism. Conversely, we might not see anything particularly interesting in the ordinary, everyday lives of white, middle-class males. Political values can also affect both the methods of investigation we employ and our interpretation of results (Morawski, 1987 – for broader discussions of these issues *see* Bloor, 1976; Mulkay, 1979 and Latour, 1987). However, the fact that science claims to be solely interested in the truth makes it, at the same time, a powerful political resource. For if 'scientific' evidence can be put forward to support one's own political viewpoint, then our opponents have little choice but to sit down, shut up and 'face facts'.

It could be argued that the history of sex difference research represents one of the more politically transparent areas of scientific investigation. As Helen Thompson Woolley (1910) commented in her review of the early work in this area:

> There is perhaps no field aspiring to be scientific where flagrant personal bias, logic martyred in the cause of supporting a prejudice, unfounded assertions, and even sentimental rot and drivel have run riot to such an extent as here. (p. 43)

By and large, the bias of the early work on sex differences was towards the existence of a biological basis. Rose, Kamin and Lewontin (1984) note how many nineteenth-century anthropologists were 'obsessed' with the relationship between intelligence, sex and brain size. These anthropologists were convinced that in just the same way as the (supposed) superior intelligence of the white races was underpinned by a larger, more powerful brain, so it was with men's supposedly greater intelligence. Rose quotes one of these anthropologists, called McGrigor Allan, who, in 1869, declared that 'the type of the female skull approaches in many respects that of the infant, and still more that of the lower races'. Many of the early experiments seemed to be bear out this hypothesis, with women's brains being found to be, on average, 142g (5oz) lighter than those of men. However, it was later pointed out that this difference is explicable purely in terms of the overall size difference between the sexes. Yet even when this relationship between body size and brain size became clear, those involved in this research merely proposed new hypotheses identifying alternative areas of the brain as the probable source of men's superior minds.

In direct contrast, most if not all of the modern tests of intelligence start with the assumption that there is *no* overall difference between men and women. Indeed, in the process of selecting appropriate questions for these tests, any item which produces a sex difference in terms of people's ability to answer correctly is labelled biased and withdrawn. Not surprisingly, this has led some to cry 'foul', seeing it as a blatant example of where egalitarian political values interfere with the discovery of real differences between the sexes (e.g. Moir and Jessell, 1989). In reality, of course, it is impossible to say whether these alterations are introducing a new bias or successfully ironing out an older one.

Debates about which, if either, sex is the most intelligent are clearly more than just academic. Those early attempts to prove men's larger, more power-ful brains were just as much about justifying men's dominant position in society as trying to discover the 'natural' order of things. Likewise, other arguments claiming inherent or natural differences between the sexes are very often part and parcel of more general political debates about how society should be organised. For example, the claim that women are naturally more subjective, empathetic and emotional than men, leads very neatly into the argument that they are best suited to childcare rather than 'hard-headed' decision-making. In a similar vein, Steven Goldberg (1973) has argued that men's inbuilt aggressiveness or 'dominance tendency' leads to the inevitability of patriarchal societies (literally, societies where there is 'rule of the father'). It follows, Goldberg insists, that there is little point in trying to stop men dominating affairs as they are essentially pre-programmed to do so.

It is not surprising that feminists and others in sympathy with the Women's Movement have sought to challenge such arguments. They have done this in a wide variety of ways. For example, some feminists have responded by denying the existence of psychological sex differences. They have argued that it is not that women are more emotional than men, it is just that men tend to hide or deny their emotions. Alternatively, a number of feminists working from within a more radical tradition have accepted the idea that men and women are psychologically distinct, but have argued that, as the less aggressive, more caring and co-operative gender, women are morally superior and thus better suited to govern (cf. Jaggar, 1983). Different again are the arguments of those who, while recognising the existence of psychological sex differences, contest their origins. For example, they might agree that men are more assertive and independent than women, but argue that this is a product of a lifetime's learning or socialisation, rather than a reflection of natural or inbuilt differences. This perspective implies, of course, that with the appropriate changes to the cultural 'curriculum', tomorrow's men and women could be brought up to be more or less the same (*see* Box 1.1).

In Box 1.1 Sandra Bem accords a completely different interpretation to sex differences which have a supposedly natural basis compared with those of entirely social origins. For Bem, natural sex differences are to be accepted happily. If women, for example, really are 'designed' with childcare in mind, then she would gladly take up her role as mother and homemaker. What she objects to is that women are being forced or coerced into such a role without

---

Box 1.1: The politics of sexual determination

'I am a feminist. This does not mean I think there are no biologically based sex differences in behaviour. Likewise, it also does not mean I think we should try to manipulate the culture so as to eliminate whatever biologically based sex differences there are. It does mean, however, that insofar as possible, we should let the distribution of activities and roles across males and females reflect nothing but biology. That is, we should try to arrange our social institutions so that they do not themselves diminish the full range of individual differences that would otherwise exist within each sex. If, under those conditions, it turns out that more men than women become engineers or that more women than men decide to stay at home with their children, I shall live happily with those sex differences as with any others that emerge. But I am willing to bet that the sex differences that emerge under those conditions will not be nearly as large or as diverse as the ones that currently exist in our society.'

(Sandra Lipsitz Bem, quoted in Myers, 1988)

---

any genuine biological justification. However, while Bem sees the question of whether or not men have an innate tendency to dominate others as dictating the appropriateness of political action, other more radical feminists view the same issue as merely influencing the type of response necessary to attain sexual equality. For example, in *The Dialectic of Sex*, Shulamith Firestone (1971) suggests that the source of women's subjugation was their exclusive capacity for child-bearing. In effect, she accepts the existence of a natural, biologically-based inequality between men and women. Yet, far from resigning herself to her biological fate, she advocates that women should use technologies of artificial reproduction in order to free themselves from the 'tyranny' of their own biological constitution.

Firestone's position is more radical than most. Indeed, when her book was published her views on this issue aroused a great deal of adverse comment from both pro- and anti-feminists alike. As far as some were concerned, any strategy which went against the grain of nature appeared ill-founded. For others, the policy seemed little short of suicidal. According to their reasoning, human beings have evolved over the course of millions and millions of years into the forms best suited to survive. Human nature (whatever that is) is a success story; a winning formula. Any attempt, therefore, to deny or artificially alter that nature would appear to be at best risky, and at worst potentially catastrophic, for it is to attack the very thing which has helped the human species to succeed (*see* later section on sociobiology for more on evolutionary theory).

Viewed in these terms, it is easy to see why debates about what is, and what is not part of human nature are so highly charged, for the very survival of the species seems to be at stake. However, in practice the driving force behind much of the work in this area has as much to do with power as with knowledge, for if people are prepared to accept inequalities only where they are seen to be based upon some kind of natural order, it is not surprising that different groups in society will be concerned as to how the boundaries are drawn. This in turn helps to explain why, despite an inordinate amount of research and theorising, we are no nearer a consensus today than we were 100 years ago.

While keeping this caveat firmly in mind, it is time to look at the arguments themselves; but where to begin? One possible strategy would be to dive straight into the sex difference literature and to see for ourselves what evidence there is to support the idea, for example, that men are naturally more ambitious than women or that women have a greater sense of loyalty than men. Instead, we shall begin our investigation by examining the basic assumption upon which all questions of this sort are predicated; namely, that there is something concrete which fundamentally differentiates males from females.

Male-female: the lowest common denominator

It hardly needs to be said that sex difference research is generally founded on the assumption that there are, at the end of the day, two different sexes. Most of the work seeks merely to find out whether or not a particular attribute or skill co-varies with biological sex (i.e. whether one sex is *consistently* bigger, friendlier or more violent, etc. compared with the other). This means, of course, that just as with the early experiments on the weighing and measuring of men's and women's brains, no matter how many times researchers fail to find significant sex differences (as has occurred more times than not), this in no way threatens to undermine the starting assumption of a male/female dichotomy.

Since the mid 1970s, a small number of studies have actually challenged the assumption of the male/female dichotomy. Anthropologists (Ortner and Whitehead, 1981), social constructionists (Lorber and Farrell, 1991) and ethnomethodologists (Kessler and McKenna, 1978) have all sought to question whether the distinction between males and females is not itself a social and conventional construct, rather than something simply given to us by nature. Such challenges must be taken seriously, for not only do they threaten to undermine the whole enterprise of sex difference research, but they also carry with them profound political implications. So let us put our assumptions aside for the moment and ask the question boldly: What evidence is there for a fundamental, irreducible difference between men and women?

At first this might seem like an extraordinarily easy question to answer, for as ordinary members of our culture we generally have little difficulty in distinguishing men from women, boys from girls. So how do we do it? How do we decide? Suzanne Kessler and Wendy McKenna (1978) argue that in ordinary, everyday life we make judgements or attributions of gender on the basis of a whole range of social cues. We make our decisions, for instance, on the basis of the person's name (e.g. 'John' or 'Julie'), their clothes, the way they walk, talk, and so on. In normal circumstances this process of gender assignment goes pretty smoothly. 'John', for example, typically appears in trousers, spreads himself out on the sofa and spends long periods of time talking about last Saturday's football match or of problems with his carburettor. 'Julie', on the other hand, wears dresses and skirts, sits with her knees together, and does most of the washing-up. However, the point is that while such cues might be quite reliable guides to a person's sex (assuming for now the distinction is valid), they work purely by convention. In other words, there is no real reason why 'John' has to be a boy's name, or why men have to sit with their legs wide apart. In another time or place there is no reason why these same signs of gender could not signify the exact opposite (just as earlier this century the names 'Leslie' and 'Tracy' were usually used for boys).

Even so, there is a big difference between acknowledging the fact that we normally make decisions about other people's sex on the basis of certain arbitrary criteria, and arguing that there are absolutely no sex differences which stand outside of social conventions. Ordinary people are aware of the fact that social cues can sometimes be confusing or misleading (such as with drag artists and transvestites). Nevertheless, this does not mean that they are unsure about the nature of sexual difference *per se*. Indeed, people *do* know what the difference is (or at least think they do). It is just that, under normal circumstances, they do not have ready access to the information that would conclusively decide the matter; namely, a knowledge of the person's genital anatomy.

In the vast majority of the world's cultures the definitive basis for the distinction between male and female is the possession of a penis or a vagina. Certainly in the West it provides the basis by which a newborn baby's sex is determined at birth. If the infant has a penis, it is designated 'male'; if it possesses a vagina, it is designated 'female'. Occasionally the appearance of a baby's genitals may lead to some ambiguity and confusion. However, in most cases it is obvious to which sex category the infant belongs. While there is no necessary connection between the possession of a penis and conventional signs of masculinity, it is generally true that these factors go together or co-vary. In other words, babies born with a penis tend to be given a boy's name and are encouraged to take up boys' interests, and so on. Consequently, when we see 'Bill' the postman cycling down the street, we take it for granted that he has a penis somewhere under his uniform. Moreover, were we to discover somehow that his gender display (the range of available social cues) was *not* in 'alignment' with his genital anatomy, this would almost certainly come as something of a surprise.

For example, about two years ago I came across a greetings card whilst browsing through the shelves at a local gift shop. The card featured a picture of an attractive woman talking on the telephone in some high-rise New York office (the Empire State Building is visible through the window behind her). The woman is wearing a wide-brimmed hat, tweed jacket and a pouting, seductive kind of expression. Her jacket is open, however, and reveals a pair of naked female breasts adorned only by a long string of pearls. The card was designed to be folded horizontally across her middle, half way between her breasts and her navel. It therefore invites the (male?) recipient to open the card out in order to reveal the lower half of the semi-naked woman's body. However, upon so doing, the viewer is confronted with a startling contradiction. 'She' also has a penis! What makes this image particularly surprising (and therefore all the more effective as a card of this genre) is that there is a non-alignment, not just between the penis and the more conventional signs of femininity (such as the make-up and jewellery), but also between different *bodily* signs as well. Most obvious of all, the person has *both* a penis *and* a pair of breasts.

This is not to say that social cues are always necessarily less reliable than (non-genital) bodily cues. For instance, chest hair as a bodily sign of maleness is almost certainly less reliable than, say, the person's first name, given the proportion of men with quite a smooth, hairless torso. The point is that while there are no inherent links between genital type and conventional symbols of sex, the relationship between different bodily signs is thought to be much more concrete and much less easily manipulated. A person born with a penis still has to be given a boy's name and has to learn, to some extent at least, the appropriate ways of sitting, talking, and so on. However, he does not have to choose to develop facial hair or refuse to develop breasts. These things just happen to him.

Of course, this does not mean that it is impossible to make choices about the constitution of one's body. The above greetings card, for example, almost certainly depicts a transsexual who is mid-way through a change from man to woman. Such a person is born with a penis, but chooses to undergo a variety of medical and surgical treatments in order to assume the bodily appearance of a woman. This being the case, it could easily be argued that every man, in a sense, does have to choose whether or not to remain male. However, this is still not the same as arguing that penises and vaginas are entirely conventional signs, taken up or abandoned like articles of clothing. It does raise, however, an interesting issue about the attribution of sex to someone who has had their genitals surgically altered, for if it is genuinely the case that a person's sex is ultimately defined by the type of genitals they possess, this implies that it is quite possible to change sex. However, it seems likely that the experiences of many transsexuals would suggest otherwise. For example, when a post-operative transsexual called Renée Richards (alias Richard Raskind) attempted to compete on the women's tennis circuit, the Women's Tennis

Association banned 'her' on the basis that she was not really a woman. She was seen instead as a man who had had his genitals cut off. This implies that for some people at least, maleness does not stop with the penis. Instead, it can be thought of as just another sign of maleness; more reliable than most perhaps, but not the *thing* itself (*see* Box 1.2).

Box 1.2: Sex in sport

'The issue of sex testing has been around for as long as women have been involved in modern sporting competition. In the 1964 Olympics, for example, each competing country had to certify that their women athletes were genuinely female. However, due to allegations that some countries were submitting fraudulent certificates, the following Games saw the introduction of physical examinations of all female athletes by neutral members of the Olympic organization's medical team. Not long after it was decided that this test was also unsatisfactory as it failed to detect those men, who by a mixture of surgical and hormonal treatments, sought to unfairly enhance their country's medal chances by "passing" as women. As a consequence, the sex chromosome test was introduced into the Olympic Games in 1972, having already proved "successful" in the 1967 European Track and Field competition where Eva Klobukowska – a medal winner in the 1964 Olympics – was found to possess male sex chromosomes.'

(Taken from Kessler and McKenna, 1978)

According to biological scientists, the presence of a penis is not the absolute or 'acid' test of maleness. Indeed, like all the other bodily signs of maleness, its appearance is determined by something else which goes much deeper; indeed, into every cell of a person's body. Like the name which runs through a stick of seaside rock, there is no possibility of cutting away or removing a person's sex, for even the smallest sliver of their skin or bone carries the same indelible proof of their membership. The average human body is made up of many trillions (1×10^{12} or $1\,000\,000\,000\,000$) of different cells with almost every one containing an identical set of 46 chromosomes arranged into pairs. Each of these chromosomes, in turn, is made up of a string of thousands of different genes, which can be usefully, if somewhat euphemistically, thought of as the 'blueprints' for the constitution of the entire human organism. Of the 23 pairs of chromosomes, 22 are called autosomes. They regulate and control most of the physical characteristics of the individual human being. The twenty-third pair are the sex chromosomes, and it is these, the biological scientists assure us, which determine the person's sex.

Just as with the genital definition of sex, virtually the entire human population can be subdivided into either one of two chromosomal configura-

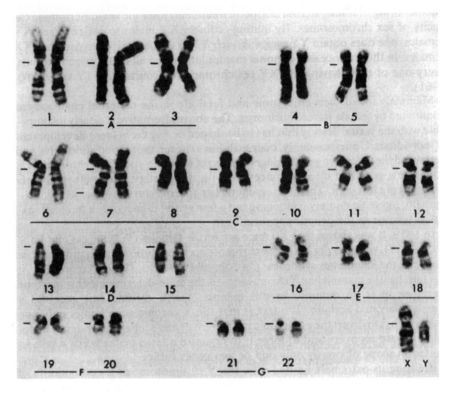

Figure 1.1 The chromosomes of a human male
Source: Ohno, 1979, p. 24

tions. Around 50 per cent of people have sex chromosomes shaped like two 'X's standing next to each other. The remaining 50 per cent possess a pair consisting of just one X-like chromosome and a much smaller 'Y' shaped partner (*see* Figure 1.1). It is these two different chromosomal configurations ('XX' and 'XY') which give rise to two quite distinct lines of physical development; one that we would recognise as female (XX), the other male (XY).

As most people know, a new life begins with the fusing of a sperm and an egg (or ovum). However, it is less well known that these two sex cells contain precisely half the genetic material of a normal cell. This is achieved by a special form of cell division (called meiosis) which sees all 23 pairs of chromosomes split apart to form two new cells each with 22 autosomes and just one sex chromosome. In the case of the female ovum this chromosome has, of course, to be of the X variety. However, in the case of male sperm production, the subdivision of normal XY cells results in half of them carrying an X sex chromosome, and the other half carrying a Y. This means that it is always the sperm which determines the sex of the offspring, for if an X-bearing ovum fuses with an X-bearing sperm then the resulting zygote will normally develop along the lines of a female. Alternatively, if the ovum fuses with a sperm carrying a Y sex chromosome then the result will be an XY zygote which, again under normal circumstances, develops along male lines (the probability of each outcome being roughly 50:50 – see Box 1.3).

Studies of the early development of the human embryo suggest that the process of sexual differentiation begins about six or seven weeks after conception. Moreover, the key factor determining the particular course of development appears to be the presence or absence of a Y sex chromosome.

> In the presence of the Y chromosome cell division in the zygote appears to be speeded up and the medulla or inner portion of the embryonic gonad proceeds to differentiate into a testis. . . . If this fails to occur then the cortex or outer part of the primitive gonad differentiates into an ovary. (Hutt, 1972 p. 22)

After this point, most of the remaining stages of sexual differentiation appear to be under the control of the hormones secreted by the ovaries and testicles. For example, in the case of the developing testis, the hormones secreted are predominantly androgens, which stimulate the development of a set of ducts (called the Wolffian ducts) into the male reproductive organs (i.e. vas deferens, epididymis, seminal vesicles and prostate gland). At the same time, these

---

Box 1.3: The lesser-spotted sex chromosome configurations

While the XX and XY chromosome configurations are by far the most common, it is not unknown for different arrangements to exist, such as XXX, XXY, XYY and X on its own (sometimes denoted XO). Within the biological and medical sciences, these conditions are generally regarded as chromosomal abnormalities in the sense of something having gone wrong. For example, people with the chromosomal configurations XO and XXY are described as suffering from Turner's syndrome and Klinefelter's syndrome respectively. However, it could be argued that these conditions represent instances of third and fourth kinds of sex. That is, they can be seen as challenging the assumption of a sexual dichotomy.

Yet the fact that 97 per cent of XO embryos spontaneously abort and that the remainder grow up to be infertile (as do those with an XXY configuration), seems to favour the position of the biological scientists. Certainly from a Darwinian point of view, it is true that if an organism is incapable of transmitting a copy of its genetic codes to the next generation it represents the shortest possible evolutionary cul-de-sac. Nevertheless, as Kessler and McKenna (1978) point out, it still requires someone to make a decision whether or not, for example, an XXY individual is an abnormal male, female or something else altogether.

hormones inhibit the development of a different set of ducts (known as the Mullerian ducts) which, had they been stimulated, would have developed into the female reproductive system (i.e. the fallopian tubes, uterus and vagina).

The development of the Mullerian ducts is the usual pattern of events in female embryos whose primitive gonads are changing into the predominantly oestrogen-producing ovaries. However, it can also occur in male (XY) embryos if, for some reason, the concentration of androgen produced by the young testis is not sufficiently high. This means that it is quite possible for a new-born baby to have all the outward signs of being female despite almost every cell in 'her' body containing an XY set of sex chromosomes. In such cases, the attribution of sex to the individual will depend upon whether we take an anatomical or a chromosomal definition. In the event, it is likely that the anatomical definition will apply insofar as the new-born child will appear to be a perfectly normal baby girl. However, because it is true that in the overwhelming majority of cases a person's anatomical sex is determined by the constitution of their sex chromosomes, it would appear reasonable to consider the chromosomal definition as the more fundamental.

At this point it worth restating the significance of all of these debates about whether or not the categories 'male' and 'female' correspond to objects which exist 'out there' in the material world. The first point to note is that the whole enterprise of sex difference research effectively hangs upon the assumption that there is a fundamental, irreducible difference between men and women. Without it such studies become meaningless. Second, and more important perhaps, it can be argued that just as the differences between men's and women's bodies have a fundamental biological origin, so might any differences between the ways in which the two sexes think and act.

Non-physical sex differences

While most of the work looking into the physical differences between men and women has been conducted under the umbrella of the biological sciences, since the late 1890s psychologists have spent an enormous amount of time and effort investigating the extent to which the two sexes differ on a wide variety of behavioural and attitudinal measures. They have asked questions to determine which sex is the most aggressive, compliant, dextrous and reliant ... the list goes on and on. Yet, as mentioned earlier in the chapter, it has proved notoriously difficult to produce clear empirical support for most of the stereotypes held about men's and women's psychological differences (as listed in Table 1.1). Indeed, Segal (1990) notes that in their exhaustive review of psychological sex difference research, Eleanor Maccoby and Carol Jacklin (1974) showed that the existence of sex differences in behaviour had been systematically exaggerated, and similarities minimalised [with] no consistent sex differences in traits like achievement motivation, sociability, suggestibility, self-esteem and cognitive styles [and only] small but fairly well established differences in verbal and spatial ability, mathematical reasoning and aggressiveness. (p. 62)

There can be little doubt that part of the reason for the 'systematic exaggeration' of sex differences lay with political interests getting the better of proper scientific procedure, but it was also a consequence of more innocent factors, such as a tendency of scientists and publishers to be more interested in 'positive' results (i.e. where statistically significant differences had been found) and a misapprehension that a 'highly statistically significant' sex difference necessarily implied a big difference. (In fact, it refers to the *consistency* of differences between groups; such that if, for example, all the girls in a school scored half of 1 per cent higher than the boys, this would be considered a highly significant, albeit small difference.)

Of the four 'small, but fairly well established' sex differences mentioned above, by far the strongest evidence surrounds the hypothesis that males are significantly more aggressive than females. Indeed for some, the debate is as good as closed.

[F]or regardless of how aggression is defined and measured, males of all ages show a consistent tendency to be more aggressive than their female peers.... Males are more apt to express their their hostile feelings in daydreams and fantasies, in socially disguised forms of dominance and competition, and in direct physical attacks. This greater male aggression is expressed not only in a variety of behavioural modes but also in a variety of situations and cultures. (Bunker-Rohrbaugh, 1981, p. 38)

Certainly it is not easy to find disconfirming evidence. While a few studies have found no significant difference between levels of male and female aggression, there have been hardly any which have suggested females to be the more aggressive sex (Maccoby and Jacklin, 1974).

Of the three remaining 'intellectual' sex differences, the most compelling case is for a male advantage in visual-spatial skills. Men have been found to do consistently better in experiments which require the subject to imagine how a three-dimensional shape would appear if rotated in space (Fairweather, 1976). Similarly, men excel at tasks which require them to find a basic shape concealed within a more complex drawing (called the 'Embedded Figure Test' or EFT). According to Hyde (1981) the magnitude of this difference is such that around one quarter of all females score higher than the average (mean) male. Since the early 1970s, men have also consistently out-scored women by about 50 points on the mathematics section of the Scholastic Aptitude Test. However, there is a good deal of evidence to suggest that this advantage may be largely a consequence of the visual-spatial processes involved in solving many mathematical problems – such as in graph reading and geometry (Maccoby and Jacklin, 1974). Many researchers thus argue that it is inappropriate to list this as another independent sex difference.

The evidence to suggest that women have greater verbal abilities than men seems even more contentious, for while some studies have found that girls develop both 'high' and 'low' level verbal skills earlier than boys (e.g. comprehension and verbal fluency respectively – Maccoby and Jacklin, 1974), others have claimed these differences to be either extremely small or non-existent (Hyde, 1981). Moreover, there have been a few studies claiming that males have a slight advantage in verbal skills (e.g. Fairweather, 1976; Brimer, 1969).

Understandably, the overall failure to find clear-cut non-physical differences between the sexes was taken by many as proof that, psychologically speaking, males and females were pretty much the same. However, there have been others who have argued that the conceptual and methodological problems associated with sex difference research serve mainly to conceal rather than exaggerate the existence of differences. Alice Eagly (1983) insists that if a study 'fails' to come up with statistically significant results, this does not necessarily mean that there is no sex difference present. Rather, by adding together the results from several compatible studies (i.e. those measuring the same variable) she claims that it is sometimes the case that the *overall* or composite picture turns out to be statistically significant. The research into the relationship between conformity and sex provides a case in point. While Maccoby and Jacklin (1974) reported that the majority of studies looking at this question came up with no significant findings, according to Eagly, studies which have used these statistical methods of aggregation (e.g. Cooper, 1979; Eagly and Carli, 1981) have 'established' that women are more easily influenced than men (*see also* Glass, McGraw and Smith, 1981, and Hyde, 1990 for more detailed discussions of these so-called meta analyses).

Eagly also argues that while it is true that a highly statistically 'significant' finding may refer to a very small difference between men and women (in absolute terms), it is quite wrong to assume that this is always the case. For there have been some studies, she points out, where the magnitude of sex differences has been proved to be quite substantial (e.g. Eagly and Carli, 1981; Hall, 1984). Finally, on a more general level, Eagly challenges the overall thrust of Maccoby and Jacklin's conclusions by suggesting that sex difference research, if anything, tends to confirm rather than refute many popular conceptions about sex differences. She suggests that while the issue of stereotype accuracy needs to be looked into further, the evidence suggests 'that laypeople, once maligned in much feminist writing as misguided holders of stereotypes, may be fairly sophisticated observers of gender' (Eagly, 1994).

Clearly, debates about whether or not psychological sex differences exist are still very much in progress, but if we presume for the moment that such differences do exist, how can we be confident that they have a biological basis? Maccoby and Jacklin (1974), for example, suggested that sex differences in visual-spatial abilities could well be a product of cultural rather than biological factors. Indeed, no such differences were found between Eskimo males and females. It seems possible, too, that boys may receive more visual-spatial 'training' as part of their normal socialisation, ranging from sport to choice of toys and games. Similarly, Eagly argues that men's greater powers of persuasion stem merely from the fact that typically they occupy the most powerful roles in society (Eagly, 1983). This encourages people to associate masculinity with power, prestige and authority, making them more likely to interpret men as knowing what they are talking about. The same kind of arguments could be made for the social origins of male aggressiveness.

Trying to work out whether men's and women's behaviour is a consequence of social or biological forces (or both) is a serious analytical problem which has been approached from a number of different angles. One line of research bases itself upon the assumption that while cultures may vary considerably, all human beings share the same fundamental biological make-up. Hence, if we compare the behaviour of men and women across a wide range of different cultures (e.g. from tribes in Borneo to groups in Switzerland), anything which has a genuinely biological basis should emerge as a constant or universal feature. Conversely, anything which varies across different cultures (like sex differences in visual-spatial abilities) is less likely to have a biological cause.

Studies of this kind have revealed that while every known culture makes some kind of distinction between male and female, the behaviours associated with the two sexes vary considerably.

> In some cultures, for example, men weave and women make pots, whereas in others these roles are reversed; in some parts of the world women are the major agricultural producers, and in others they are prohibited from agricultural activity. (Hargreaves, 1986, p.17)

According to Hargreaves, the only roles which do appear to be universally linked to one sex or the other are those 'concerned with child-rearing, hunting and war-making'. This has often been taken as evidence of men's natural tendency to aggress. However, as Archer (1976) and Gilmore (1990) point out, universal patterns of gendered behaviour may represent nothing more than common practical solutions to universal problems. In other words, the fact that men tend to do all the hunting and the fighting might reflect, not that they are pre-programmed to do so, but part of a division of labour which sees women largely occupied with having and nursing the children.

Obviously, we cannot just assume that all cross-cultural consistencies in sex-related behaviour originate from biological sources. Yet it is equally wrong to take the absence of clear cross-cultural patterns in sex-related behaviour as meaning that there are no biological forces at play, for there is no logical reason why biological factors need always find expression. Instead, they may be 'masked' or overridden by social or cultural influences operating in a different 'direction'. For instance, the celibate and the hunger-striker represent just two examples of where what many people believe to be natural instincts are successfully overridden by social and political beliefs.

A second avenue of research consists of a series of studies with new-born babies and young infants. The assumption here is that while a person may be a product of both social and biological forces, social influences must come later (i.e. post natally). Therefore, by studying the behaviour of males and females in the very earliest days of their lives, any observable sex differences are most likely to be a consequence of biology rather than social upbringing. However, as with the cross-cultural studies, very few behavioural sex differences have been found using this line of work. Maccoby and Jacklin (1974) found only that baby boys tended to be slightly more irritable, and girls slightly more responsive to tactile and oral stimulation. Yet this has not stopped some from claiming these to be the foundations for much more marked gender differences in later life (e.g. Garai and Scheinfeld, 1968; Bardwick, 1971; McGuiness, 1976).

Archer and Lloyd (1985) see the entire rationale of this project as fundamentally flawed. They point to studies which have shown how differently adults treat boys and girls, even from the first day of their lives (e.g. Rubin et al., 1974; White and Woollett, 1981; Culp et al., 1983; Block, 1978). Parents project gendered identities onto their children, seeing baby boys as bigger, tougher and more active. They also reinforce stereotypical gender behaviour in a myriad of more or less subtle ways. For example, Rheingold and Cook (1975) found that the bedrooms of children only days old were filled with gender-specific items: floral wallpaper and doll's houses for the girls, bold stripes and toy cars for the boys. Therefore, it becomes virtually impossible to decide whether a particular behavioural sex difference is the product of biological factors or differential parental treatment.

A third line of investigation takes in the ethological work of Konrad Lorenz (1967), Robert Ardrey (1966) and Desmond Morris (1967). These researchers argue that we can discover the contours of human nature by studying the behaviour of our near and distant evolutionary cousins. In other words, if we can find close parallels between animal and human behaviour, we can be confident that there may be some common evolutionary mechanism underlying both. For example, it has been noted many times that in most animal species it is the male who is the more aggressive. From elephants down to sparrows, it is generally the male who does the fighting and, where relevant, the hunting. Similarly, it is widely recognised that the male of the species is generally more active in finding a mate. Again it is he who attracts the female with his brighter colours and elaborate courtship rituals.

The major problem with ethological studies concerns the validity of extrapolating from animal behaviour to that of human beings. Can the 'territorial' behaviour of football hooligans really been seen in the same light as the male robin redbreast attacking a red Post Office van (Morris, 1977)?

Can the wearing of a trendy shirt be likened seriously to the male peacock fanning out his tail? As Reynolds (1976) comments, it is one thing to draw parallels, but quite another to say that the two forms of behaviour are one and the same thing.

Despite the fact that none of these approaches provides us with anything like conclusive evidence of a biological basis to male (or female) behaviour, there are large bodies of work which simply presume such a link exists. Instead of seeking to discover if men's behaviour is a product of their biological make-up, this work looks to explain why and how it occurs. It is to this distinction between *functional* and *causal* types of accounts (Janson-Smith, 1980) that we now turn our attention.

Sociobiology and the functions of sex-related behaviour

In 1975 Edward Wilson, the father of sociobiology, defined the discipline as 'the systematic study of the biological basis of all social behaviour'. Like the ethologists mentioned above, sociobiologists treat human beings as just another species of animal. Moreover, they adopt the basic principles of Charles Darwin's theory of 'natural selection' to explain the structure of human societies in terms of their evolutionary functions.

'Evolution' refers to the gradual change in either plant or animal species over the course of geological time. The driving force of this change, Darwin argued, is the nature of the environments in which these species live. If any given species is to survive, it must be able to cope sufficiently well with the environmental conditions to allow successive generations of organisms to be produced: if this cannot be achieved, the species will quickly become extinct. So, for example, if the environment is very hot, the only organisms which will be able to thrive are those which can in some way control their own temperatures. Similarly, the only types of species which will be able to survive on a food source which is found high in the tree-tops will be those that are able to fly, climb or stand very tall.

Whether a given organism possesses wings or long legs depends largely upon the nature of its genes, the genetic make-up of a parrot being quite different from that of a giraffe. However, one of the most important principles in understanding the evolutionary process is that while the genetic constitution of individuals within a species will obviously be similar, they are by no means the same. For example, if we were to look closely at a field full of cows, we would notice that they vary in size, shape, colouring, and so on. Similarly, within the human species it is the existence of these types of variations that enables us to recognise each other as different individuals. The significance of this variation in evolutionary terms is that any given individual will, according to its particular genetic constitution, be more or less well equipped or adapted to survive in its native habitat. For example, those individuals who are 'built' to be the better flyers and climbers will get to the tree-top food quicker: if there is not always enough food to go around, the poorest flyers and climbers end up going hungry. More to the point, the 'fitter', well-fed individuals stand a better chance of living long enough to reproduce, thereby passing on copies of their 'successful' (genetic) formulae. Therefore, over the course of successive generations there is what Darwin called a natural selection towards ever more environmentally suited or adapted individuals.

Broadly speaking, genetic variation occurs via two mechanisms. One occurs if the normal process of cell reproduction for some reason malfunctions. Indeed, this is the only way in which novel characteristics can emerge in species which reproduce asexually (for otherwise the offspring has a 'carbon copy' of its parent's genetic profile). The second occurs in species which reproduce sexually where the genetic material of the offspring originates from two different parent organisms (in the form of the sperm and the ovum – *see earlier*). Not only is the genetic profile of the offspring, therefore, different from each of its parents, but it is also different from virtually every other member of the species. In evolutionary terms, this high level of variability is extremely advantageous, for it dramatically increases the probability of a significantly better suited or more adapted individual being produced.

Sociobiologists argue that the evolutionary advantages of sexual reproduction account for why so many animal species (including humans) have evolved two distinct sexes. What is more, they employ precisely the same kind of functional arguments to account for a whole variety of different sex-related behavioural characteristics; including, most contentiously, men's aggressive and philanderous activities.

Beginning with the observation that, in most animal species, the males appear more aggressive than the females, the sociobiologist's first thought is to how this behaviour might improve the species' chances of survival. One of the most straightforward explanations is that aggression enables an individual organism to defend itself from attack. Another is that many species need a certain level of aggression to be effective as hunters. A third, more convoluted explanation, is that aggression serves to reduce the risk of vital food supplies becoming depleted by forcing the species to spread itself over a wide area in order to minimise the chances of dangerous confrontations. But why, we might ask, it is only the males of most species that have evolved these aggressive tendencies? Surely the same evolutionary pressures have existed on females? To this, sociobiologists respond that males and females have evolved together as a team, and because females spend much of their adult lives either having or nursing babies, the aggressive jobs of hunting and fighting have necessarily fallen upon the male.

In the area of sexuality, the pattern of behaviour which sociobiologists seek to explain is the tendency of men to be more promiscuous or sexually forward compared with women. Wilson (1975) argues that men adopt a sexual strategy based on infidelity and philandering while women favour 'coyness'. Leaving aside the question of whether there are invariant differences of this kind across human populations, such variations could be explained, Wilson suggests, in terms of the differential 'investments' which males and females have in their offspring.

> There is a basic asymmetry between male and female. The female knows that the young she bears are hers, and therefore worth her time and effort, while the male will never be quite sure. A female will be interested in two things – whether a male is carrying 'good' genes, and whether he is prepared to help her with the rearing of the young. The male however has different ideas. Because he is not limited by carrying and later nursing the young, his capacity for reproduction is far higher than the female's. His initial investment in the offspring is small, a teaspoon or so. As, in evolutionary terms, he is interested in getting the maximum number of children (thus passing on as many copies of his genes as possible) he will 'ideally' want to mate with as many females, and evade as much parental responsibility, as he can. (Janson-Smith, 1980, p. 67)

Not surprisingly, there has been a great deal of fierce criticism aimed at sociobiological theories of sex-related behaviour. For example, when Randy Thornhill and Nancy Wilmsen Thornhill published an article entitled 'The evolutionary psychology of men's coercive sexuality' (*see* Box 1.4), it met with a wave of adverse reaction. As far as many were concerned, their work served, not simply to explain men's sexual coercion, but to justify it. For like other sociobiological accounts, it not only re-cast an oppressive form of behaviour in a much more positive light (as 'adaptive'), but it also represented this negative characteristic as a natural quality of men; something which they could not help but embody.

Box 1.4: The 'evolution' of rape

'Because of the different ways that selection acted on the sexes during human evolutionary history, evolutionary psychologists believe human sexual psychology is dimorphic, that is, the respective adaptations differ in men and women . . . . The evolved sex difference in mating strategy leads to differences in how men and women feel about whether, when, and how often it is in their interest to mate. Because women are more selective about mates and more interested in evaluating them and delaying copulation, men, to get sexual access, must often break through feminine barriers of hesitation, equivocation, and resistance . . . . According to the rape-adaptation hypothesis, during human evolutionary history there was enough directional selection on males in favour of traits that solved the problem of forcing sex on a reluctant partner to produce psychological inclinations specific towards rape.'

(Randy Thornhill and Nancy Wilmsen Thornhill, 1992)

Apart from any moral or political objections, sociobiological explanations can also be attacked on a number of other grounds (*see* Caplan, 1978
and Ruse, 1979 for comprehensive reviews). For example, Allen *et al.* (1977)
note that geneticists have long since abandoned the idea that each bit of the
human body is controlled by its own corresponding gene, and yet sociobiologists continue to assume such a link exists between genes and various
aspects of social behaviour. Others have argued that, as a scientific theory,
sociobiological accounts are unverifiable (e.g. Burian, 1977). This is because
they typically begin with certain empirical details or facts about the world,
and then work backwards to develop an explanation of why these conditions
came into existence. Hence, it is meaningless to judge sociobiological accounts according to their predictive value, for they *pre*-dict nothing. Furthermore, as a number of commentators have pointed out, it is often just as easy to
produce a sociobiological theory which accounts for a hypothetical situation
(such as women being the more aggressive sex) as it is for situations which
actually exist.

Despite these criticisms, sociobiological theories continue to feature in
contemporary work on sex-related behaviour. It is important to stress that
sociobiologists themselves vary from those who stress biological factors to
the exclusion of other forms of explanation to those who take a much more
qualified and muted approach, believing that evolution has a part to play in
determining human behaviour along with cultural and social factors.
However, we will leave these accounts of why men and women might have
evolved different ways of thinking and acting, to concentrate instead upon
explanations of how biology might influence behaviour.

Genes, hormones and the 'causes' of sex-related behaviour

Raymond Montemayor (1978) claims that people have believed in some kind
of bridge between the body and the mind for at least 2000 years. For example,
he notes how during the late nineteenth century Sir Francis Galton claimed
men of genius to be of bigger than average build (Galton, 1896/1962).
However, studies which merely look for the existence of co-variations between, say, biological sex and specific patterns of behaviour tell us little or
nothing about how one factor influences the other. They shed no light on how
a man's body can force him into thinking and behaving in a specifically
'masculine' way. Fortunately, however, there are some theories which do
offer something of an explanation.

If psychological and behavioural sex differences really do derive from
physical sex differences, it would seem logical to suppose that ultimately they
both have the same origins. This means that, directly or indirectly, psychological and behavioural sex differences might also result from the two different sex chromosome configurations XX and XY. In the next few sections we

will review three theories of how such a mind-body bridge may be constructed.

The first and most straightforward theory of a mind-body bridge assumes that the ways in which people think and behave are just as much under the control of genes as is the constitution of their physical body. According to this view, people are born clever, criminal, extroverted, and so on. It is not surprising, therefore, that it is an extremely controversial theory which even some of the most committed biological determinists disavow (e.g. Corrine Hutt). However, recently there have been widely reported claims in the media that scientists have 'discovered' the genes which are responsible for shyness, homosexuality and violently aggressive behaviour (*see* Box 1.5).

Box 1.5: The aggressive gene

In the 18 June 1993, edition of *Science* (Volume 260, No. 5115, pp. 1722–3) Virginia Morel reports upon the findings from a study by Han G Brunner of a large Dutch family with a history of violent menfolk. One had raped his sister, another two were compulsive arsonists, and a fourth had responded to a reprimand at work by attempting to murder his employer. Apparently, scientists had first encountered the family when, in 1978, one of the female members sought genetic counselling, worried that there may have been some genetic defect within the family. However, the story continues, it was only with recent developments in molecular biology that her question could be properly answered.

Basically, the scientists compared the 'genetic fingerprints' of the violently aggressive men with those belonging to the more 'normal' men in the family to see if there were any systematic differences. What they claim to have discovered is that all of the violent men share a similar genetic defect which interferes with the production of an enzyme responsible for breaking down a number of neurotransmitters. As a result of this defect, certain 'brain chemicals' rise to unusually high levels of concentration which, it is suggested, could cause a person to respond 'excessively, and at times even violently, to stress'.

However, because the condition is rare, it is highly unlikely that this theory could account for every act of aggression. Indeed, in the *New Scientist* report of the same study (Volume 140, No. 1897, p. 6), behavioural geneticist Gregory Carey is quoted as saying 'It may be that this gene is responsible for one in a million cases of aggression in the general population'.

Because aggressiveness represents one of the few traits that psychologists have consistently picked out as differentiating men and women, the supposed discovery of an aggressive gene is particularly interesting; it raises the question of how a specific gene, passed down from one generation to the next, can affect only one half of the population. At first sight, the most obvious solution to this puzzle is that the aggressive gene must be carried on the one chromosome which women do not possess; namely, the Y chromosome. However, genetic scientists have argued that this is quite unlikely as the small Y chromosome carries very few functional genes. Indeed, paradoxical as it might seem, they suggest that the aggressive gene is most likely to be carried on the X sex chromosome.

According to their hypotheses, the aggressive gene disproportionately affects men in precisely the same way as a number of other so-called sex-linked conditions such as red-green colour blindness and haemophilia. Statistically speaking, 1 in every 20 people carries the gene which produces red-green colour blindness. However, while 1 in 20 men suffer from red-green colour blindness, this is true of only 1 in 400 women (Patt and Patt, 1975). The reason for this imbalance is that the gene for red-green colour blindness, which is carried on the X sex chromosome, is what genetic scientists call recessive. This means that it will become effective only in the absence of any corresponding dominant genes. The point is that while women have a 95 per cent chance that their other X chromosome will carry the dominant gene for normal colour vision, men, with their single X chromosome, do not. (N.B. This is why the probability of a woman being colour blind is 5 per cent of 5 per cent, or 1 in 400).

The idea of an aggressive gene is appealing in a number of different ways. First, it is a simple, straightforward notion. Men, it says, are more aggressive than women because of the way they are made. No amount of cursing, cajoling, or indeed, cutting will change it. Second, it is a theory which can make sense of why some families seem to be much more aggressive than others. Third, and most mischievous, it is also a theory which sees the problem of male violence as something 'given' to men by women (carried on the X chromosome that mothers donate to their sons).

In spite of these various appeals, genetic theories such as this are open to the same charge of naïvity as has been lodged against sociobiology (*see above*). In other words, they assume that a neat one-to-one relationship exists between a specific gene and an equally specific form of social behaviour. However, genetic scientists have found that some of the most simple physical features of the human body (such as hair and eye colour) are determined, not by one, but by a number of different genes. In addition, genetic theories appear to ignore, or at least underplay, the contingency of human behaviour: an individual has either got it (e.g. aggression) or they have not. The situation in which an individual finds himself (or herself) can only, at best, dictate whether or not these predispositions are activated. As such, the theory denies the possibility of personal change: there can be no such thing as a 'reformed character'.

Nevertheless, as we have already mentioned, debates about the genetic basis of human behaviour are far from going out of fashion. In laboratories all over the Western world, research continues into the connections between these microscopic pieces of material and complex forms of social activity.

Even so, it is a relatively minor area of investigation compared with that which places sex hormones centre-stage in the determination of sex-related behaviour.

Most of the effects of sex hormones on the physical development of human beings are, by now, well documented. They are thought to influence not only the development of the male and female reproductive systems (as already explained), but also the development of 'secondary sexual character- istics' during early adolescence (such as breasts in women and facial hair in men). However, there remains one much more controversial claim about the physical effects of sex hormones: they also stimulate sex differences in brain physiology and functioning, which then go on to produce differences between men's and women's behaviour.

Several studies have outlined general physiological differences between men's and women's brains (e.g. Treadwell, 1987; De Vries et al., 1984; Naftolin, 1981). These include variations in the thickness of the brain's cortex or outer layer, the volume and organisation of a whole variety of different nervous structures such as neurons, synapses and dendritic spines, and the thickness of the tissue connecting the two hemispheres of the brain called the corpus callosum (see Toran-Allerand, 1984). According to many of these studies, the sex differentiation of the foetal brain depends upon its exposure to androgens in a way similar to the differentiation of the repro- ductive tracts. However, others have suggested that the differentiation of the brain is less dichotomous; rather, it operates on a kind of sliding scale where the greater the exposure to male hormone the more 'male-typed' the de- veloping foetus' brain becomes.

In their popular account of these physiological differences, Ann Moir and David Jessell (1989) argue that a wide range of sex differences in perception, priorities and behaviour can be attributed to the different 'wiring' of men's and women's brains. To support this claim they draw upon evidence from experiments using a sophisticated brain scanning technique called Positron Emission Tomography (PET). PET monitors the metabolic activity of the brain as it functions, allowing researchers to see which parts of the brain are used for different kinds of activities. This technique has shown, for instance, that the left hemisphere of the human brain appears to deal more with language and numerical skills, whereas the right hemisphere seems more concerned with musical awareness, pattern perception and imagination (Tor- tora and Anagnostakos, 1984). Moir and Jessells' argument rests on the premise that men's and women's brains are not subdivided by function to the same degree. (N.B. They are by no means the originators of this idea. Indeed, research into sex differences in brain functioning dates back to the early 1970s – see McGlone, 1980.)

For some time researchers have claimed that sex differences in behaviour result from the fact that, while in men, the right hemisphere of the brain (the site of visual-spatial skills) dominates over the left (the centre of verbal abilities), in women the situation is reversed. Many researchers now believe that these differences develop post-natally (Nicholson, 1979). Some claim that, in infancy, both sexes can perform verbal and spatial skills with equal competence. However, with age, their brains begin to divide themselves into separate areas of specialisation. In girls, the left hemisphere starts to take over the control of verbal processes while relinquishing the control of visual-spatial tasks. In boys, the exact opposite occurs (i.e. right hemisphere special-ises first to become more efficient at visual skills and less efficient at verbal skills). After this, in both sexes, the opposite side of the brain begins to take up the control of those activities abandoned by the other. However, according to the proponents of lateralisation theory, the male brain achieves a more profound degree of specialisation.

Moir and Jessell (1989) argue that the greater 'compartmentalisation' of the male brain has two main consequences. First, it enables men to perform concurrent tasks more easily. That is, as long as the two tasks do not draw upon the same area of the brain, a man can cope better with trying to do two or more jobs simultaneously. The drawback (and second consequence) is that because all of these different areas of the male brain are cut off from each other, they remain relatively unable to 'communicate' with one another. Moir and Jessel see this as explaining, for example, the difficulty which many men have in trying to talk about their emotions. If only men's emotional and language 'centres' could make better contact with each other (something which the authors suggest can occur under the chemical effects of alcohol), men could 'loosen up' much more easily.

Clearly such explanations are crude in the extreme, and no doubt do the credibility of a highly complicated and experimental area of scientific investi-gation a great disservice. Nevertheless, they do point to the need for concrete explanations of how sex differences in brain physiology affect men's and women's behaviour. Even if we accept the claim that there are differences between men's and women's brains (something that a number of other researchers would want to dispute – see Segal, 1990), we still need to understand how this connection works. The problem is that our understand-ing of the functioning of the human brain is far from comprehensive. Further-more, much of the research on brain lateralisation and psychological skills has produced contradictory or inconclusive results. As a consequence, there is still a tendency to assume that just because the brain is the chief adminis-trative organ of the body, any sex differences there *must* have an impact on men's and women's social behaviour, yet this is inadequate. While it may appear more plausible, such an assumption is no more justified than another claiming behavioural sex differences to be a product of penises and vaginas – both are purely correlational.

Theories about the influence of sex hormones on behaviour are not restricted to arguments about their effects upon the development of the foetal brain. Indeed, for a long time people have assumed that hormones have a profound effect upon men's and women's day-to-day behaviour. For example, it is not uncommon to hear people arguing that women's behaviour is closely bound up with the monthly ebbing and flowing of a few key hormones. However, research into the effects of different sex hormones has produced far from clear, unambiguous results. Part of the problem stems from the fact that much of the research has been conducted, for obvious ethical reasons, using animals rather than people, the issue being that even if, for example, a female rat *does* exhibit more typically male-type behaviour after being injected with a high dose of androgen (Blizard, 1983), this does not necessarily mean that the same would be true for a female human (*see* Herbert, 1976; Gray and Drewett, 1977). Furthermore, in the studies that have used human subjects (e.g. looking at the relationship between patterns of behaviour and hormone levels from blood samples), the findings have been complex, if not downright contradictory. For example, in surveying the evidence for a relationship between aggression and the male hormone testosterone, Archer and Lloyd (1985) note that while there have been several studies which have claimed a positive finding (such as Persky, Smith and Basu, 1971 and Olweus *et al.*, 1980), there have also been a number claiming the opposite (e.g. Kreuz and Rose, 1972 and Doering *et al.*, 1974). In other areas, too, the results have been far from straightforward. For instance, Jacklin *et al.* (1988) found that while higher levels of neonatal androgens correlated negatively with low spatial ability scores in girls (tested six years later), no such correlation existed for boys. More complicated still, some experiments have found neonatal progesterone levels positively related to physical strength and negatively related to timidity in boys, but negatively related to strength and unrelated to timidity in girls (Jacklin *et al.*, 1983; Jacklin *et al.*, 1984).

One way in which researchers have attempted to sort out this mass of confusing information is by positing a kind of two-stage theory of hormonal influence. The first stage consists of a kind of critical period of development (Levine, 1966) during which time some limits and potentials are 'set down' for later life. It is like the creation of the circuit-board along which the electricity will later run. Once the hot metal has solidified, the pathways are fixed, once and for all. The second stage refers to the effects of hormones once this critical period has passed. So, for example, a dose of testosterone may have quite a different kind of effect on the 'male brain' (having perhaps already been primed for aggression, etc.) as compared with the female brain.

There are two main sources of evidence for this type of theory. The first comes from experiments with animals (with all their attendant problems of extrapolation). The other consists mostly of studies which look at atypical human populations such as people with genetic conditions associated with abnormal prenatal hormone levels (such as Turner's syndrome and Klinefelter's syndrome – *see* Box 1.3) and those who, for a variety of reasons, were exposed to exogenous hormones while still in the womb. Some of these studies emerged with positive findings; for example, Money and Ehrhardt (1972) claimed that girls whose mothers had been exposed to androgens while pregnant tended to engage in higher than average levels of rough-and-tumble play. Similarly, Yalom, Green and Fiske (1973) suggested that boys whose diabetic mothers had been treated with high doses of oestrogen to prevent miscarriage appeared to be less assertive, athletic and interested in male-type activities compared with control groups.

However, these studies are also not without their problems. For example, Singleton (1986) notes that they suffer from a number of methodological weaknesses, particularly the tendency to rely on extremely small sample sizes and on interview rather than observational data. Furthermore, it could be argued that these behavioural and psychological 'abnormalities' result, not directly from the hormones themselves, but from atypical schedules of social reinforcement which follow as a consequence of their physical effects. For example, imagine a male who, as a foetus, was exposed to exogeneous oestrogens. Let us say, for the sake of argument, that he grows up to be more sylph-like than his brothers. As a consequence, he might be treated as something of a 'mummy's boy' who is more sensitive, cerebral and less inclined to enjoy sports and other kinds of physical activity. There has been no shortage of people willing to argue that a male's behaviour is more a consequence of his upbringing rather than his physical constitution. The problem with trying to substantiate such a claim is that in the majority of cases, a man's gender identity and his biological sex are, so to speak, in alignment. However, there have been a number of studies which exploit those rare occasions where, for some reason, a person has been assigned to a sex category which contradicts the facts of their biological constitution. The all-important question being, do these people grow up to be masculine or feminine?

Once again, the evidence is mixed. In his review article of 84 cases of hermaphroditism Albert Ellis claimed that upbringing was the major determinant (Ellis, 1945). Money and Ehrhardt (1972) came out with similar conclusions from their review of studies on sex hormone anomalies (*also* Hampson, 1965 and Lev-Ran, 1974). Kessler and McKenna (1978) argue that in many cases where an individual's gender identity is challenged, say, by the development of irreconcilable secondary sexual characteristics, the person opts for 'corrective' surgery. In other words, they do not change their gender identities to fit the facts of their bodies, but seek instead to remake their bodies in line with their existing self-image (*see also* Stoller, 1974).

Yet, at the same time, there have been others who have challenged the notion of psychosexual neutrality. For example, Imperato-McGinley *et al.* (1979) report the cases of 37 boys from the Dominican Republic who, because of a rare genetic disorder, were pronounced girls at birth. The fact of this genetic disorder emerged with the onset of puberty when the 'girls' began to develop male-typed secondary sexual characteristics. Apparently instead of seeing their bodies as having somehow gone wrong, they came around fairly quickly to the idea that they were really males. Accordingly, they began to adopt characteristically masculine patterns of sexual interest and activity (*see* Zuger, 1970 and Hutt, 1978 for further critiques).

Dissolving the nature-nurture dualism

Reading through the above, one cannot help feeling slightly frustrated at the inconclusiveness of all this research. Hundreds upon hundreds of experiments, surveys and other types of studies have been undertaken and yet still we seem to be no closer to knowing whether there is a biological basis to psychological and behavioural sex differences. In part, of course, this is due to the high level of political interest in the whole debate (as discussed at the beginning of the chapter), for this ensures that as soon as somebody claims to have discovered some positive findings, a whole band of others set out to discredit them. However, others have argued that the *impasse* is also a consequence of the embracing of a false dichotomy or dualism between nature and the environment.

Segal (1990) argues that from its start, modern psychology has framed its study of sex differences within the terms of the nature-nurture debate. In other words, it has always seen men's and women's behaviour as being determined by two independent factors. Up until now, this chapter represents a continuation of that tradition insofar as it seeks to investigate just one of those influences (i.e. the natural or biological). This is not to suggest that the nature-nurture debate is a question of either/or. Even sociobiologists such as Edward Wilson acknowledged the importance of culture or society in the development of the human species. However, what the framework does presuppose is that the two factors can be separated out and measured against each other to see, perhaps, which is the major determinant.

Probably the most common version of this additional model of influence sees biology as defining the limits or parameters of human behaviour (e.g. Hutt, 1972). Men, for example, are said to have a greater natural propensity for aggression; whether or not they display this capacity depends upon the situation or environment. Nevertheless, the potential is always there. Most advocates of this model see the two factors as acting unidirectionally, with society 'amplifying' or elaborating upon the themes set by nature. However, it also includes those accounts which see the potential for cultural forces to counteract or nullify biological dispositions.

Attempts to expose the nature-nurture framework as conceptually inadequate have come from a wide range of academic quarters. Arguing that human behaviour is not the product of some straightforward addition or mix of biological and social components, they offer a much more sophisticated, interactional model of biological/environmental influence. For example, Paul

Hirst and Penny Woolley (1982) argue that cultural factors have played a significant part in the evolutionary history of the human species. According to them, the key moment in human evolution started when people began to walk on two legs rather than four; in so doing, they freed their hands to become 'tool manipulators'. The usefulness of these primitive tools created an evolutionary 'pressure' towards selecting those individuals with better hand-eye co-ordination, stereoscopic vision and dexterity. At the same time, the creation of effective weapons (such as spears and clubs) reduced the selection pressure for powerful jaws and teeth. We come to see, therefore, that while biology influences culture (we need gripping hands to hold a spear) the reverse is also true. One is always part and parcel of the other (*see also* Box 1.6).

Box 1.6: Dissolving the dualism

'Currently in Puerto Rico hundreds of girls have started to experience an accelerated process of sexual maturation from the age of six months. There are cases of 4 year olds showing full breast development and menstruating. This is thought to be the result of the use of oestrogen in animal feed for chickens – now the staple diet of a large number of Americanized Puerto Ricans. The effect of these biological changes is utter confusion of the children, their peers and adults regarding the appropriate behaviour and expectations, so that they are caught in the limbo of child-woman. However, it is not the biological changes that have unilaterally altered the childrens' views of themselves or their social relations; that is, biology has not had a direct determining effect. It is because of the ways that adult women's sexuality signifies that the effects are as they are. Yet the effects of the oestrogen in the diet – the biological reality – cannot be denied or disregarded. The problem is at the same time both a biological one and a social one. Furthermore, the changes can be reversed with a chicken-free diet; a move contested by the corporations – mainly American – which control agribusiness there. The problem therefore is also economic and political.'

(Henriques *et al.*, 1984, pp. 21–2)

Evidence of the inter-relationships between biology and culture is all around us. For example, it is well documented that since the introduction of a more Western-style diet into China, the average height of the Chinese population has risen by at least 5cm (2 inches). This demonstrates that one's stature is by no means 'natural'. Instead, it is always a (partial) product of the culture in which one lives. A similar conclusion is reached when one considers notions of the 'body beautiful'. For example, in Western cultures the current ideal of the male body has it as rigid, hard and machine-like (Easthope, 1990). In cultivating such bodies, therefore, men are quite literally *embodying* cultural values.

To conclude, there has to be some kind of biological basis to masculinity.

The gross physical facts of their penises, beards and biceps cannot be entirely irrelevant to the study of men. However, a man is much more than just flesh and blood; he is an object full of social significance; full of meaning. So in asking 'what is the biological basis of masculinity?' one poses a false question. It requires us to separate what cannot be separated: men are the product of a complex system of factors and forces which combine in a variety of ways to produce a whole range of different masculinities, and it is the purpose of the remainder of this book to examine some of the aspects of this complex network.

Chapter 2

Psychoanalysis and the emotional life of men

In this chapter we turn away from biology to the second perspective on masculinity we wish to develop – the arguments of psychoanalytic theories. Although psychoanalysts have some interest in the physical basis of masculinity, their starting point is not genes and hormones but feelings, thoughts, fantasies and self-experience. Psychoanalysis suggests that if there is a distinctively masculine kind of subjectivity, we should not look to evolution and natural selection for explanations but to family life and the boy's early experiences of social relationships.

Psychoanalysis was devised by Freud and his co-workers in the late nineteenth and early twentieth centuries. It is a theory and set of practices intended for clinical use and suited for work with patients in consulting rooms. However, despite these origins in clinical psychology, psychiatry and medicine, psychoanalysts claim to have discovered general principles which apply to all human minds. The goals of psychoanalysis throughout its history have been broad – to investigate systematically mental structures, the organisation of emotion and action, and to explain the origins of our psychic life. In theory, psychoanalytic techniques could be used to make sense of any man's life: whether patient or non-patient, contented or disturbed, analyst or client.

The beginning point for psychoanalysis is the lived, raw experience of individuals as this is presented to their conscious awareness. Patients in therapy 'free associate' describing how things appear to them, ideally without censorship of any kind. Although psychoanalysis begins with this record, the 'tangled mass of syntax, memories, movements, affects, and fantasies' (Stoller, 1985, p. 2) which makes up the contents of a person's mind at any given moment, it does not end there. The psychoanalyst tries to interpret the free associations, searching for patterns of cause and effect. The analyst might focus on repetitions in people's life histories over time or on repeated patterns in their perceptions of others, including the analyst, which might relate to early childhood experiences.

Psychoanalysts do not take a person's free associations at face value as an accurate record. Our experience of ourselves is seen as incomplete, full of self-deception, defences, and 'not knowing'. Self-knowledge is difficult to obtain, not just because we may lie to ourselves about our real motives, but because only part of the reasoning behind our actions may be conscious. Freud, and subsequent psychoanalytic theorists, suggest what is often described as a depth analysis of the human psyche. They propose that there are layers to subjective experience and, thus, different levels of awareness of emotions and motives. At any moment, some feeling states and wishes will be repressed, and these may only be recovered to conscious awareness with difficulty, if at all.

Psychoanalysis in this way upsets a collective Western self-image of ourselves as lucid and rational beings acting reasonably from clear and comprehensible motives. The reversal of this image may be particularly disturbing for men since it is men, above all, who have tried to establish themselves in recent history as the rational sex. For this reason and because psychoanalysis frequently focuses on primitive emotions and fantasies, sexuality, rage, anxiety and terror, it presents a radical challenge to accepted accounts of human social life.

To discover what such a perspective might have to say about men and masculinities, it will be necessary to work from a number of angles. Psychoanalysis has a long history. It is not a unified or homogeneous body of thought. We will need to look at the classic Freudian account of male development and then compare that with more recent psychoanalytic evaluations of men found in the 'object relations' branch of psychoanalysis. We will need to look, too, at work which links psychoanalytic concepts with notions of discourse and power relations. One of the difficulties with reviewing psychoanalytic accounts of masculinity is that they range from some of the most horrendously difficult, unlikely and abstruse arguments found in the social sciences through to theories found in popular and 'coffee table' books on men which are accepted as obvious. Psychoanalysis reaches widely varied audiences.

Despite the divergencies, this body of work holds some assumptions about men in common. There is no such thing as *one* masculine type for psychoanalysis. However, there are assumed to be some core psychological conflicts which men typically resolve in contrasting ways to women. These conflicts concern intimacy and independence, how to relate to other people, sexuality and the process of becoming a sexual being (*see* Box 2.1 for representations of these dilemmas found in two popular psychoanalytic texts on men).

Analysts Hudson and Jacot (1991) argue that the 'most masculine men' typically 'conceive of people as though they were inanimate and of inanimate objects as though they were people' (p. viii). They suggest that men are more likely to invest bodies of ideas, technologies, machines, science, and abstract sets of symbols with the kind of personal energies and passions women often

---

Box 2.1: Men and the trouble with feelings

'Trouble with feelings is what brings a lot of men into therapy. When I first met Sam he told me he had a problem with the relationship he had been in for a few years. He wanted some help from a therapist. He was extremely curt and addressed me as if I were some kind of management consultant; he needed to turn over a few ideas in his head and then see how they resonated in me. He wanted plenty of feedback, he told me. He wanted directions from me: if I were the expert, he said, then all I had to do was hand out guidance and all he had to do was follow. Then his relationship would improve.

It was, I felt, a very "masculine" approach he brought to therapy. Sam's attitude, business-like and to the point, would not allow us to become close. No feelings would get in the way of our "business". And yet it was precisely because of his detachment from his feelings that he had come to be sitting opposite me in the first place.'

(Heather Formaini, 1991, *Men: The darker continent*, p. 11)

'Win or lose, a man will carry the scars of this battle [with his mother] for life. "Most if not all the men I meet exhibit some fear of closeness or intimacy with women," says psychotherapist Tom Ryan. "But the fear and the wish exist simultaneously. All men who fear women are obsessed with concerns about masculinity. A man's sense of his maleness is always less secure than a woman's experience of her femininity." The quest for manhood, then, is determined from infancy as an oscillation between these two poles. The endless jar between the lust for freedom and the lust for intimacy form the inveterate yin and yang of the adult male.'

(Rosalind Miles, 1992, *The Rites of Man*, p. 40)

---

invest in relationships. Men are thought to be more anxious than women about the threat of engulfment by other people, and to be more likely to strive for separation, control, activity, and distance.

Regardless of theoretical orientation, and regardless of the way masculine internal conflicts are described, all psychoanalysts argue that the causes for these conflicts lie, in some way, in the events of childhood where the pattern and structure of the mind become laid down. The explanation lies within, what Hudson and Jacot (1991) describe, as the mental 'architecture' of men. Different modes of masculinity are seen by psychoanalysts as representing a range of uneasy balances or compromises between conscious and unconscious desires, arising because of commonalities in the treatment of male children.

Freud and the Oedipus complex

To understand Freud's analysis of male development, we need, first, to have a more general understanding of his view of childhood. Freud assumed that children come into the world with certain innate drives which push the child towards particular forms of action and physical satisfaction. Children are not like pieces of plasticine which can be modelled easily into any shape; they are active in their own socialisation. For this reason, Freud saw the process of raising a child, male or female, as inevitably a violent business, full of conflict, censorship and repression, since the child, in all key respects, begins life as an animal impelled by strong desires and instincts (Hirst and Woolley, 1982). Childhood involves a struggle in which 'the child must [learn to] swallow his/her desires in the face of the power of the real world' (Frosh, 1987, p. 36). To become civilised adults, children must move from their original primitive and anarchic state to a situation where strong desires can be held in check and aimed at socially sanctioned goals. Becoming human involves a conflict between two sets of forces – the child's drives and the inhibitions which arise from interactions with parents and others who act as representatives of society and the 'reality principle'.

Freud's theory does not suggest, as the biological perspective suggests, that male children have a built-in predisposition to behave in masculine ways, or an innate potential for some kinds of sex-related behaviour. The instincts he perceived in the infant were not particularly masculine or feminine, simply drives to satisfy hunger or needs for physical security, and, more controversially, a set of sexual and aggressive drives. Masculinity and femininity derive from the way these innate drives towards different forms of pleasure and varying forms of satisfaction are strategically handled by human communities in the shape of the parents.

What kind of sexual drives might a small child possess? Children are viewed, in Freud's classic phrase, as 'polymorphously perverse', meaning that the sexual instinct is generalised and attuned to all forms of sensual gratification (Coward, 1983, p. 192). Children are not naturally heterosexual and focused on the opposite sex, or even naturally homosexual, they are simply sexual and driven towards pleasurable, sensual (erotic) experiences in a number of body sites, receiving pleasure from eating, for example. Childhood sexuality is a form of sexuality which has not yet been organised into conventional social forms or into deviations from these.

In the first stages of childhood, both the sexual and aggressive instincts become focused around what Freud describes as the 'oral' and 'anal' stages of development – meaning simply that, initially, both parents and children will be predominantly concerned with feeding and weaning, and, then, with training in bowel and bladder control. In both stages the child has to learn to give up certain kinds of pleasures in return for increasing control and other kinds of bodily pleasures, and in both stages, there can be conflicts between parents and children over this renunciation and control. The oral and anal stages establish a certain pattern of authority, dependence, and independence between parent and child which is vital for adult personality. Although the sexual or life instincts along with aggressive responses are at the core of the child's pleasures and pains at these stages, neither the oral nor the anal stage is the key, in Freud's view, to the establishment of masculinity.

By the age of three, Freud suggests, the early physical processes of maturation are more or less established, and from about three to five the focus of the child's instinctive strivings shifts to more obviously sexual interests and to interests in relationships within the family. This is what Freud calls the 'phallic' or 'Oedipal' stage, the central stage in the development of masculinity. For the male child, the onset of the phallic stage may be correlated with an increasing interest in the genitals which can manifest itself in a higher frequency of masturbatory-type activities and in the predominance of exhibitionistic and voyeuristic actions. Crucially, since the mother is usually the primary care-taker and the main focus for the child (both male and female), these new sexual interests are directed at the mother.

Freud argues, that boys originally love their mothers because mothers are the main source of satisfaction for their needs for food and comfort, but, at this stage, the interest in the mother becomes such that it runs up against the universal incest taboo found in all human societies, and the imperative that sexuality and the desire for close physical relationships be directed outside immediate family groupings. The boy's conscious and unconscious fantasies and desires at this stage to annexe his mother, to keep her for himself, and his subsequent resentment and rivalry with his father are socially inappropriate signs of immaturity which need to be firmly suppressed. The boy must learn to direct his attentions away from his mother to attain an appropriate genital heterosexuality ('genitality') which eventually will be directed at other women: he must learn to move from the world of women towards the world of men. According to Freud, it is the presence of the father which is vital in mediating this shift.

Freud argues that, at the phallic stage, the penis begins to become symbolic for the boy of his identity and self-hood. The boy begins to fear damage and imagine harm which might occur to this symbol of himself. These unconscious fears of castration become particularly salient as the boy becomes aware of sexual difference and the fact girls and women appear to be without a penis. Indeed, the boy becomes anxious that his main rival, the father, may do the same to him and his fear of damage becomes acute. For Freud, this anxiety is sufficient to explain why boys at this age begin to turn away from their mother, repressing their desire for her and begin, instead, to turn to the father, identifying with the father's power, and idealising his characteristics.

'Identification' and 'introjection' are key concepts here. By identification Freud means that the boy comes to incorporate or introject his image of his father within himself as an internal voice (the 'super-ego') setting standards and ideals for behaviour. The father, you could say, becomes an internal conscience, sometimes harsh and punishing. As Stephen Frosh (1987) notes, Freud describes this as like the development of a garrison in a conquered city –

where social norms, conventions, ideals and mores, embodied in the father, come to act within the psyche of the boy as a voice within his head as he identifies with male authority. The child, ideally, begins to gain the potential for self-discipline at this stage and acquires the capacity to monitor and internally criticise his own behaviour.

This developmental sequence was thought to impart male sexuality with a particular flavour. Freud argues that, for many men, sexual desire and love can become separated too easily – the familiar Madonna and Whore syndrome.

> Where [men] love they do not desire and where they desire they cannot love. They seek objects they do not need to love, in order to keep their sensuality away from the objects they love. (Freud, 1912, cited in Rutherford, 1992, p. 44)

This separation arises because adult heterosexual desire carries overtones of the boy's first erotic choice of his mother. This desire, however, is repressed. When sexual desire and love come together for men, the mixture is too uncomfortably close to the early response to the forbidden object, the mother; hence men's anxieties concerning relationships and the development in some cases of the strategy of separation of loved objects (Madonnas) from desired objects (Whores). Freud also argues that it was because of this developmental history that sexual impotence or failures to perform become such a common male sexual problem and fear. In these cases unconscious anxiety concerning castration overwhelms male desire.

Overall, Freud had a very positive view of masculinity, commensurate with the views of his historical period (Mitchell, 1975). For Freud, men are the superior sex. He argues that not only are men more active, assertive and aggressive than women, they also possess a capacity for idealism, civilisation and 'world-building' not associated with the feminine (cf. Frosh, 1987, Ch. 2). Femininity, in Freud's view, is not only an inferior identity, a failed form of masculinity, but also a less secure and integrated psychological state. Men have the capacity to look outwards, beyond the domestic circle, to subjugate and discipline their passions, and the ability to direct their energies towards higher values and causes. Men can defer immediate gratification and the spontaneous expression of impulses in favour of rational planned action orientated to the future. Men, however, are also intensely competitive and rival each other.

This combination of idealism, competitiveness, assertiveness and emotional detachment is due, Freud suggests, to the experience of castration anxiety and the way in which the boy was stimulated to identify with his father and build a super-ego, or a strong conscience. Women's consciences, Freud claims, never quite acquire the same creative, outward-looking focus. As we shall see, this highly positive account of masculinity and misogynistic view of femininity have been substantially modified in psychoanalysis in recent years. As a consequence, theories of male development have diverged, too, from Freud's classic account.

It is difficult to know what status to give to Freud's account of the Oedipus complex. We could take it literally as a description of the concrete events of childhood, and, if we take this view, we might expect boys of a certain age to talk about their fear of castration, to demonstrate their sexual interest in their mother, and we should be able to witness overt behavioural signs of their phallic preoccupations. Many critics of Freud take only this literal reading, and find his theory difficult to stomach as a consequence, since it seems to assume a kind of active childhood sexuality and eroticism, and a preoccupation with the penis, quite at odds with our cultural emphases on the innocence of children and on their protection from sexually explicit acts and material. Indeed, some find Freud's story of castration anxieties and sexual fixations on mothers simply too fantastic to believe.

However, as Jennifer Sommerville (1989) has pointed out (*see also* Box 2.2, for another reading), it is important to recognise that Freud was describing what he believed to be a largely unconscious process – a process involving desires and fantasies which may be deeply repressed. Freud does not argue that mothers typically act in sexually seductive ways towards their male children or that fathers overtly threaten their sons with castration; he does not suggest that the average family is a scene of such primitive desires and threats. He describes what he saw as the unconscious fantasies of the small boy which

---

Box 2.2: The Oedipus complex as parable?

Stephen Frosh argues that an alternative way of making sense of Freud's argument is to treat his account as a parable – as a symbolic and metaphorical story concerning the tasks confronting male children in patriarchical (male-dominated) societies.

'... the father in the Oedipal structure is not just (or even) the child's real father, who may be threatening or appeasing, appalling or absent; he is the symbol of patriarchical authority and hence of all social authority under patriarchy, he stands in the position of the originator of culture and of sexual difference, of what is male and female, allowable and forbidden ... The real father slips away in this; what emerges instead is a description of the impossibility of interpersonal relationships (child with object) that are not already structured by something outside them, the "law" which society operates ... The Oedipal matrix is thus a symbolic matrix, not something that can necessarily be observed in the surface interactions between parent and child. It is the realisation by the child of the sexual and power structures of reality, of how the world is organised. What makes society human, what makes the child human rather than animal, is just this realisation.'

(Frosh, 1987, pp. 48–9)

have a reality and power of their own. These fantasies connect with and are stimulated by actual family events and family structures, but they are also a transformation of actual social reality. The primitiveness, urgency, and immense anxiety belong to and are generated by the unconscious.

As critics of psychoanalysis (e.g. Eysenck, 1985; Kline, 1981) have been quick to note, the emphasis in psychoanalysis on an unconscious or psychic reality, which may differ from actual social reality, means that psychoanalytic concepts can never be verified or tested properly. Psychoanalysts can explain, for example, cases where boys show signs of castration anxieties and yet also argue that Freudian theory is still valid, even if there are no overt behavioural signs whatsoever of boys' fears. This problem, as we shall see, plagues other psychoanalytic accounts, too.

Object relations theories of male development

There were always those who dissented from Freud's view of masculinity as the superior pattern for development, and femininity as the deviation, such as Karen Horney, Helene Deutsch and even one of Freud's closest colleagues Ernest Jones (Sayers, 1992), but not until the 1960s and 1970s, partly under the influence of feminism, was there a wholescale revision. Psychoanalysts began to suspect that perhaps it was men, rather than women, who were best described as the more insecure and fragile sex. Perhaps it was femininity which formed the basic pattern, with masculinity as a distortion of 'normal' development?

The American psychoanalyst Ralph Greenson was one of the first to develop these themes. Greenson (1968) noted how Freud's view of masculinity seemed to be directly contradicted by the research findings emerging from studies of transsexuals. Most of those who wished to change their sex through surgery, drugs and cross-dressing were men not women. Why would this be so if masculinity was a more secure and established identity than femininity? Why were men demonstrating the most radical forms of dissatisfaction with their sexual identity (cf. Stoller, 1975)? Tom Ryan, writing in the 1980s, similarly notes that there are typically many more men than women in psychotherapy because of some conflict about their gender identity. How, too, could psychoanalysts explain men's greater propensity to violence, perversity and sexual disorder (Miles, 1992; Stoller, 1985)? There can be no doubt that, in terms of every relevant statistic, men are more violent than women (see Box 2.3). For considerable numbers of men, internal conflict seems to become translated into the abuse of women and children, rape, and other virulent misogynies. Psychoanalysts noted also that the female sexual 'pervert' is rare; it is men who become voyeurs, exhibitionists, and fetishists, who are considerably more likely to engage in necrophilia, coprophilia,

---

Box 2.3: Male violence

'Some fifty millions have died at the hands of psychiatrically normal males since 1900. We are the death sex.'

(Phillip Hodson, 1984, cited in Miles, 1992, p.15)

Rosalind Miles comments:

'Not all violence is "sexual" in the sense of an act designed to produce sexual gratification or release. But all violence is sexual in the basic meaning of the word, determined by sex as breasts or testes are. Women may get angry, threaten and scream, lash out in fury or seek murder and revenge. Only men habitually prey on those weaker than themselves, stalk the night in search of the lonely victim, hunt one another in packs, devise initiation rituals, exquisite tortures, *pogroms* and extermination camps, delight in "Russian Roulette" ... and all the world's never-ending games of fear, pain and death.' (1992, p.15)

'Not every man carries within him the seeds of the sadist or tyrant: most men never set foot on the path that leads a bright youth to the adult destiny of a Caligula, a Doctor Mengele, or an Idi Amin. But today and throughout history "becoming a man" is inescapably involved with violence at some level with violence, either as perpetrator or victim. "Masculinity is *predicated* on violence", says London psychotherapist Adam Jukes, leader of a team working with violent men, and author of the long-term study *Men Who Hate Women* (1990). "It's part of the formation of every male as they grow up. If you're not "a man", what are you? The fear of that fear is at the core of male identity: it's quite peculiar to people with penises. 'Masculinity' is our escape from that".'

(Miles, 1992, pp.17–18)

---

sado-masochism and paedophilia. It is as if male sexuality is more easily diverted from the path towards mutual and equivalent relationship with another adult.

Rosalind Miles' rather 'purple' account of masculinity and violence in Box 2.3 underestimates female violence (cf. Campbell, 1984), which does exist, but we can see that supposed masculine qualities, once celebrated, have a Janus face. The 'dark side' of masculinity became more obvious to psychoanalysts. Assertiveness, detachment, competitiveness were seen to have their parallel in problems with relationships and pathological forms of sexuality. Psychoanalysts also began to note that masculinity seems to have a permanently defensive flavour about it. Men seem never to be sure whether they are masculine enough. Male identity becomes an accomplishment, which men strive to act out, but one which – perhaps paradoxically – is defined most clearly in the negative. Masculinity is the absence of femininity; it is *not* femininity. It becomes the product of a constant struggle against effeminacy (cf. Hunter, 1992), and this struggle appears to make men uncertain about their status as men.

In revisions of the Freudian account greater attention was paid to the role of the mother in male development, turning, too, to family relationships at a much earlier period of childhood than the phallic stage stressed by Freud. A period which became particularly crucial was that between the ages of 18 to 36 months. Nancy Chodorow (1978) argues, for example, that a basic and unalterable sense of core gender identity as masculine or feminine was established at that time. Typically, by age two and a half, most small boys display a conviction that they are masculine, a certainty which is expressed in distinctive body movements or the patterns of kinesics (gestures, stance, and action patterns) characteristic of each sex (Stoller, 1985). After this age, as case studies of hermaphrodites suggest, it appears to be increasingly difficult to change an individual's sense of their gender identity (Money, Hampson and Hampson, 1955 – *see also* Chapter 1). What happens at this stage which might also explain the more defensive and insecure nature of masculinity? The new explanations which emerged stressed not the inhibition of un-acceptable drives and instincts and the active role of the child, but placed more emphasis on the environment, particularly the emotional and relational structures experienced by the growing child.

Ralph Greenson argued that boys typically begin life completely and fully identified with their mothers and, thus, in relation to the feminine. Men with very few exceptions are reared by women. The boy's first model and first experience is thus of femininity not masculinity. 'All men have spent a significant formative part of their lives totally in the care of women who wiped their bottoms, fed their mouths and their egos, and held their hands whenever there was danger or difficulty' (Cooper, 1986, p. 113). Greenson pointed out that boys, unlike girls, must, thus, go through two separate further stages in developing a gender identity. They must first *dis-identify* from their mother and from the feminine model, and then *counter-identify* with their father. Girls, on the other hand, require none of this dislocation. Their first experience and their first identification, later continued, is with the femininity embodied in their mother.

> Initially, while symbiotically connected to their mother, both son and daughter perceive their father as 'other'. But then, as the male gender identity crystallises, the son sees that 'other' (his father) as 'same', and what was 'same' (his mother) as 'other'. That is to say, the son experiences a reversal – one of similarity-in-difference and difference-in-similarity – which his sister does not. (Hudson and Jacot, 1991, p. 40)

Put this way then, it becomes obvious that there might be more things which could go 'wrong' in the development of conventional masculinity than in the development of conventional femininity. Masculinity is now thought in this psychoanalytic account to involve a less stable and more complex psycholo-gical process than femininity. Boys may fail, for instance, to make the dislocating move from mother to father, they may lack adequate male role models, and they may also fail to counter-identify with their father.

Femininity in this approach is seen, as it is in biology, as the 'normal' or 'basic' human condition, with masculinity requiring something extra – masculinising hormones and the Y chromosome in the case of the developing foetus or maternal dis-identification in the case of the developing male child. Just as it is well known that male children are more vulnerable to mishap in their biological and physical development, perhaps the same applies in their psychological development.

Greenson's theory has many similarities with Freud. Both see masculinity as involving a reaction against femininity and the mother. However, for Greenson, the boy needs to move away, not because of his forbidden sexual desire for the mother, but because he identifies from an early age with her as a person. Whereas Freud places most emphasis on the force of instincts and drives and the blocks to these, object relations theorists (who are interested in the child's relations with its 'objects' or people in its environment) place most emphasis on the way the mind is built up from the internalisation of very early relationships.

In contrast to Freud, object relations theorists, such as Winnicott, Fairburn and Guntrip whose work developed in the 1950s and 1960s, envisage (in some ways) a more peaceful beginning to human life and hold a more optimistic view of the outcomes (cf. Greenberg and Mitchell, 1983). These theorists argue that an individual's sense of self, including both our conscious and unconscious subjective experiences, are formed through early family relationships within the 'interpersonal field' provided by the family or family substitutes. The unconscious is structured not by instincts or by inbuilt and pre-existent drives, but through the mental residues of these early relationships. The unconscious, in other words, is composed principally through social influences from the beginning. Stephen Frosh has provided a clear description of the object relations argument.

> Whereas Freud places sexual and aggressive instincts at the centre of mental life, object relations theorists emphasise the relational context of development. For them, the crucial point in considering individual psychology is not the biological 'drives' that underlie behaviour, but the quality of the relationships that are available to a person, and have been available during the formative period of very early life. These early relationships are understood to lay down basic psychic structures and internalisations which provide the template for later relationships; the quality of the early environment is thus crucial for the future conduct of a person's life. (Frosh, 1987, p. 4)

Let us look now at the boy's experience of identification, dis-identification and counter-identification in more detail. Psychoanalysts who observe the interaction between mothers and babies in the first few months of life argue that this relationship tends to be quite unlike any other human relationship in its emphasis on 'merger' and 'symbiosis'. It is distinguished by the extreme dependency of the child upon its mother, by the degree of sensitivity most mothers show to the child's needs, by the blurring of identity between mother and child, and by the potential for absorption of each in the other.

The British object relations theorist Donald Winnicott (cf. Greenberg and Mitchell, 1983, ch. 7; Frosh, 1987, ch. 4) argues that at birth the baby's sense of self is best described as 'undifferentiated'. The baby, whether male or female, experiences true symbiosis with the mother. He or she has, initially, no sense of where the mother ends and self begins, no sense of what is 'me' and what is 'not me', and only a limited or non-existent grasp of the properties of objects and its own powers in relation to these. A sense of self emerges, however, through early interactions with the primary care-taker (which is usually the mother). The child learns through frustrations and delays in the gratification of needs and, as the mother begins to turn her attention to other matters, that there are boundaries to their experience which define where self ends and the world begins. Babies learn that they are not omnipotent, but dependent. Indeed, at around six months, anxiety at separation when the mother is absent becomes possible, although it was not evident before, because the child can now perceive the mother and itself as distinct individuals.

This process of separation and gradual individualisation is one which all humans are thought to experience. It is a process which psychoanalysts see as pivotal in the development of self-esteem, a self-concept, a sense of physical security, and a self-confident and optimistic attitude to life. For boys, however, it is suggested that individualisation has this further dimension of a much stronger dis-identification from the mother as core gender identity begins to form.

What encourages the boy to dis-identify? Different theorists favour different explanations of this point. Hudson and Jacot (1991), for instance, argue that there may be a biological impetus: boys, they suggest, are constitutionally more restless, less tolerant of frustration, more active, possibly more aggressive, and less attuned to eye contact with others. As these traits become evident, the distance between sons and mothers becomes more strongly established.

Nancy Chodorow (1978) and Christiane Olivier (1989) argue that it is the reaction of the mother to the boy which is crucial in driving the boy to dis-identify. Chodorow argues that mothers have very different conscious and unconscious expectations of their male and female children, and consequently build relationships with sons which differ from those with daughters. Baby boys may not yet know that they are male, but their mothers know, and this knowledge will structure responses to sons in complex ways. Robert Stoller (1985) points out that this knowledge will have effects on many levels – at the conscious verbal level in the way mothers talk about and talk to their sons, but also, non-verbally, in patterns of holding babies, stimulating and playing, responding to upsets, and so on.

Chodorow argues that mothers experience quite different kinds of

attachment to their male and female children. Daughters tend to be perceived
as an extension of the mother, as 'like me', and this leads to some distinctive
problems and pathologies in feminine psychology (cf. Eichenbaum and
Orbach, 1982, for a discussion of the psychology of women which results).
Sons, on the other hand, are perceived from the beginning by their mothers as
different, as 'other', as 'not like me', as a masculine opposite. Since many
mothers have also internalised the negative stereotypes of women in society,
the 'otherness' of male sons is frequently more highly valued than the
perceived similarity of daughters. Mothers may also have a more sexualised
relationship with their male children, simply because of this sense of dealing
with a male rather than a female counterpart. Mothers treat male children as
though they were already masculine, and thus, says Chodorow, they become
so.

It is not only mothers, however, who reinforce masculine separateness.
As psychoanalysts point out, family relationships are usually triangular –
mother plus child plus father (Ross, 1986). Boys as they grow are, as Freud
originally pointed out, in competition with their fathers for their mother's
attention and care. The relationship with the father, therefore, can have a
double-edged quality. On one hand, the father can be vital in helping the boy
disentangle himself from identification with his mother by providing an
alternative model; yet on the other, this identification can be based on rivalry
and fear of punishment if the attachment to the mother is too great (Cooper,
1986).

As Stephen Frosh (1987) points out, the picture painted in object relations psychoanalytic theory of the child's early relationship with the mother
suggests the child, perhaps particularly the male child, will experience a
strongly conflicting (ambivalent) set of emotions. The child is driven by a
fantasy and sometimes a reality of total unity and perfect gratification, but
mothers are also experienced as all powerful and engulfing, as denying and
frustrating since no mother can fulfil all her baby's demands. The nature of
the relationship produces:

> ... an extreme degree of intensity, ensuring that the mother-child relationship
> will centre on the axis of separation/engulfment throughout life. The father, on
> the other hand, is conventionally more distant from the start, treating his child
> as separate and perceived as outside the boundary of the mother-child unit. So
> fathers are important figures in encouraging the ability to differentiate between
> self and others, and between people . . .. The separateness of the father enables
> the child to treat him as a genuinely distinct object with attributes of his own . . ..
> (Frosh, 1987, pp. 180–1)

Feminist psychoanalysts such as Nancy Chodorow argue that boys'
ambivalent perception of their mothers as both gratifying and engulfing is
one reason why men sometimes idealise but also denigrate women, and why

there is often a fear of powerful women combined with exaggerated admiration. Femininity is associated in both sexes with feelings of powerlessness and is experienced as a backward state to be transcended. Children grow away from the world of their mother, towards the public world of their father. Mothers become the objects against which children must struggle and fight to assert themselves. Chodorow argues, quoting the anthropologist Margaret Mead, that the experience of being mothered induces misogyny in both women and men and a contempt for femininity.

> One result for children of both sexes is that since 'it is the mother's and not the father's voice which gives the principal early approval and disapproval, the nagging voice of conscience is feminine in both sexes' (Mead, 1949). Thus as children of either sex attempt to gain independence – to make decisions on their own that are different from their upbringing – they must do this by consciously or unconsciously rejecting their mother (and people like her) and the things she is associated with. (Chodorow, 1989, p. 34)

This rejection is much more profound in boys, since their striving for independence involves patterns of identification directed away from the mother. The consequence is to reinforce the devaluation of women and apparent dread of the feminine found in patriarchical ideology.

In summary, we can see how this perspective explains why masculinity is typically defined in popular culture and by men in defensive terms – against femininity – and why men often find it easier to say what masculinity is *not* rather than what it positively is. Masculinity becomes, from this viewpoint, a struggle against the feminine, a struggle in which men are vulnerable because of their initial identification with their mother.

Case histories of men in conflict

In this section we will try to expand upon these psychoanalytic claims in more detail, illustrating the ways in which these concepts have been applied to make sense of a range of men's lives. We will begin first with Dave's story (*see* Box 2.4) as told by his psychotherapist Tom Ryan.

In analysing this case Ryan argues that Dave's behaviour indicates the simultaneous presence of a strong wish and a strong fear. The wish is for intimacy and closeness with women and for surrender and union in a relationship, but, perhaps because this wish is so strongly felt, it is combined with a pervasive fear about the disintegration of the masculine self, expressed as a fear of being dominated, trapped and swallowed. In the past Dave has coped with this conflict by avoiding women who remind him too strongly of motherly femininity and by oscillating behaviour – moving towards his female partner combined with movement away and retreat. Both movements rest on real emotions and desires, but since these emotions and desires are contradictory, his behaviour, also, is contradictory. He is in a no-win situ-

---

Box 2.4: Dave's story

'Dave, a thirty year old professional man, came to therapy because of his inability to commit himself to a relationship without feeling anxious and fearful. According to him, when demands for commitment were made of him, he retreated, fearing that he would be controlled or swallowed up by his partner. His most recent relationship actually survived for several years, but repeated discord and separations left him feeling lonely, depressed and despairing. Away from his partner he felt love and affection for her, but while with her, especially during moments of intimacy, he experienced feelings of irritation and anxiety. A pattern developed whereby when he felt entrapped he behaved in a contemptuous or rejecting manner, inducing his partner to reject and leave him. The pattern of rejection, separation and reconciliation was repeated innumerable times until Dave's partner finally decided to disengage herself from the relationship. Dave is attracted, for what at first seem to be aesthetic reasons, to women of "angular and athletic" build. He wishes his partners to be "firm and sharp". In other words there must be no hint of softness or largeness, particularly in the breasts – what Dave calls "the motherly type". On occasions when Dave has seen or been with a "fat" or "large" woman, he experiences a sensation of being lost or enveloped by their "layers of flesh"...'

'As with all men who fear intimacy with women, Dave is obsessed with concerns about masculinity. Even though his appearance and build do not strongly deviate from what is culturally considered to be masculine, he believes himself to be weak and small, a poor specimen of a man. He is plagued by the need "to prove himself" but always fears that he could never measure up to, or defend himself from, attack.'

(Ryan, 1985, pp. 22–3)

---

ation where it is impossible for him to gain what he wants, since his two strongest desires clash head-on.

Ryan argues that all men, because of the process of dis-identification and counter-identification, share some of Dave's ambivalence about intimacy. Many men, however, are able to form satisfactory committed relationships. So what is different in Dave's case? To explain this Ryan looks to the details of his particular childhood history. How was the general dynamic of masculine development played out in Dave's early life? Ryan notes that, unlike his brothers, Dave strongly identified with his mother. He felt protective of her, he shared her interests, identified with her temperament, and enjoyed doing things with her. Dave's father, on the other hand, was strong and aggressive, prone to outbursts, against which Dave felt his mother needed protection. Dave's brothers seem to have strongly identified with the father and Dave was considered a sissy by both his father and his brothers. Dave had a recurrent experience of being made to fight battles rather than retreat, since for the father and brothers nothing was worse than cowardice or not being able to stand up for oneself.

One can see from these circumstances why Dave is, first, so fearful of losing what he sees to be his masculine self, and, second, why his desire for relationships with women might be so strong that he finds it necessary to be on constant guard against what he sees as 'submission'. Perhaps because it would be so easy for Dave to establish intimacy and revert to a familiar model from his earlier relationship with his mother, his fear of doing so is even more intense. Ryan's example begins to suggest why even brothers who share what seems to be the 'same' family can follow very different masculine paths in later life.

This example also suggests the fragility of a masculinity defined mainly as the absence of, or the opposite to, femininity. Would Dave be so concerned about 'losing' a masculine self in relationships with women if there was some other conception of masculine identity available in our culture? Masculinity defined through difference with femininity will always be insecure and in danger of being 'lost', since a 'collapse' into femininity is always possible. The polarising of differences between masculinity and femininity in cultures such as ours makes it more difficult, some psychoanalysts argue, for men to accept their actual, real and authentic selves, needs, and desires (Formaini, 1991; Metcalf and Humpheries, 1985). Masculinity becomes an 'impossibility' in this situation; a standard men aspire to, a fantasy of conduct and behaviour which can never be realised in practice because constantly men will be defeated by their actual humanity and mix of feminine and masculine capacities.

In Dave's story, as it is narrated by Ryan, we can see one possible masculine response to heterosexual relationships. This story is not so unusual. Other psychoanalysts such as Robert Stoller have chosen to focus on much less conventionally masculine men and boys to clarify the origins of male behaviour. Stoller argues that one way of understanding 'normal' or conventional gender development is to examine cases of deviance from everyday patterns. Stoller's focus in much of his research has been on patients with various gender disorders. He has studied, for example, patients with biological disorders such as hermaphrodites, people with chromosomal abnormalities such as cases of XXY or Klinefelter's syndrome, and those with hormonal disorders (see Box 1.3, Chapter 1). His main psychoanalytic work, however, has concerned children, particularly male children, and their parents, principally mothers, who have been concerned about their femininity.

Stoller's work began with an intensive analysis over a long period of time with one family with a 'very feminine boy'. Stoller argues that from this experience he was able to develop a series of hypotheses about the family dynamics involved in the development of transsexualism which were then tested out with a further 15 families with feminine boys who came for treatment or for evaluation. Stoller points out that his sample is small and inadequate, since psychoanalysis is a time-consuming process which can take many years. He presents his claims as requiring collaboration and confirmation from other sources, but, he also argues that his transcripts of analytic consultations give an in-depth picture of not only the family dynamics involved in the very rare cases of 'gender disordered' boys but indications of what more usually happens in the familial production of masculinity.

Rather like Freud, Stoller stresses the role of conflict in male development. Conflict occurs in the first two years of life when dis-identifying from the mother, occurs again when the male child discovers the anatomical difference between the sexes, and is renewed when the boy enters into competition with his father and is forced finally to distance himself from his feelings for his mother. Following Freud, Stoller argues that individual minds typically grow and form through the experience of frustration, of renunciation of desires, pain and trauma. Humans become civilised through struggle, and need to be goaded to develop and mature. Usually, Stoller claims, boys develop within these conflict situations what he calls a vigilant attitude, a 'symbiosis anxiety', or 'barrier to symbiosis' in relation to their mother. This psychic structure allows boys to perceive themselves as having a separate body and identity with their mother and other people mentally placed on the outside of self. Stoller describes this resistance to merging as a piece of 'neurosis' boys acquire which pushes them to develop in the expected way.

Stoller's most controversial claim is that in the early history of very feminine boys and male-to-female transsexuals what is striking is the absence of this kind of conflict. He describes these boys as suffering from a 'developmental arrest' which is the source of their femininity. Stoller's patients suffer, he says, from a 'deficiency disease'; a deficiency of the normal goading to mature through frustration, and thus from an absence of symbiosis anxiety in relation to their mother. These boys end up wanting to be like their mothers, as opposed to the usual case where the boy sees himself as separate and different from his mother, initially wanting to possess or 'have' the mother and, when this wish is thwarted, turning attention to having and possessing other women in later heterosexual relationships.

Although men who wish to change their sex suffer a great deal from social disapproval and, as they get older, from the strangeness of their social situation, Stoller argues that this conflict and the struggles it generates are not basic to their personality. These are not disturbed or neurotic individuals: disturbance is a later addition, not part of their basic or core character. Stoller reports that the transsexuals he has studied are always entirely convinced that they are really female and that the problem lies not in them – not in their identity – but in the mistaken nature of their genitalia. Their belief is that their body should be changed and never their sense of gender. Stoller comments that it is difficult to persuade male-to-female transsexuals to enter psychoanalysis, and thus to investigate their backgrounds, since from their point of view there is nothing wrong with their character or personality, simply with their body.

What is the origin, then, of this lack of conflict, this confident sense of being a woman in a man's body? What does Stoller see as the origin of the behaviour of the boys he studied?

> Each of the boys, anatomically normal, was graceful, charming, and feminine in appearance and carriage. Each liked to dress all day in girls' clothes and to play exclusively with girls in girls' games; each wanted his body changed to be female. His parents said he had been this way since the beginning of any behaviour one could judge as masculine or feminine, starting around a year of age. (Stoller, 1985, p. 28)

Stoller points to a constellation of factors which seem to distinguish nearly all the families he could investigate with very feminine boys. First, he argues, these tend to be families with absent and/or uninvolved fathers. The fathers are often distant and passive, uninterested in their family, often away. Usually these fathers leave for work before their children are awake and return after they are once again in bed. At weekends, these fathers are typically involved in hobbies which effectively remove them, with the encouragement of their wife, from family life.

In contrast to the fathers, however, the mothers tend to be extensively and massively over-involved in the life of the male child. One might anticipate that very feminine boys might be raised by mothers who desire daughters above all else, but Stoller argues this is not the case. These mothers, he says, are women who are typically heavily invested in the idea of masculinity and dismissive of femininity. Women who are overjoyed to have a son and who treat this son as an extension of themselves. The son is seen as 'an ideal product of her body' (Stoller, 1985, p. 31), as 'the beautiful phallus for which she has yearned since her sad, hopeless girlhood … from her own body has been produced … the perfect penis' (p. 30). Typically, Stoller claims, during their own girlhood, the mothers of very feminine boys wished to be male and grew up in family situations absorbing the message that to be female is to be worthless. Despite this preference for all things male and despite their idealisation of masculinity, these women eventually accept their femininity at puberty, and without much enthusiasm or investment in romance, marry and have children. The choice of a passive and distant male partner unconsciously acts out this devaluation and suspicion of their own heterosexual femininity, but with the birth of a son, these mothers feel they have produced an idealised version of what they would like to have been.

Stoller suggests that other patterns also recur in the families he has investigated. Not all the sons of these mothers become very feminine; only one seems to be 'chosen', and what seems to mark out these particular boys is their beauty and physical perfection. It is as if the dynamic works only if the mother can see the baby as a perfect object; male babies perceived as ugly are treated quite differently. Stoller also reports that all the mothers he worked with commented that their son's eyes were large and beautiful and the mothers felt constantly drawn to long periods of intense eye-to-eye contact. What, then, is early life like for these ideal sons?

> With this cure for her lifelong depression in her arms, she is not about to let go of it. There is nothing complex about this motivation: when she holds the baby, she feels marvellous; when he is out of reach, she feels less so; and if he were out of sight, she would be anxious. Therefore, she simply acts on her desire and keeps him unendingly in contact with her, skin-to-skin, day and night, with as little interruption as she can manage. Father may be driven from the marriage bed, the infant taking his place for extended periods.... When one hears of a mother and infant in a blissful relationship in the first months of life, one thinks that this is normal, even ideal. One does not expect it to go on day and night with the mother trying to keep it from being interrupted, and certainly one does not expect it to persist for years. But in these families, we observe it still active when the children come to us, usually around age four or five. (Stoller, 1985, pp.30–1)

If the father remains unavailable and does not intercede between the mother and the boy, the consequence is a boy whose core gender identity seems to be female, who remains, in some sense, merged with the mother and convinced that he is really a woman. This, in Stoller's view, is the explanation of the psychodynamics of male-to-female transsexualism. He sums up his main conclusions from 25 years of research on gender in this phrase: 'the more mother and the less father the more feminine the boy'.

Critics of psychoanalysis often comment unfavourably on the slipperiness of psychoanalytic predictions, since both a thing and its opposite may be attributed to similar dynamics. As we have just seen, Stoller attributes the genesis of femininity in boys to over-intrusive mothers and absent fathers. Yet, in other psychoanalytic writing, we find the claim that displays of 'excessive masculinity' or male machismo are due to the same broad family pattern of intrusive mothering and inadequate fathering. John Munder Ross (1986) in his explorations of 'martial masculinity' argues that exaggerated masculine performance, characterised by tyrannical and aggressive behaviour, misogyny, and a rigid and artificial valorisation of all things masculine, can be traced similarly to deviations and disturbances in the usual or ideal pattern of family dynamics in early childhood. For Ross the best outcome of the developmental process is the formation of a man who is masculine yet capable, without excessive fear and anxiety, of recognising his 'ambisexuality', his capacities for fathering, for caring and loving, his desires to be passive and cared for, his desires for merger in sexual passion, while respecting the separateness and otherness of women.

The potential for this kind of man – the ideal father – is present, Ross believes, in the usual process of masculine development, although often subverted. Ross's reading of the developmental sequence seems to borrow both from Freud and object relations theory. He traces out a sequence beginning with the male infant's gradually developing sense of self as separate from others and, thus, capable of holding wishes towards these others. The boy's wish, says Ross, developing what, by now, is a familiar psychoanalytic argument, is to possess the mother and to maintain union with her. This wish, however, is frustrated by the triangular nature of family relationships as the boy begins to realise this wish cannot be enacted. In Ross's scheme, like Freud's, more emphasis is placed on the role of the father in frustrating the boy's wish to remain merged with the mother, than on either the boy's own tendency to dis-identify which Hudson and Jacot stress, or the mother's actions in defining the boy's difference which are emphasised by Chodorow.

Ross argues that, faced with the void of the loss of the mother, the boy develops two compensatory strategies. First, boys begin to identify with their father, taking on their father's traits and masculine characteristics more generally. Second, boys begin a secondary identification with their mother, with their mothering and femininity. The final masculine character structure, therefore, in Ross's view, is a compromise between a strong wish to merge with the mother, a defense against this usually expressed as a castration anxiety and fear of father figures, an identification with masculine and paternal traits, and a secondary identification with the mother's personality and characteristics.

The healthy man, according to Ross, is one who resolves all these elements in constructive ways, allowing him to adequately father his own children and engage in positive reciprocal sexual relationships. Unhealthy men, such as the excessively masculine type Ross focuses upon, fail in a constructive resolution. Their tendency is to over-play the masculine identification, over-repudiating the feminine aspects of their own personalities, along with femininity in general. These men cling to what Ross describes as 'phallic nuclei' in their mental structure.

Some of the themes Ross picks out can be seen in the extract in Box 2.5, a detailed case study of a man called HL. These extracts come from a period five years into the therapy, as HL is becoming aware of his defences against femininity, and illustrate some of HL's free associations concerning his own sexuality, his fears of having children, and reactions to his girlfriend, S.

Box 2.5 demonstrates the unmediated nature of material derived from free association in psychoanalytic sessions. It also demonstrates the irrationality and the primitive nature of fantasies and fears which psychoanalysts argue are characteristic of all our mental life, although usually disguised in conscious and 'civilised' self-presentation. Ross suggests that HL's hypermasculinity, his adoration and yet fear of strong male figures, is a defence against his primary identification with his mother – HL's emphasis on the 'paternal threat of castration' is a way of not recognising his underlying and more basic desire for 'reabsorption' and union with women. Ross suggests that what is crucial in producing this pattern in HL's case is his experience of

Box 2.5: The case of HL

'In part, he was afraid of punishment for finding a woman who loved him. Having intercourse in his sublet, he was literally afraid the landlord or perhaps a neighbour would become enraged and castrate him ... More than this, the uninterrupted intimacy was in itself terrifying. As Loewald (1951) long ago suggested, the threat of paternal castration served to fend off reabsorption. Cloacal fantasies abounded as HL became more interested in his girlfriend. And the patient, who had propped his feet on the analytic couch in the position of women during delivery, confessed that he was afraid that her womanliness was catching, that the secretions from a vagina he would have felt more secure in sadistically "scraping out" or "plugging up" would somehow contaminate him. When her sexual demands threatened him, he verbally abused her to hide his fears ... Gradually, however, he acknowledged his love of her, his fascination with oral sex. In the past masturbation fantasies had involved a sequence wherein cunnilingus was followed by a reassuring near-rape. Fitfully he spoke of "playing with her" pillow-like breasts, of his urge to melt into her, of his relish in the smells which had hitherto repulsed him. Even more tentatively, he admitted that on occasion, ejaculating, he had "squealed like a fuckin' baby". With this fatherly ambitions also began to emerge.'

'In the next session: "I didn't work on Saturday and stayed with S. S and I are getting closer. She cried after intercourse. It scared me – I still don't stay in for long. She wants to marry me. But I got no good models of marriage ... I don't want to bend over backwards no more – to submit ... Being stubborn is masculine. I wanna be Superman ... With my coat behind me, I felt like Superman with his cape. Women are supposed to be gentle ... passive. Female activity turns me off. Again I think about having kids ... I'm a baby inside and it scares me. S's breasts are so big; I sometimes think I like playing with them better than anything. How can you be a father if you're weak? ... Sometimes I think my treating S mean is a big coverup. I don't want to show her my fears. I'm real soft inside and care for her, and I get so scared for her ..."' [*Weeps*]. (Ross, 1986, pp. 57–8)

his mother who was intrusive and engulfing and yet hostile to HL, and HL's experience of his father as ineffectual and weak in contrast to the mother. Ross argues that the unavailability of the father is the trigger for the production of martial masculinity. The boy over-compensates by creating an internal phallic illusion of strong masculinity warding off a deep fear of femininity.

Although, superficially, Stoller and Ross seem to be describing similar family dynamics (intrusive mothers and absent fathers), while prescribing very different outcomes, the two accounts can be reconciled. Ross is attempting to sketch out the nature of the conflict that Stoller identifies as creating the 'symbiosis barrier' evident in normal masculinity. His concern is with what happens once the boy disengages from primary identification with the mother and the various compromises and trajectories which will emerge through different early histories. Stoller is describing what he sees as the rare cases in which primary identification with the mother is never disrupted and, hence, what occurs when the sequence of normal conflict between wishes for an object, defined as different from self and fear of the father, cannot unfold.

Social relations, discourse, power and the male self

From a feminist point of view, what is worrying about some of this work, particularly Stoller's, is the implicit devaluation of femininity which seems to continue some of Freud's misogyny. The assumption in the work of Hudson and Jacot, Robert Stoller, and John Munder Ross seems to be that the main contribution of research and therapy should be to restore atypical men to 'normal masculinity'. While not exactly celebrating men as the superior sex, these analysts point to the beneficial aspects of conventional masculine psychology. In this context, Stoller, as we saw, talks of 'feminine men' as suffering from a 'deficiency disease' or as experiencing a form of 'developmental arrest', which suggests his own valuation of femininity versus masculinity and the desirability of boys becoming 'men'. Ross talks, perhaps more even-handedly, of healthy men acknowledging both the feminine and masculine aspects of their character.

For feminist psychoanalysts such as Nancy Chodorow (1978; 1989) and Christiane Olivier (1989), what is much more salient is the damage men do to women, children, themselves, society and the environment. From this point of view, the problem is precisely 'conventional' or 'normal' masculinity. These psychoanalysts also have been concerned to stress the relationship between patterns of masculinity and general social inequalities between women and men. Male emotional development has to be seen, they argue, in the context of male power in patriarchal societies.

In this section we look at a range of theories of masculinity and male sexuality which have tried to examine the connections between the events psychoanalysts study, and broader social relations and patterns of ideology. We begin with Wendy Hollway's (1983; 1984; 1989) intensive and perceptive studies of British couples talking about their relationships. One of Hollway's concerns is the way men talk about, understand and position themselves in their relationships with women. She sees the patterns in men's understanding of relationships as cultural and social in origin, but believes these patterns also indicate the operation of unconscious and irrational defence mechanisms such as 'projection' and 'splitting' described in psychoanalytic theory. Men's talk about relationships is revealing, in Hollway's view, about the construction of broader power relations in society and

---

Box 2.6: Dependency, needs and male vulnerabilities

MARTIN: People's needs for others are systematically denied in ordinary relationships. And in a love relationship you make the most fundamental admission about yourself – that you want somebody else. It
seems to me that is the greatest need, and the need which, in relationship to its power, is most strongly hidden and repressed. Once you've
shown the other person that you need them, then you've made
yourself incredibly vulnerable.

WENDY: Yes, I agree. But I think there is a question about how much you show
yourself to be vulnerable.

MARTIN: But you do, just by showing that you are soft on somebody. It seems
to me that when you have revealed that need, you put yourself in an
incredibly insecure state. You've before managed by not showing
anyone what you're like. By showing them only what is publicly
acceptable. And as soon as you've shown that there is this terrible
hole in you – that you want somebody else – then you're in an
absolute state of insecurity. And you need much more than the
empirical evidence that someone likes you ... You become neurot-
ically worried that you're not accepted. Now you've let them see a
little bit that's you. It'll be rejected. It is not so bad when a false
exterior is rejected. The insecurity gives someone else power. I don't
mean any viable self-exposure. I just mean any little indication that
you like the other person.

(Hollway, 1984, pp.246–7)

---

concerning male solutions to the problem, resonating back to childhood, of
how to express and recognise desire for the other.

Hollway argues that although men are frequently reluctant to admit to
and, indeed, often suppress recognition of their desires, men's wants are not
so dissimilar to those expressed by women. Like women, men want relationships, they want to be looked after, they want reciprocity, safe havens, loving
and being loved in return. Hollway argues that men differ because they have
an equally strong investment in not 'voicing' these desires, or in voicing them
in particular ways, since, from childhood, need is associated with these
feelings of intense vulnerability. Some of this conflict over voicing need for
the other is evident in the extract in Box 2.6 from one of Hollway's interviews
with a man she calls 'Martin'.

So, given these sorts of conflicts, how does the voicing of needs in
relationships work out in practice? Hollway argues that if we examine talk or
discourse about relationships in British (and probably other Western so-

cieties) we find several common themes which construct different male sexual identities. First, there is what Hollway calls the 'male sex drive discourse' which is the argument that men are driven to have sex in a way that women are not, that men should, therefore, initiate sex, pursue women, and be active. In this way of talking, male sexuality is presented as an impersonal need, not a matter of romance, intimacy and dependency, but a matter of responding to physiology and the sexual signals of women's bodies. In adopting this way of voicing, men can present themselves as motivated, not by need of the other, but as driven by biology. They are still vulnerable to rejection, but rejection has a different significance. A second, highly prevalent, way of making sense of sex is one Hollway calls the 'have and hold discourse'. Here the emphasis is on commitment, relationships, sexuality as a sign of romantic involvement linked to marriage. Typically women are presented as the subject of this discourse and men as the object. Meaning that, for women, sex is often defined as an indication of love and commitment. They accept this discourse, and speak from it, whereas men frequently define themselves as outside the discourse, as the object of women's strategies to obtain commitment. The third discourse identified by Hollway is much more historically recent – a 'permissive discourse', where sex is presented as a matter of pleasure, with both men and women seen as having a right to sexual expression. Sex is seen as natural but also as no big deal, enjoyable, but separate from commitment and marriage. This discourse is one, Hollway argues, that men generally find more congenial than women.

Hollway's point is that sexuality and relationships gain their meaning in a cultural and symbolic context. There is no essence to sexuality, nothing it 'really' is, rather sexuality is largely a matter of how we understand it. However, we do not have a free choice in this understanding, since to a large extent our understandings will mirror the understandings collectively shared in our culture. Hollway argues that men and women are socialised into quite different paths through the available discourses – these paths, in effect, protect male power (allow men to assume the most powerful positions and identities) and result in men suppressing the needs they share in common with women.

The consequence, says Hollway, is that when men talk about themselves, their sexual experiences and their relationships, a type of 'splitting' and 'projection' is evident. Although expressing feelings, giving support, being dependent, being independent, expressing strength and weakness, rationality and emotion are general human capacities; men typically project weakness, irrationality, dependency, the expression of feelings onto women. Projection involves seeing in another person emotions that rightfully belong to oneself, but which are unacceptable in some way. It is not we who are angry, for example, but the other person, or, 'I don't need her, she needs me'.

In relationships it becomes not men who need support but women. It is not men who have feelings and are in some way 'weak', but women because of the identities and discursive positions men adopt. What happens, says Hollway, is that emotions which are not necessarily contradictory and opposite – one can be both independent and dependent, strong and weak, give support and express feelings – are seen as split and specialised, with one job for women and one for men. Hollway's argument is that men have a considerable investment in misrecognising their needs, taking up certain voices and projecting other voices onto women. Men gain a great deal from splitting and projection, but they must also suppress a great deal.

In Martin's response (*see* Box 2.6) and in Dave's story presented earlier (*see* Box 2.4) we can see one possible masculine response to heterosexual relationships. But 'moving away' is only one solution. Psychoanalysts argue that another typical male response, given masculine socialisation, is to 'move against' the other and female partner, finding a form of safety in domination, power and control. Stephen Frosh (1993), following Jessica Benjamin (1988), argues that many men experience not just intimate relationships but sexuality in itself as degrading, dangerous and threatening. Domination of the other is a way of obtaining emotional expression, care, attention and intimacy – the benefits of relationships – but minimising the experience of dependency and vulnerability in relation to the other person. As Frosh points out, however, even when dominating, men are still dependent since, ironically, the master needs the slave to confirm he is the master.

> Sex is a threat to masculine autonomy, because it generates and is built around relationships characterised by dependence. This is true even in the most sadistic of contacts: the search for the recognition of the other is that much more desperate, the need to prove oneself separate and in control is so much more out of control. In a reciprocally sado-masochistic relationship the confusions of mastery and dependence are even more obvious. And in 'ordinary' non-abusive sex, dependence on the other for pleasure and for a pleasured response is acute, intense and paramount. So why is this such a problem for men? (Frosh, 1993, p. 47)

Frosh argues that, in part, dependency is such a problem for men because masculine ideology, established in society and culture, idealises rationality, independence, lack of emotion, hard-headedness and free self-assertion – qualities which are usually presented as incompatible with dependency on others, but also because masculinity, from childhood, is the impossible struggle away from dependence and oneness with the mother.

Frosh suggests that these specifically male fears and dreads also explain why some men come to sexually abuse and violate women. Male violence against women can serve as a defence, he argues, against men's fear of their needs for women. It can be an expression of a man's rage at himself for being so 'weak' as to need others. Similarly, male sexual abuse of children can be understood within this framework as a way in which men might indulge pressing sexual and emotional needs, without confronting the threat posed by adult women.

Sex ... becomes an enormously important channel for the expression of emotion, which is denied any other channel; but it is also a terrifying threat. This is because it makes the man dependent on the other and also represents the overwhelming of control by desire. Masculine sexuality may then, if alienated enough, seek the least threatening, the most controllable of objects – which may not be the adult woman. (Frosh, 1993, p. 53)

Equivalent analyses can be offered to explain male promiscuity and the 'Don Juan' or 'Casanova' pattern of repetitive infidelity or one-night stands where the man moves rapidly from woman to woman.

Through the work of the German writer Klaus Theweleit (1987; 1989) we can see how psychoanalytic explanations such as these have been extended from the individual to the collective, from the patient in therapy to groups of men. Like John Munder Ross, Theweleit is concerned with the manifestations of aggressive 'martial masculinity'. His focus is on the psychoanalytic correlates of Fascist culture with its celebration of militarism, heroic youth, strength and might, male bonding, and the transforming power of violence. What, Theweleit asks, is the psychology of Fascism, the psychology of the 'soldier male' who turns to Fascist symbols for his self-definition? Why do some men find military discipline, guns, uniforms, marching in step with other men, and the development of a machine-like body and mind so appealing?

The materials for Theweleit's analysis were not the usual psychoanalytic ones of individual case histories, but an archive of the writings, novels and memoirs of a group of soldiers (the Freikorps) who played a crucial role in 1920s' Germany in putting down the workers' rebellions of the period, in subordinating communism, and in the subsequent rise of Nazism and a Fascist state. Although there are differences between the ideology of the Freikorps and Hitler's National Socialism, some themes persisted as well as some of the personnel; former Freikorps members became influential figures in Nazi Germany of the 1930s and 1940s. Theweleit argues that the autobiographical and biographical writings of this group of men reveal their habitual unconscious concerns. These writings include anecdotes and descriptions of particular campaigns and events, celebrations of Freikorps ideology, as well as descriptions of the men's emotions and feelings when faced with the attacking mass, and by collective protest on the streets of Germany. Theweleit argues that Fascistic attitudes and a military stance – redemption through battle – become a solution to the psychological conflicts to some extent shared by all men, but experienced particularly vividly by these men, concerning attempts to define the boundaries of the body, femininity and masculinity, separateness, fusion, individuality and action within a collective mass.

Like Ross's patient HL, the men of the Freikorps seem to be simultaneously attracted and disgusted by femininity which they associate with formlessness, engulfing floods, and radical otherness. Their response is to reinforce the masculine in the face of this experience of difference. Masculinity comes to be associated with the trained, disciplined and armoured body, with complete self-control and a rigid stereotyped response. As Benjamin and Rabinbach (1989) note, quoting Theweleit (1989), the soldier male experiences the threat to his trained and disciplined 'mechanised self' as coming both from the outside in the form of crowd, the undisciplined, rebellious, communist mass, and from his own softer, unregulated, uncontrolled human insides.

Militarism and Fascist ideology are used to bolster what Theweleit calls the 'muscle physis' of the Freikorps soldier. The muscle physis being a system of self-regulation arising from an implacable dread of outside life, which threatens to fragment the disciplined body's 'wholeness' and integrity. The Freikorps soldiers' most intense wish is to be 'men of steel' where 'the most urgent task of the man of steel is to pursue, to dam in and to subdue any force that threatens to transform him back into the horribly disorganised jumble of flesh, hair, skin, bones, intestines, and feelings that calls itself human' (Theweleit, 1989, p. 160).

Theweleit argues that war, violence and blood-letting begin to take on a particular significance to these highly constrained and self-contained soldier males as a place where a limited explosion of feelings becomes possible. 'Only in the explosion of war itself can redemption from constraint and control be risked: war is a kind of rebirth, the apocalyptic moment of battle when "the man longs for the moment when his body armour will explode" (Theweleit, 1989, p. 179). In killing there is a transgression against the boundaries of the other while the inner cohesion of the self remains intact.' (Benjamin and Rabinbach, 1989, pp. xvii–xviii)

Here again, therefore, is the same notion of masculinity as the development of a neurosis, or defence against femininity, feeling, human weakness, fragmentation, lack of individuation, lack of boundaries, and symbiosis. Theweleit argues that the soldier males of the Freikorps sought fusion through the military troop (male bonding) as a reaction against fears of internal dissolution, internal lack of control and fusion with the maternal. He does not specify, however, how this response is created *en masse* in the Freikorps and whether it is necessary to assume that all these men experienced the same basic family dynamics to result in this pattern. As Benjamin and Rabinbach (1989) point out in their introduction to Theweleit's work, it is also not clear whether Theweleit sees most men as sharing the same fantasies, attempting to approximate, to a greater or lesser extent, to 'men of steel', or whether fascination with these symbols emerges at some historical junctures rather than others as a consequence of patterns in child-rearing found in certain social groups.

Box 2.7: Psychoanalysis and its critics

'... with the exception of some inspired but fairly restricted conquests, psychoanalysis is neither a natural or a human science, but a self-confession by the bourgeoisie of its own misery and perfidy, which blends the bitter insight and ideological blindness of a class in decline.'

(Timpanaro, 1976, p. 224, cited in Frosh, 1987, p. 11)

'[Freud] was, without doubt, a genius, not of science, but of propaganda, not of rigorous proof, but of persuasion, not of the design of experiments, but of literary art. His place is not, as he claimed, with Copernicus and Darwin, but with Hans Christian Anderson and the Brothers Grimm, tellers of fairy tales.'

(Eysenck, 1985, p. 208, cited in Frosh, 1987, p. 6)

'... there is something very puzzling about this new psychoanalytic approach to masculinity ... No mention is ever made of men's power in the outside world. No sustained analysis of male violence, or of child sexual abuse, is attempted. Indeed, there is a disturbing and, for feminists, provocative tendency in object relations psychoanalysis ... to suggest that "women are the powerful sex", but they "give away" their power to men.'

(Segal, 1990, p. 76)

Evaluating the psychoanalytic perspective

The comments from Timpanaro, Eysenck and Segal (*see* Box 2.7) capture some of the exasperation critics often display in relation to psychoanalysis. They also point to three main themes in contemporary assessments of psychoanalytic achievements – a critique of the social theory implicit in some forms of psychoanalysis, a critique of the validity of psychoanalytic methods, and feminist concerns which we have noted already about psychoanalytic misogyny.

Eysenck and others (e.g. Kline, 1981) have argued that one of the major difficulties with psychoanalysis is the unscientific nature of its claims about areas such as masculinity. A more scientific approach, Eysenck argues, would make concrete predictions about observable events, would design experiments to test hypotheses, and would collect data in a more systematic fashion, focusing on quantitative and numerical records. Psychoanalysis proceeds, according to this view, too extensively on the basis of intuition, argument, interpretation and hunch, developing unwarranted generalisations from individual stories to people as a whole.

In response to these claims, psychoanalysts argue that this kind of criticism misses the point and ignores the distinctive gains which emerge from the emphases on free association and interpretation we described in the introduction to this chapter.

> The object of psychoanalytic knowledge is subjectivity, the flowing, changing, productive and disjointed experience that each of us has of ourselves and the world and the pattern of linkages that this subjectivity has with external events. The criteria for evaluation of the correctness of theories in this area cannot be solely empirical or observational, because such approaches operate on the wrong level to conceptualise and measure subjective experience. Other criteria that deal with personal *meanings* are the appropriate ones for investigating the persuasive and conceptual power of psychoanalysis. (Frosh, 1987, p. 9)

Whether you are persuaded by this argument will depend largely on how you view the nature of science and the development of appropriate methods for the social sciences. There certainly is a tension in psychoanalysis between analysing the individual case and proposing broad principles. As we have seen, some psychoanalysts do attempt to talk about the psychology of men in general, yet every case history also reveals the complexity of individual subjectivity and the idiosyncratic nature of early family experiences. Sometimes, as we have seen, simple formulae contradict each other when we compare, for instance, Stoller's claim that 'the more the mother and the less the father, the more feminine the boy' with Ross's apparent argument that 'the more intrusive the mother, the less present the father', the more 'martial' the man. It is not clear whether psychoanalysis can claim to have discovered a principle of male subjectivity (or set of principles), or whether its goal should be the more restricted one of providing tools and concepts for understanding varying individual cases.

Marxist and other social theorists, such as Timpanaro (1976), have argued that one of the main difficulties with psychoanalysis is that it tends to create mysteries where there are none. Timpanaro notes that psychoanalysis has a preference for complicated and laborious explanations of human motives, matching its suspicion and distrust of the more contingent ordinary explanations for their actions which people provide in everyday life. According to Timpanaro, phenomena such as ambivalence which could easily be explained by the contradictions in people's social position, and phenomena such as wishful thinking, which may simply compensate for areas of disadvantage and deprivation in people's lives, are instead understood as the operations of the unconscious. In a similar vein, clinicians from other theoretical schools such as family therapy have argued that psychoanalysis places too much emphasis on the past history of the individual rather than their current relationships. Individual problems, in their view, can be understood only in their immediate social context. Timpanaro and others (e.g. Leonard, 1984) have also pointed out that Freud and other psychoanalytic theorists tend to work with relatively undifferentiated models of society, described simply as 'civilisation', for example. There is no analysis of the different social circumstances of varying social groups. Diversity, in general, poses some troubling issues for psychoanalytic theory. One issue is simply the commonality of the kind of family patterns psychoanalysts assume. If the dis-identification thesis, for example, is to stand as a broad explanation of masculinity, psychoanalysts have to assume that something like the nuclear family is the basic male (and female) experience, but do family relationships fall so neatly into the pattern of caring mother and more distant and detached father, and how has this family model changed historically?

> My own mother worked her twelve-hour professional day within a week of my birth. Cooking, cleaning, empathic skills – she has none, though she is an excellent surgeon and acclaimed gynaecologist. And as I have sought sympathy for my own 'unnatural' childhood, I have found everywhere evidence of the amazing diversity buried within the ideology of the familial: fathers who were present and caring, 'working' mothers who were strong and powerful within the home, daughters who bonded tightly with fathers or older brothers, mothers who could not love their sons, mothers who never accepted their daughters, mothers who identified with their sons, and so on. As Liz Heron comments ... 'Each story belongs somewhere inside that general pattern (the public image of "the family"), yet none of them quite fits'. (Segal, 1987, p. 140)

Class and ethnic divisions are another important source of diversity. It is often unclear, for example, whether psychoanalysts commenting on men and male experience are referring exclusively to white, middle-class, hetero-sexual, able-bodied men (cf. Timpanaro's concept of a class 'in decline'), or whether they assume that masculinity has a common genesis and shape and thus the experiences of black men in different class positions, for instance, can be incorporated into their models (cf. Clatterbaugh, 1990, ch. 7; Spelman, 1988). Again, the issue which needs to be confronted is the extent to which variety and diversity among men compromise the search for a common psychology of masculinity.

In her more recent writings, one feminist object relations theorist of masculinity and femininity (Chodorow, 1989) has acknowledged these kinds of limitations in her earlier work, and has supported some of the points made by critics (*see* Box 2.8).

One way of making sense of diversity is to note that people in different social positions are inserted into very different power relations which con-dition their experiences and relationships: we will return to this point in Chapter 4. Indeed, many feminist critics have argued that one of the major problems with most psychoanalytic theories, with some notable exceptions (e.g. Hollway, 1984; 1989), is that they have almost entirely neglected inequalities in power, not just across the range of social divisions, but more crucially for gender development, between the majority of women and the majority of men.

As Lynne Segal notes, it seems strange that men, the most socially powerful group, should be described as 'vulnerable', 'fragile' and 'wounded'. Many feminists have noted the extent to which object relations theories effectively blame mothers for the children's psychological ills, holding mothers to impossible standards for caring and maximising their already

Box 2.8: Dealing with diversity

'Like all theoretical approaches within the feminist project, psychoanalytic feminism does specific things and not others. First, like the theory from which it derives, it is not easily or often historically, socially, or culturally specific. It tends towards universalism and can be read, even if it avoids the essentialism of psychoanalysis itself, to imply there is a psychological commonality among all women and among all men. Psychoanalytic feminism has not tried enough to capture the varied, particular organisations of gender and sexuality in different times and places, nor has it made the dynamics of change central. The dominant theoretical lexicon of psychoanalysis included gender but not class, race, or ethnicity. Accordingly psychoanalytic feminism has not been especially attuned to differences among women (and men) – to class, racial, and ethnic variations in experience, identity, or location in social practices and relations. Feminist theory and practice, of course, need to be culturally and historically specific, and it would be useful if psychoanalysis had the data and theory to differentiate genders and sexualities finely across history and culture. Psychoanalytic feminism would also be considerably enriched by clinical, theoretical, or psychoanalytically informed phenomenological and experiential accounts of gender identity, self, and relation among women and men of colour and of non-dominant classes.' (Chodorow, 1989, p. 4)

highly active sense of guilt. Mothers are powerful in family life, but in a context where women as a whole are powerless in society, and the flavour of this dilemma has perhaps not been adequately captured in psychoanalytic accounts of family life (cf. Woollett and Phoenix, 1991; Walkerdine and Lucey, 1989). Segal argues that without some sense of the powerlessness of women, their level of social disadvantage, and their devalued state in patriarchal societies, it is inexplicable why men should display the flight from femininity, and dread of femininity described in some psychoanalytic accounts of masculine experience. Perhaps, Segal suggests, men fear the feminine not because of the experience of an engulfing mother, but because they rightly perceive the association between femininity and powerlessness.

Some psychoanalysts have responded to these critiques while accepting part of their import by making a strong distinction between form and content. Chodorow (1989), for instance, argues that the *form* of the human mind may be pretty much as psychoanalysis describes and pretty much universal. That is, people everywhere will have conscious and unconscious motives and fantasies, and, says Chodorow, everywhere the basic emotional lives of individuals will be structured through their early experiences of family life. The *content* of those minds, however, and the content and shape of early object relations will vary according to local circumstances and the family lives people can construct within those circumstances.

This seems a much more satisfactory argument. Psychoanalysis is seen as providing some of the intellectual tools to analyse masculinity and gender development, but these analyses will need to state their boundaries of applicability clearly. We move from attempts to provide universal theories of masculinity to plural accounts which mesh with the psychoanalytic stress on the individual case history. Chodorow's final argument for psychoanalysis is negative rather than positive, but it is perhaps difficult to refute her logic.

> Until we have another theory which can tell us about unconscious mental processes, conflict, and relations of gender, sexuality, and self, we had best take psychoanalysis for what it does include and can tell us rather than dismissing it out of hand. (1989, p. 4)

Chapter 3

Learning to be manly:
the case of the male sex-role

masculinity
formed at
an early
age.

According to those working within the psychoanalytic tradition, the reproduction of masculinity is, by and large, a family affair. As we have seen, the
gender identity of each and every male is assumed to be determined, primarily
at least, by the pattern of relationships that he experiences early in his life. By
the time the boy is old enough to make his way out into the wider world, his
gender 'personality' is as good as fixed. At most, society influences the
development or socialisation of the male individual indirectly, by helping to
maintain a sexual division of labour which sees (or at least *has* seen) fathers
thrust out into the public realm of paid employment while mothers are left
behind to tend to the home and, most important, the children. However, there
are other theories of male socialisation which, while not denying the importance of the boy's relationships with his parents, see the family as just the first
of many agents which act on the individual, shaping his identity through the
course of his entire life. It is to these alternative theories of masculine
development that we now turn our attention.

David Lee and Howard Newby (1984) define socialisation as 'the business of learning the normative standards of society' (p. 265). Socialisation
describes the process whereby members of the species *homo sapiens* become
people: individuals who obey laws, vote in elections, marry, go to schools and
universities, hold down jobs, believe in God, and so on (Dahrendorf, 1973).
If society is also largely responsible for making males manly, then it follows
that somewhere among this gigantic curriculum there must be a particular
sub-set of lessons about the meaning of masculinity. These normative standards would tell us, for example, how a man should dress, how he should
behave in public, the things he should and should not think. Collectively they
would constitute what many social scientists have termed the male sex-role.

Role theory is an established social scientific perspective. Its precise
origins, however, are somewhat difficult to ascertain, for not only do the
roots of the theory appear to go a long way back into the history of the social
sciences (e.g. to the work of the famous sociologist Emile Durkheim in the late

nineteenth century), but they also seem to emanate from a number of disparate areas. In a detailed account of this complex history, Biddle and Thomas (1966) argue that the main foundations of a coherent theory of social roles were laid down during the 1930s by George Herbert Mead (1934) and Ralph Linton (1936) (a sociologist and an anthropologist respectively). Certainly for the next 40 years, role theory became an increasingly popular theoretical resource for many social scientists. Nowhere was this expansion of interest more apparent than in the psychological study of gender socialisation. Wesley and Wesley (1977), for example, calculated that from 1965 to 1975 the number of sex-role type studies increased by a factor of ten. Furthermore, 1975 saw the foundation of an academic journal dedicated entirely to the study of sex-roles (and called, appropriately, *Sex Roles*).

Certain academics argue, then, that men are socialised into the 'male sex-role'. Yet what do they mean when they say this? How does the role perspective theorise men and masculinity? In the next section we will look at these important issues.

Masculinity as performance

Role theory, as the name suggests, is founded upon a theatrical or dramaturgical metaphor in which all social behaviour is viewed as a kind of performance. Positioned at the 'intersection' of psychology and sociology, role theory draws attention to the fact that most people, for most of the time, behave in ways which are socially prescribed (Hargreaves, 1986). Very rarely are they genuinely 'doing their own thing'. Instead, role theorists suggest, they are like actors on a stage, playing out parts which have been assigned to them. Viewed in these terms, masculinity becomes seen as an act rather than an essence. It exists as a set of lines and stage directions which all males have to learn in order to perform.

Role theorists have suggested that social roles can be broken down into two constituent elements: social positions and social expectations. In complex societies like Britain and the USA there is a wide variety of different types of social position. For example, there are occupational positions, such as welder, teacher, priest; others which relate to cultural and leisure pursuits, such as choir singer, football referee, beer drinker, as well as positions in a kinship network, such as son, father and uncle. Each of these different positions carries with it a particular set of expectations about behaviour. For example, anyone adopting the position of a football referee is expected to be firm and fair in applying the rules of the game. Alternatively, priests are expected to be humble, approachable and trustworthy; while fathers, in the eyes of their children at least, should be big, strong and good at fixing things. All of these roles, like actors' roles, are relatively impersonal. Irrespective of who is playing the part, the expectations will almost always be the same. Furthermore, the role never 'dies' with the actor ('The King is dead. Long live the King'). As long as there is someone else to take over the part, the show goes on.

Erving Goffman was an eminent American sociologist who spent much of his academic life looking at the structure of social interaction from the perspective of the dramatic performance. In a series of brilliant analyses he demonstrated how the activities of ordinary people could be understood in terms of a range of different 'scripts', 'props' and 'stage directions'. Yet while emphasising the way in which people's lives are structured by social roles, Goffman did not mean to imply that all human behaviour is completely determined: some roles demand a closer adherence to the script than others. For example, those who play the roles of bride and bridegroom at a wedding are required to follow a tightly choreographed sequence of 'lines' and movements. The groom cannot kiss the bride before they have made their pledges, and the couple cannot exchange rings before entering the building. Yet upon leaving the church they are much freer to 'improvise' with their new roles of husband and wife. In other words, Goffman's point was that while social roles sometimes represent fairly rigid prescriptions with little scope for adlibbing, at other times they provide little more than a broad outline for action with the details of behaviour being improvised from situation to situation.

Goffman (1959) tried to show how people actively bring social roles, and thus social structures, to life. He said that inevitably we 'realize' our characters in society and depend on socially-shared roles and rules to make ourselves intelligible. For example, when patients enter a doctor's surgery they expect, not only that the doctor has a special kind of knowledge, but that he or she will be ready to display it. If, therefore, the doctor decided to cease playing the role of physician and took up instead the part of a chat-show host, the consultation would be likely to end both quickly and in a great deal of confusion. Bringing a role to life, Goffman noted, involves, consciously or unconsciously, intentionally or unintentionally, displaying oneself as a particular kind of person or social actor for an audience, and being recognised by that audience. Actors have stagecraft and learn acting techniques, and Goffman was interested in trying to describe some of these features in the everyday performances of ordinary people. How does the bank manager convince others that he or she is to be trusted and has authority? How does the doctor display an image of competence and compassion? How does the teenager 'act out' adolescent rebellion?

By now it should be clear how the theatrical metaphor used by role theorists can help illuminate various aspects of social life in a way which might prove useful for studies of masculinity. However, as Ralf Dahrendorf (1973) points out, it is important to remember that analogies work at a distance from reality (if I say 'Your eyes are crystal pools' I do not really mean it!). So while it may be useful to treat masculinity as if it were a mass of different but often inter-related performances, it is a mistake to imagine it as nothing more than a sham or hollow pretence.

> Whereas the unreality of events is assumed in the theatre, it cannot be assumed with respect to society. Despite the theatrical connotations of 'role', it would be wrong to see the role-playing social personality as an unreal person who has merely to drop his mask to appear as his true self... The characterization of man as a social being is more than a metaphor. His roles are more than masks that can be cast off, his social behaviour more than a play from which audience and actors alike can return to the 'true' reality. (Dahrendorf, 1973, pp. 13–14)

There cannot be many applications of role theory which highlight the validity of Dahrendorf's argument more clearly than the case of sex-roles. For while people might sometimes experience a kind of distance between themselves and the roles they are playing, very few would be actively conscious of having to work at being a man or woman (although *see* Box 3.1). Most people do not have to think about their gender performances. Indeed, it is unlikely that they would see their gendered behaviour as a performance at all. They would sense themselves as 'being' masculine rather than 'playing' masculinity.

In response to this conceptual ambiguity, David Hargreaves (1986)

Box 3.1: Gender performances

While gendered behaviour may be performed in most circumstances without a second thought, Kessler and McKenna (1978) demonstrate through their interviews with transsexuals, that it is still very much a role which needs to be thoroughly learned and rehearsed. It is just that most people become expert well before they are in a position to reflect upon the process. However, consider the case of 'Robert', who, as a female-to-male transsexual, had to go through an extended period of 'retraining'.

'Robert looked masculine as a teenager. He was not certain he was a transsexual at that time and tried to live as a female. Because it was upsetting when he was mistaken for a male, he tried to do what had to be done to be taken as female. He learned to walk in a feminine way, avoided wearing pants [i.e. trousers – NE], and in general tried to look like a female (for which he had the corresponding genitals). Although he was usually accepted as a female and would not have been considered by most people as "passing", in his words he "faked being a woman". He had to concentrate his energies on being seen as female. When he later began living as a man he no longer saw himself as passing. That, to him, was just being natural. In the social construction sense, however, he was not doing anything more or less to be taken as a man than he had done to be taken as a woman.'

(Kessler and McKenna, 1978)

draws a distinction between three different 'levels of role assimilation': identity, role-taking and role enactment. Sex-role *identity* operates, he explains, at the most basic, subconscious level. A person internalises the sex-role to such an extent that it usually becomes indistinguishable from his or her sense of self. At the other end of the scale, sex-role *enactment* involves a very self-conscious and superficial activity, such as might describe the way in which a drag artist plays at or pretends to be someone of a particular gender. In between these two extremes, sex-role *taking* refers to the way in which people take on prescribed sex-roles in the course of everyday life. Hargreaves provides the example of a policewoman who has to display 'masculine' behaviour when dealing with offenders, and 'feminine' behaviour when dealing with victims.

When looking at the process of male socialisation from the perspective of role theory several key issues or debates emerge (not least the one about whether or not it is possible to maintain an absolute distinction between the role players and the parts they perform). However, for the moment we will postpone the discussion of such detailed and specific arguments until after we have provided a more general outline of the ways in which the concept of the social role has been applied to the topic of men and masculinity. Consequently, in the next section we will be examining some of the work which has sought to describe the nature of the male sex-role, going right back to the pioneering efforts of Terman and Miles in the 1930s. We will then go on to consider different theories of how the male sex-role is 'taken up' or internalised; starting with the work of Talcott Parsons, then moving on through the efforts of social learning theorists and cognitive developmentalists to the more recent work in gender schema theory (e.g. Bem, 1981; 1987). The final section of the chapter will consist of an evaluation of the usefulness of the concept of the role in studying men and masculinity, focusing in particular upon the critiques provided by Arthur Brittan (1989), Bob Connell (1987) and Michael Kimmel (1987b).

Describing the male sex-role

According to Joseph Pleck (1981), sex-role theory not only increased its influence from the 1930s through to the 1970s, but for the greater part of this period represented *the* dominant paradigm in American psychology. The first landmark in the development of this approach, he argues, was the publication of Lewis Terman and Catherine Miles's book *Sex and Personality* (1936). Pleck notes that the book emerged at a time when there was a widespread concern about the state of American manhood. Americans had been shocked, for example, to discover that nearly 50 per cent of their World War I recruits were declared unfit for military service (Filene, 1975). They were also disturbed by the growing number of men who were 'dropping out' of society in response to the pressures of having to provide for their families (Demos, 1975). The feeling was that men were losing their manliness. Indeed, in 1910, the Boy Scouts of America was formed with the expressed aim of recreating a new generation of masculine males.

> The Wilderness is gone, the Buckskin Man has gone, the painted Indian has hit the trail over the Great Divide, the hardships and privations of pioneer life which did so much to develop sterling manhood are now but a legend in history, and we must depend upon the Boy Scouts Movement to produce the MEN of the future. (Quoted in Hantover, 1978, – emphasis in original)

Terman and Miles's main contribution to the development of a role perspective on men was to conceive of masculinity and femininity as two opposing types of personality, located on either end of a single bipolar dimension. Masculinity and femininity were seen as variable and flexible states, unlike biological sex. A biological man might express a quite feminine personality and vice versa. Between the masculine man and the feminine woman there could lie a broad landscape of intermediate states.

> [A]long with the acceptance of M/F types of the sort we have delineated, there is an explicit recognition of the existence of individual variants from type: the effeminate man and the masculine woman. Grades of deviates are recognized ranging from the slightly variant to the genuine invert who is capable of romantic attachment only to members of his or her own sex. (Terman and Miles, 1936 – quoted in Pleck, 1987a)

Terman and Miles's insistence that gender personalities do not necessarily follow from biological sex opened up the field for role theory and encouraged speculation about the social basis of masculinity and femininity. Despite this, they adopted a far from neutral stance in relation to the effeminate man and the masculine woman. As their terms 'deviate' and 'invert' signal, Terman and Miles were convinced that men and women were psychologically healthy to the extent that they displayed the characteristics 'appropriate' to their biological sex. The fact that American men seemed no longer to be living up to the masculine ideal was seen as an indication that something was going drastically wrong.

Terman and Miles's other major contribution was the development of the first psychological measure of gender (the M/F test – see Box 3.2) through which the supposed demise of American manhood could be scientifically monitored. It became a landmark in psychometric testing, providing the basis for a number of later and more general personality tests (such as 'Minnesota Multiphasic Personality Inventory') which were eagerly taken up by 'people-processing' institutions such as the armed forces, mental hospitals and prisons (Pleck, 1987a).

Box 3.2: Terman and Miles's M/F test

'In order to construct their M/F dimension Terman and Miles went around trying to gather a list of those characteristics which seemed to differentiate one sex from the other. At the end of this process, they were left with two equivalent forms, A and B, each consisting of 456 items. A person completing the "M/F test" was instructed to work their way down these two forms, choosing just one term from each pair of stimulus words (e.g. "blue" or "pink"; "wrestling" or "sewing"; "football" or "hopscotch" etc.). Having done this, the person's gender score is calculated by sorting through their answers and awarding +1 for each male-type response and −1 for every female-type response. Needless to say, highly positive scores indicated a very "masculine" personality, and highly negative scores indicated a very "feminine" personality. Having administered their M/F test to a large number of subjects, Terman and Miles found that the average score for males was +52 and the average for females −70.'

(Brown, 1986)

While Terman and Miles's work has been criticised on a number of different fronts, the assumed relationship between sex, personality-type (M/F) and psychological health has attracted an especially high level of attention. One source of criticism, Pleck (1987a) notes, emerged from the anthropological studies conducted by Margaret Mead (e.g. Mead, 1935) which suggested that the content of gender personalities varies from one culture to the next. This implies, of course, that there is nothing essentially masculine about behaving in a domineering and aggressive fashion, for in another culture the same kind of behaviour might be viewed as typically feminine. It is quite wrong, therefore, to label the effeminate male as sick, although how and why he has come to contravene his own culture's sex-role definitions remains a live issue.

During the 1970s there were at least two other challenges to Terman and Miles's basic assumptions. One came from a small group of male writers who claimed that the masculine man was the epitome of psychological damage rather than health (we will be looking in detail at the arguments of these so-called 'men's liberationists' later in the chapter). Another, more well-known critique appeared in the work of Sandra Bem (Bem, 1974). Bem's central argument was that masculinity and femininity were independent rather than oppositional states. To be a masculine man, she said, does not necessarily mean that the man must lack most or all feminine traits. Rather, she insisted, not only is it possible for a person to be both highly masculine *and* highly feminine, it is positively advantageous for someone to be so. For these androgynous personalities (derived from Greek terms *andro* – meaning male and *gyne* – meaning female) have a much more comprehensive range of qualities from which to draw in the course of their everyday lives (*see* Taylor and Hall, 1982 for a critique of Bem's concept of androgyny).

Many also noted that Terman and Miles's M/F test described not the actual personalities of typical men and women, but people's ideas or expectations about how they ought to behave. Gender personalities were conflated with gender stereotypes (this is a theme to which we will be returning). Most of the more recent attempts to describe the male sex-role see themselves as tapping explicitly into commonly held stereotypes about men and women, masculinity and femininity. For example, Williams and Bennett (1975) asked university students to sort 300 adjectives into two groups: those that were typically associated with men and those that were typically associated with women. Their results showed that not only could the vast majority of terms be positively assigned to one or other of the sexes, but that there was also a high level of agreement about how they should be allocated (Archer and Lloyd, 1985).

Of the studies focusing more specifically on describing the male sex-role, several have tried to reduce the mass of different sex-related traits down to a handful of core norms and expectations. Pleck and Sawyer (1974), for instance, suggested that the male sex-role could be summarised by the dual maxims 'get ahead' and 'stay cool'. Similarly, Brannon (1976) saw the role as consisting of four basic clusters:

(a)   'no sissy stuff' – the avoidance of all feminine behaviours and traits;
(b)   'the big wheel' – the acquisition of success, status, and breadwinning competence;
(c)   'the sturdy oak' – strength, confidence and independence;
(d)   'give 'em hell' – aggression, violence and daring.
        (*See also* Fasteau, 1974; Pleck and Thompson, 1987.)

Yet despite all of the different ways in which the male sex-role has been conceived, studied, and subdivided, there still appears to be an overriding consensus concerning the meaning of masculinity. According to most of these sources, masculinity is widely associated with aggressiveness, independence, self-reliance, and so on. In comparison, social scientific work looking into how males come to take up or 'internalise' the male sex-role shows nothing like the same level of agreement. Instead, as we will see, we are faced with a number of quite different theories of male socialisation.

Theories of sex-role assimilation

The key figure in the development of sex-role theory during the middle part of the twentieth century was the renowned sociologist, Talcott Parsons. Parsons belonged to the functionalist school of sociological thinking (the dominant paradigm during the 1950s), which, broadly speaking, saw the functioning of society as analogous to that of a living organism. The basic presupposition is that societies, just like plants or animals, have certain basic needs, and in the same way that all the various parts of a living organism work together to help satisfy these requirements, so must every element of society. According to this logic, therefore, the two sex-roles must have developed along the lines they have, because in some sense they contribute to the 'ecobalance' of the social system. The question is, what particular functions do they serve?

Parsons argued that societies require two quite different, indeed contra-dictory, types of social activity, to which he assigned the labels 'instrumental' and 'expressive' (Parsons and Bales, 1953). Men, he argued, tend to be more instrumentally oriented; that is, good at making tough decisions and getting things done. In comparison, women were seen as better suited to expressive sorts of activities; creating things, caring for others and generally greasing the wheels of social interaction. Together, Parsons figured, they appeared to form a perfectly complementary partnership. (Note a certain resonance here with some of the sociobiological theories discussed in Chapter 1.)

In offering an explanation of the origins of male and female sex-roles, Parsons stands apart from most other theorists of gender socialisation. Yet, if anything, he is remembered more for his attempt to provide an account of how people were 'fitted' or socialised into these structures (Parsons, 1942). At first sight this might appear strange since Parsons drew heavily on classic Freudian theory (in particular Freud's ideas concerning the resolution of the Oedipal complex – see Chapter 2). What was particularly noteworthy about this effort was the way in which Parsons managed to fuse Freud's psycholo-gical account of how the male sex-role is reproduced from one generation to the next with the functionalist explanation outlined above. As such, he pro-duced what is still one of the few genuinely socio-psychological explanations of how people become gendered.

In many ways Parsons deserves his reputation as one of the most impressive theorists of gender socialisation. Yet despite his intellectual achievements, by the early 1960s, social scientists had all but dispensed with his work and were busy looking around for alternative theories of sex-role assimilation. One of the main reasons for Parsons's fall from grace was that psychology, as a discipline, was striving hard to prove its 'proper' scientific credentials (vis à vis physics, chemistry and biology). To this extent, psycho-analytic accounts were widely perceived as failing to meet even the most elementary standards of good scientific theory. The most basic hypothesised structures (id, ego, superego and the unconscious) were unobservable and hence unmeasurable; the validity of the primary mechanisms (repression, identification, etc.) was untestable, and the overall logic was thought by many to be quite unbelievable. What was sought in its place was a theory which 'focused firmly upon overt influences and overt behaviour' (Connell, 1987).

Without doubt, social learning theory represents the most widely known alternative framework for understanding the processes of gender socialisa-tion. Based upon the principles of conditioning and reinforcement, social learning theorists such as Walter Mischel and Albert Bandura argued that people acquire and perform sex-typed behaviour, like any other, through a combination of observation, imitation, indoctrination and conscious learning (Mischel, 1966; 1970; *see also* Bandura, 1977; Bandura and Walters, 1963 for more general descriptions of social learning theory).

> From the cradle to the grave [a male] is inculcated with expectations, beliefs and values designed to make him conform to extant gender divisions. A boy will be expected to do things that boys do, and not things that girls do – he is not encouraged to play with girls' toys, just as he is not supposed to be timid when playing with other boys. (Brittan, 1989)

As far as Bandura was concerned, psychoanalytic concepts such as repression and fear of castration were unnecessary in explaining the take-up of sex-roles. For him, the process of gender socialisation was a fairly obvious or explicit process which could be described quite easily using no more than a handful of straightforward concepts. He maintained, for example, that young boys were simply taught to behave in 'sex-appropriate' ways through the administering of punishments and rewards. In this respect, the principles were no different from those used by dog owners trying to teach their new puppies to sit and walk to heel. In addition, social learning theorists assumed that sex-appropriate behaviour would emerge in the young boy as he first observed and then imitated the actions of his father (*see* Figure 3.1).

Figure 3.1 Sex-role identification
Drawing © Opie, 1978, *The New Yorker Magazine*, Inc.

Social learning theorists identified a number of important 'socialising agents' which worked together to encourage conformity to sex-role norms. Indeed, there is now a great deal of experimental evidence which shows how parents, teachers, peer groups and the media utilise an array of techniques to encourage sex-appropriate behaviour. Fagot (1974) found, for instance, that while parents tend to reinforce the assertive behaviour of young boys by responding to their 'demands' (i.e. cries, whines and screams), they generally manage to suppress the same kind of behaviour in their daughters by ignoring such outbursts. Similarly, the findings of Rheingold and Cook's (1975) study of children's bedrooms (discussed in Chapter 1) also demonstrates how parents can help to reproduce gender stereotypes (*see also* Fling and Manosevitz, 1972; Fagot, 1977; Lewis, 1975; Snow *et al.*, 1983).

Studies which have revealed the pressures to conform to sex-role norms within the classroom include one by Fagot (1977), who found that nursery school teachers tended to discourage each sex from engaging in activities

---

Box 3.3: Teaching gender at school

'Just like parents, elementary school teachers when asked will state that they treat all their students fairly, regardless of their sex. Research findings indicate, however, that in practice, teachers typically interact differently with their male and female students. For one thing, most teachers continue to use various subtle forms of sex segregation in their classrooms. For example, they seat girls on one side of the room, boys on the other; or they ask girls and boys to form separate lines; or they organize teams for a spelling competition according to students' sex. It is also not uncommon for teachers to assign girls and boys different classroom chores; for instance, girls may be asked to dust or water the plants, whereas boys carry books, rearrange desks, or run equipment.

'But [this is] neither the only nor the most significant way that teachers treat their male and female pupils differently. It also appears that teachers respond more to boys than girls, in both positive and negative ways. For example, one recent study of fourth, sixth and eighth-grade classes in the Washington D.C. and New England areas found that "teachers were more likely to provide remediation and challenge for male students. They gave boys more help in finding errors and correcting problems. They were also more likely to challenge a male student to achieve the best possible academic response." Other studies confirm these findings. Boys get more praise for the intellectual quality of their work, whereas girls are praised more often for the neatness of their work. In addition, teachers typically provide boys with detailed instructions for completing a complex task, but they are more likely to simply do the task for girls, thereby depriving girls of the valuable experience of independent learning through doing.'

(Renzetti and Curran, 1992)

stereotypically associated with the other. For example, boys would be steered away from the toy dolls while girls were kept from playing with the construction kits (*see* Box 3.3 and *also* Serbin *et al.*, 1973). With newspapers and magazines, films and television programmes peddling much the same kind of messages (Sternglanz and Serbin, 1974) it is not surprising, from a social learning perspective, that children even as young as three and four begin to regulate both their own and each others' gender displays (Fagot, 1977). For example, Garvey (1977) reported an occasion where a three-year-old boy was rebuked by a female playmate for wanting to pretend to cook the dinner.

A rather simplified version of this social learning theory (sometimes combined with elements of humanistic psychology) also provided the theoretical underpinning for a number of popular books on masculinity, written around the same time. For example, David and Brannon's (1976) *The Forty-nine Percent Majority*, Farrell's (1974) *The Liberated Man*, Fasteau's (1974) *The Male Machine*, Jourard's (1971) *The Transparent Self* and Nichols's (1975) *Men's Liberation* all made a similar kind of point. All of them criticised the notion that the masculine male was an image of health and happiness (as had been suggested by Terman and Miles, for example – *see above*). Instead, they saw the socialisation of males as an oppressive process which forces young boys into playing a limited and constricting sex-role.

> The new literature viewed traditional masculinity as bad for two main reasons. First, it leads men to do nasty things, like compete with each other, oppress women, destroy the environment, and ruin the Third World, notably by bombing Vietnam (that masculinity among the Vietnamese might have had a different significance did not occur to anyone). Second, men are themselves uncomfortable with it. There is 'role strain', a 'male dilemma', a 'crisis of masculinity'; men can't live up to the images. This was evidently a deeply felt point. The autobiographical sketches that peppered the 1970s books about men regularly remarked how the author had been taught the conventional male role, found it hard to inhabit, and eventually discovered the trouble was not in him but in the role. (Carrigan *et al.*, 1987)

Jourard (1974) and Harrison (1978) both went so far as to claim that the male sex-role was dangerous; pointing out that men die younger than women, have a higher suicide rate compared with women and suffer more from a whole range of stress-related disorders. Similarly, in her study of American college men, Komarovsky (1976) reported that more than 80 per cent of college seniors interviewed experienced some form of role strain; that is, a difficulty in fulfilling some or all of the expectations associated with the male sex-role (*see also* Box 3.5 below).

According to David Hargreaves (1986), Bandura went on to draw in his later work from a different theoretical tradition; namely, cognitive developmental theory. The founding father of this perspective (which can be contrasted with social learning theory) is undoubtedly Jean Piaget. Much of Piaget's work was with children; observing and recording the ways in which they perceived and categorised the world around them (Piaget, 1928; 1955). However, Piaget never really focused specifically upon the development of gender identities. Rather, this issue was taken up some time later by Lawrence Kohlberg. Kohlberg (1966) argued that the process of gender socialisation begins some time between the ages of two and five years when children learn to categorise themselves either as 'boys' or 'girls'. At first, he said, they often fail to appreciate the constancy of their membership, believing that by dressing up they can switch from one gender type to the other. However, soon they learn not only that their gender does not change with their appearance, but also that boys will inevitably grow up to be men rather than women.

Since the late 1960s the cognitive developmental perspective has become a very popular resource for psychologists working in the area of sex-role socialisation (Franklin, 1984). Some have adopted the approach wholesale, whereas others have used it to build more eclectic theoretical models. Yet this should not be taken to mean that the cognitive developmental perspective necessarily sits comfortably with all other socialisation theories. In many respects it makes claims which stand in direct contrast with those proposed by other alternatives. Hargreaves (1986), for instance, points to the marked differences between social learning and cognitive developmental accounts of the driving force or motivating energy behind the process of gender socialisation. Social learning theorists hold that the internalisation of the masculine role occurs primarily because the young boy is rewarded for performing its constituent behaviours. Conversely, cognitive developmentalists insist that, once the boy becomes aware of his gender status, the impetus for performing sex-appropriate behaviour originates from *within* the child himself. He does not need to be tempted and coerced. Rather, a supposedly natural tendency 'to ascribe worth to himself' impels the boy not only to see his own gender as inherently superior, but also to view all objects and activities associated with his gender as similarly preferable (Kohlberg, 1966 – *see also* Box 3.4).

During the 1980s probably the most significant development to the cognitive perspective on sex-role assimilation came in the form of Sandra Bem's *Gender Schema Theory* (Bem, 1981; 1985; 1987). Bem defined schemas as the internal (i.e. mental) conceptual frameworks that an individual builds up as a result of past experiences. They impose a kind of order upon the world, making an otherwise overwhelming range of seemingly disparate objects and events sensible or understandable. For example, in most Western cultures we have one schema which sees the material world as divided into the categories animal, vegetable and mineral, and another which splits the same range of objects into those that are either edible or inedible. When we go about our everyday lives we perceive the world *through* these schemas. That is, the world appears to us to be made up of rocks, plants and animals; foodstuffs and non-foodstuffs.

Gender schema theorists argue that the male/female distinction is one of

---

Box 3.4: The assimilation of sex-role stereotypes

'As early as two or three years old children possess some knowledge of sex-role stereotypes, for example about boys' and girls' preferred activities. Knowledge of sex-role stereotypes is correlated with the degree of gender identity/stability/constancy achieved (Kuhn, Nash and Brucken, 1978). By the early school years, all children possess sex-typed ideas of roles and behaviour, both of classmates, and of adults. In a study of 5–8 year olds, Hartley (1981) found that both boys and girls saw boys as being rough, noisy, untidy, immature and lacking concentration; girls saw themselves as being more gentle, and as having the positive qualities boys lacked (though the boys did not perceive girls as different in this way). In a US sample of 5, 8 and 10 year olds, Williams and Bennett (1975) compared the stereotypes held by children to those held by adults, using an adjective check-list. The 5 year olds showed appreciable similarity with the adults' ratings, and this increased by 8 years, but no further by 10 years. The male stereotype seemed to be learned at an earlier age than the female stereotype.'

(P K Smith 1986)

---

the most important classificatory systems in human social life (Bem, 1987). The social world in which children grow up, they point out, is thoroughly gendered.

> Starting with linguistic labels – including, usually the child's own name – and continuing with toys, clothes, hairstyles, parents' socialisation practices, the contents of children's books, television programmes, advertisements, school teachings and socialisation efforts, and peer socialisation, gender differentiation is everywhere imposed from 'outside', so to speak. (Zammuner, 1987)

Consequently, it is argued, children soon learn to interpret their experiences through this same system of categories; including, importantly, their own sense of self. However, Bem suggests that not all children do this to the same extent. In other words, while some individuals see themselves as entirely defined by a particular gender category (i.e. where the two concepts are virtually synonymous), others imagine there to be at least some degree of difference between the two. This, she maintains, is what differentiates 'strongly sex-typed' from 'non-sex-typed' people.

Bem assumes that the degree to which people were sex-typed could be directly measured using her Bem Sex Role Inventory (BSRI – examples of which can be seen in Chapter 1, Table 1.1). Furthermore, she suggests that the degree to which a person was sex-typed indicated something about the extent to which they tended to code or classify information about themselves or about the world in general in terms of sex-roles. In order to test this hypothesis, Bem (1981) compared subjects' BSRI scores with the degree to which they tended to recall sets of stimulus words in terms of gender. She found, as expected, that those people who were more strongly 'sex-typed' tended to recall lists of words much more in terms of tight gender 'clusters' (for a critique of Bem's methods of analysis *see* Spence and Helmreich, 1978).

In this section we have reviewed a number of different theories concerning the ways in which the male sex-role is absorbed – from Parsons' socio-psychoanalytical synthesis through social learning theory to different cognitive developmental theories. Between them they enabled the concept of the male sex-role to remain at the forefront of explanations of gender socialisation for several decades. However, in recent years the entire paradigm has come under a barrage of searching criticism from a number of different quarters. Consequently, in the next two sections we will switch from a predominantly descriptive style of analysis to one based more upon evaluation. We will begin by looking at the reasons why the concept of the male sex-role remained so popular as a theoretical resource for such a long time, before moving on to consider the trenchant criticisms which since have forced it into a period of decline.

The merits of sex-role theory

Perhaps the most obvious appeal of the role theory approach to gender socialisation is that, on a kind of common-sense level, it seems somehow right. In other words, when people think in terms of their own experiences of growing up, it is likely that the social learning theory of role assimilation, in particular, would 'ring true' in some way. Men, for example, might be able to remember occasions when, as small boys, they were told that they should be brave and strong. They might also recall being teased for doing things more stereotypically associated with girls. The theory may also appear to be supported by our experiences as parents, for there cannot be many parents who have not marvelled at how quickly their babies learn to copy their behaviour, even down to the smallest mannerism.

However, the concept of the male sex-role has more than just an intuitive appeal. Indeed, it has a number of significant theoretical strengths compared with the biological and psychoanalytical perspectives. For example, one of the main difficulties for a biological approach to men and masculinity is trying to explain the pace of historical change. Men today are in many ways quite different from their great-great-grandfathers and even more unlike men of the Dark and Middle Ages; but even though biologists can account for changes in a species in terms of the theory of evolution, there is no way in which the mechanisms of natural selection could account for developments which occur over a timescale of just a few years. Instead, these have to be explained at the level of culture or society.

Sex-role theory also avoids some of the criticisms aimed at psychoanalytic theory – as outlined in Chapter 2. First, while psychoanalytic explanations have been attacked for their untestability, there is a long and established tradition of empirical work looking into the effect of various reinforcement schedules (e.g. work of B F Skinner) and patterns of imitation (e.g. Bandura and Walters, 1963; Bandura, Ross and Ross, 1961; 1963). Second, as mentioned earlier, sex-role theory is more parsimonious than its psychoanalytic counterparts. That is, it sets out to explain only those things which can be observed, and aims to do so in the most simple and straightforward manner. Third and finally, most branches of sex-role theory see the socialisation process as something which continues to operate throughout a person's life, rather than stopping in early childhood. As such it gets away from the slightly deterministic flavour of much psychoanalytic writing.

In general terms, probably the most important strength of sex-role theory is that it forms, or at least appears to form, part of a genuinely social account of human action and development. In other words, it is derived from a broad theoretical perspective which explains any systematic differences between people's behaviour in terms of different social expectations rather than the biological factors described in Chapter 1. Moreover, sex-role theory provides us with a simple framework for understanding the relationship between society and the individual (surely one of the important and difficult theoretical tasks for the social sciences). Any adequate theory of male socialisation has to be able to explain how individual males come to 'inhabit' socially shared conceptions about what it means to be a man. As we have seen, sex-role theory accomplishes this through the notion of males internalising or being socialised into the masculine role (again, this is what Ralf Dahrendorf meant when he said that role theory sat at the intersection of psychology and sociology). As such, sex-role theory would appear to be a social psychological theory *par excellence*.

Another major strength of the sex-role perspective on men and masculinity is that it provides what Connell (1987) calls a 'politics of reform'. The point is, if masculinity is a reflection of biological forces then, as we explained in Chapter 1, the way forward for those interested in challenging the status quo is, at best, difficult and, at worst, hopeless. However, if the tendency of men to be aggressive, dominating and emotionally inarticulate is mainly a result of role expectations that define them as such, then the obvious way ahead is to change those expectations. Men simply need to be taught to be more gentle, considerate and emotionally expressive. It has been precisely this kind of reasoning, Connell points out, which has brought about the development of non-sexist school curriculae, anti-discrimination laws, equal opportunity policies and programmes of 'affirmative action'.

The positive political implications of sex-role theory also appealed to the male liberationists working during the 1970s. Writers such as Nichols (1975) and Farrell (1974) latched on to the theory claiming that men, like women, were the victims of restrictive and damaging sex-roles. Just as the female sex-role pressured women into being passive, cheerful and dependent, so men were being forced into being competitive, violent and goal-oriented. Men, Jourard (1971) complained, were caught in a particularly nasty dilemma or 'double bind'. If he fulfilled his prescribed role, then he denied himself some basic human requirements (such as the need to both give and receive love and affection). Yet if he refused to conform to the role, he risked being thought of, and thinking of himself, as unmanly (*see* Box 3.5). The breaking down of sex-roles appeared, therefore, to benefit both sexes (maybe even equally). For without them, both men and women would be free to develop to their full human potential.

Box 3.5: The male dilemma

'From about the age of seven to twelve sporting activities partly acted as masculinizing practices and played a part in developing my "masculine" identity against a background of great personal insecurity. In my case the usual problematic process of separation and individuation from my mother was made worse by an over-close attachment to her and the prolonged absence of my father. So I was all at sea with my gender identification. My ambivalence about wanting to gain independence from my mother to model myself on my father was shown in the way that, although I partly wanted to be accepted by an actively virile schoolboy culture that stressed the values of physical toughness, aggression, honour and daring at the expense of "girlish" softness and physical incompetence, another part of me felt extremely uncomfortable within conventional masculine behaviour and that part was able to use sport to express a number of choked, contradictory feelings and qualities like a sense of grace, sensuality, poise, passion and, sometimes, even delicacy.'

(David Jackson 1990)

In this way, Carrigan *et al.* (1987) point out, the men's liberationists managed to reinterpret feminism as a project parallel to their own. No longer were they seen as the *cause* of women's problems. Rather, men and women stood together, side by side, against a common enemy; namely, sex-role stereotypes.

In summary, we can see that role theory appears to have a great deal to offer. First, it seems to provide a perspective which deals sensitively with the relationship between society and the individual by illustrating the ways in which people come to embody (sometimes quite literally) the norms and values of their cultural community. In this sense it is less individualistic than psychoanalytic accounts. Second, insofar as it permits a movement away from biological assumptions about sex differences, not only does it hold the possibility of a more healthy and equitable society, but also provides broad guidelines regarding how such a goal might be achieved. Finally, compared with many other theories of gender socialisation (and especially psychoanalytic accounts), the role perspective appears plausible; fitting in with people's own everyday experiences.

Yet despite these considerable strengths, the concept of the male sex-role has been the focus of a great deal of critical attention. Indeed, some commentators have gone so far as to argue, not only that the male sex-role itself does not even exist, but also that the entire dramaturgical framework should be abandoned as 'internally incoherent'. Let us now look in detail at some of these arguments.

Problems with sex-role theory

One of the most searching criticisms of the role perspective comes in the form of Bob Connell's claim that, upon careful examination, the social basis of role theory turns out to be illusory (Connell, 1987). Role theory is generally understood as a form of social determinism. It sees people, in other words, as 'trapped' into playing sets of stereotypical roles. Role theory suggests that people are ensnared by a mixture of bribery and coercion. More specifically, they are rewarded for role conformity and punished for non-conformity. Little boys, for example, are encouraged to be competitive, assertive and brave, and ridiculed for being passive, quiet or 'soft'. But why, Connell asks, do the 'second parties' apply these sanctions? What, in other words, motivates people such as parents, nursery school teachers and workmates to pressure others (but particularly youngsters) into fulfilling the expectations associated with the 'appropriate' sex role? As Connell quite rightly points out, the motivation cannot be explained in terms of the demands of another kind of role; say, the role of 'socialiser'. For this merely displaces the problem rather than solves it (i.e. we are left asking why it is that people apply sanctions to encourage others to become sanctioners). In the end, Connell suggests, the supposed social dimension of role theory 'ironically dissolves into voluntarism' with people simply choosing to encourage conformity. The point being, of course, that individual choice is a curious basis for a social theory of masculinity.

Clearly this objection has a particular force when applied to social learning theories of sex-role assimilation. For it is this formulation which imagines parents, teachers and others reinforcing 'manly' behaviour and punishing effeminacy in boys. However, Connell's argument is less obvious in the case of both cognitive theories of sex-role assimilation and in Parsons's functionalist account, because neither relies heavily upon the concept of 'external' reinforcement. Cognitive theorists, for example, claim that the motivation to assimilate comes, supposedly at least, as much from within the individual as it is imposed from outside. On the other hand, Parsons's account of sex-role assimilation contains a kind of dual-level model of motivation where the male individual is simultaneously driven to conform to the appropriate sex-role both on account of his fear of castration and by some kind of 'evolutionary' pressure to adopt those forms of social activity (i.e. 'instrumental') which contribute to the smooth and successful working of society (this could be referred to as the 'motivation of function').

The social status of sex-role theory is perhaps more seriously challenged if we turn to the question of where sex-roles come from, for with the obvious exception of Parsons, sex-role theorists have routinely ignored the issue of *why* there is one role for males and another for females. A number of critics have suggested that sex-role theorists simply assume the existence of two sex-roles on the basis that there are two biologically distinct sexes (e.g. Connell, 1987; Brittan, 1989). This reliance upon biological categories is reflected, Connell argues, in the name of the theory itself – being a straightforward combination of two different elements, one social and the other biological.

> The socialisation case assumes that a man's and a woman's body respectively provide *different* foundations on which the social and cultural world builds its gender system. Biological differences are the starting point for the construction of an edifice of gender differences. *Roles are added to biology to give us gender* – and, once this happens, men and women acquire their appropriate gender identities. (Brittan, 1989, p. 21 – emphasis in original)

The fundamental reliance of sex-role theory upon biological categories is given particular emphasis here by Brittan's deliberate use of a common architectural metaphor. In portraying sex-roles as being built onto the foundations provided by biology, Brittan implies that sex-role theorists not only see biological sex differences as in some sense coming *before* gender differences, but that they also imagine the biological make-up of the two sexes as in some way directly influencing the type of roles which go on top of them (in the same way that one cannot erect tower blocks on shallow foundations). Again, therefore, the prominence given to biology undermines sex-role theory's claim to be a genuinely social theory.

Even more problematic are the writings of authors such as Pleck and Sawyer (1974), Nichols (1975) and others within the humanist tradition, who portray the process of role acquisition as a destructive, rather than a constructive process. According to these theorists, infants of both sexes enter into the world bearing a similar full complement of gender characteristics. Both males and females, they insist, are born with the same propensities to aggress, love, and compete; the same desires for warmth, recognition and respect. The socialisation of men and women, they argue, represents the closing down of certain propensities and the denial of particular needs. Women repress their ambition and their assertiveness, whereas men deny their sensitivity. Becoming gendered, therefore, is seen as a deeply damaging and detrimental process from which both men and women require liberation.

'We no longer want to feel the need to perform sexually, socially, or in any way live up to an imposed male role ... we want to relate to both men and women in more human ways – with warmth, sensitivity, emotion, and honesty ... we want to be equal with women and to end destructive competitive relationships with men.' (A declaration by the Berkeley Men's Centre – quoted in Pleck and Sawyer, 1974, pp. 173–4)

According to this version of sex-role theory, a person's 'authentic' or 'real' self does not have its origins in society. Rather, as with some branches of psychoanalytical theorising (notably that of Carl Jung), the account relies upon the existence of some kind of pre-social self, the nature of which must, presumably, be either biological or mystical (Segal, 1990).

It is interesting that this distinction between real, inner, or authentic selves and enacted social selves, which so undermines role theory's claim to be a thoroughly social perspective, lies at the very heart of the theatrical metaphor upon which role theory is founded. Our knowledge of the stage allows us to appreciate the difference between the actors and the parts they perform. We know, for example, that the Sylvester Stallone who played the boxer in *Rocky* was the same Sylvester Stallone who played the war hero in *Rambo*. The parts may have changed, but the person behind these roles remains the same. Similarly, in our own life we feel sure that there is a consistent self which travels from one situation to the next. We may act differently at the office compared with how we behave in our own living room, but nevertheless, most of us feel sure that we are essentially the same person in both contexts.

It is important to point out, however, that role theory does not necessarily require the distinction between essential and superficial selves. It could be argued, for example, that people are like onions, entirely made up of layer

---

Box 3.6: Man – the some of many parts?

'Whether the visage we assume be a joyful or a sad one, in adopting and emphasizing it we define our sovereign temper. Henceforth, so long as we continue under the spell of this self-knowledge, we do not merely live but act; we compose and play our chosen character, we wear the buskin of deliberation, we defend and idealize our passions, we encourage ourselves eloquently to be what we are, devoted or scornful or careless or austere; we soliloquize (before an imaginary audience) and we wrap ourselves gracefully in the mantle of our inalienable part ... Everyone who is sure of his mind, or proud of his office, or anxious about his duty assumes a tragic mask. He deputes it to be himself and transfers to it almost all his vanity ... Self-knowledge, like any art or science, renders its subject matter in a new medium, the medium of ideas, in which it loses its old dimensions and its old place. Our animal habits are transmuted by conscience into loyalties and duties, and we become "persons" or masks.'

(George Santayana, 1922)

upon layer of skins which, when peeled away, leave nothing at all. In this version of role theory there are no actors; only the parts themselves (*see* Box 3.6). Any sense of our having a 'real me' or core personality is simply an illusion produced purely by virtue of the sheer frequency of performance.

In addition to the problems associated with the notion of layers of selves, much of the male sex-role literature suffers from a fundamental confusion over the issue of what the sex-role actually represents. Earlier in this chapter we referred to a number of studies which had tried to describe the male role in terms of a few key norms (e.g. Pleck and Sawyer, 1974; Brannon, 1976). The point is, however, that the concept of the norm is itself ambiguous. On the one hand, it can be understood as 'any type of rule *that is actually recognized and followed* by a substantial portion of the membership of a group' (Lee and Newby, 1984 – emphasis added). Put another way, it describes the ways in which real flesh and blood men normally behave. Yet on the other hand, the same notion can be used to describe, not men's actual behaviour, but the ways in which society expects men to behave: here the norm stands for what is normative or ideal.

The tendency to confuse or conflate these two different meanings of the 'norms' of male behaviour has had a number of knock-on effects. To begin with, it has encouraged sex-role theorists to see any forms of activity which were at variance with such norms as, not just different, but deviant and defective. It was seen as the effect of improper socialisation; as a failure in the attempt of people to learn the parts provided for them by society. Not surprisingly, this led to the stigmatisation of those who were interpreted as being 'abnormal' – particularly lesbians and gay men (think back to Terman and Miles's M/F test which was used to sort out normal, healthy males from the sexual 'deviants' and 'inverts'). Furthermore, the confusion also served to exaggerate the extent to which men conformed to the normative standard case. Deviance took on the appearance of something unusual, despite the fact that the lives of most men in some way departed from the prescriptions of the male sex-role (*see* Box 3.7).

In addition, the tendency to focus upon the standard normative case has led to an appalling lack of attention to anything other than white, mainly middle-class forms of masculinity. For example, studies of black male roles are rare (Staples, 1978 and Franklin, 1984 – *see* Chapter 5) while gay men have been totally ignored by sex-role theorists.

Connell (1987) argues that if we can untangle the two meanings of the concept of the norm it soon becomes clear that they do not define that which is most common or standard. Instead they can be seen to represent the privileged versions of masculinity which the holders of social power wish to have accepted. This realisation, he continues, forces us into asking a whole series of important questions about whose interests are best served by particular sex-role norms. It also forces us into reconsidering the status of those

---

Box 3.7: Men – real and ideal

'That which is normative, i.e. expected or approved, is not necessarily standard, i.e. actually the way things usually happen. Perhaps especially not in the case of sexuality. Research has produced a series of upsets. The Kinsey studies are the most celebrated, finding frequencies of homosexual behaviour in the American population that normative sex role theory has never come to terms with. Data on premarital and extramarital heterosexuality make further trouble. Data on intra-family violence are also difficult to absorb: sober estimates by Straus and others that more than 50% of American families have experienced domestic violence suggests a very large gap between what is normally approved and what actually happens. Statistics on household composition show that the mother-father-two-kids-cat-and-dog nuclear family routinely invoked by priests, presidents and advertising copy-writers, is not the majority form of household now and perhaps never was. The normative pattern of husband-as-breadwinner and wife-as-homemaker, still powerful in ideology, has been undermined in fact by economics: around a third of the world's paid workers are women, while a good many men are not in the labour force. Role theorists who do close-up field research ... have to push the data very hard to get anything like the theoretical model of "roles" out of it.'

(Connell, 1987)

---

activities previously written off as 'deviant'; rather than seeing them as the result of some kind of malfunction in the socialisation process, they become reinterpretable as acts of resistance; that is, the attempts of other groups in society to redefine normality in ways more in line with their own interests (this will be one of the main themes discussed in Chapter 5).

In portraying gender socialisation as a relatively smooth and harmonious process in which males and females gradually learn to adopt those characteristics associated with their respective sex-roles, role theorists fail to grasp the extent to which the construction of gender identities is based upon the struggle for social power.

> As some critics have observed, we do not speak of 'race roles' or 'class roles' because the exercise of power in these areas of social life is more obvious to sociologists. With 'sex-roles', the underlying biological dichotomy seems to have persuaded many theorists that there is no power relationship here at all. The 'female role' and the 'male role' are tacitly treated as equal. (Connell, 1987 pp.50–1)

Role theorists not only lose sight of the fact that men, as a group, are more powerful than women, but also that the ways in which the categories of masculinity and femininity have come to be defined over the years actually function to reproduce or maintain this power difference (*see* Chapter 6). For as Michael Kimmel (1987a) points out, while masculinity has become associated with traits that imply authority and mastery, femininity is associated with the opposite characteristics of passivity and subordination. Similarly, those occupations and activities which are generally defined as male-dominated tend to be perceived (often by both sexes) as being more valuable compared with those seen as typically reserved for women (Touhey, 1974a; 1974b; O'Leary and Donoghue, 1978). What these studies show, however, is that there is nothing inherently more worthwhile about the activities associated with men. Rather, their value appears to be a product, pure and simple, of the fact that it is men who are engaged in doing them.

In failing to see gender definitions as a contested territory or ideological battlefield, the sex-role paradigm reveals a further important limitation. As a number of critics have pointed out, the approach is profoundly static or ahistorical (Connell, 1987; Carrigan *et al.*, 1987; Kimmel, 1987b). To begin with, the overriding image of sex-role socialisation is of a new generation growing up to be just like their older role models, but even where social change is recognised, it is not understood as emerging out of an often difficult and painful process of negotiation either between different groups of men and women (*see* Box 3.8) or else in the minds of individual men. Rather, as Carrigan *et al.* (1987) explain:

> Change is always [portrayed as] something that *happens to* sex roles, that impinges on them – whether from the direction of society at large (as in discussions of how technological and economic change demands a shift to a 'modern' male sex role) or from the direction of the asocial 'real self' inside the person, demanding more room to breathe. (p. 166 – emphasis in original)

Box 3.8: Resistible roles

In a paper on children's sex-role stereotypes, Vanda Lucia Zammuner (1987) describes a strand of research aimed at examining the internalisation of sex-role norms using children's preferences for certain toys, games and play activities. Broadly speaking, these studies offer children of various ages a range of sex-stereotyped toys, games etc. (such as dolls, footballs, tea-sets, and building blocks) and monitor the number of 'correct' or 'sex-appropriate' choices. Zammuner notes that while most studies find that children of both sexes make more 'correct' choices as they get older, at every stage girls are found to make more 'incorrect' choices compared with boys. She also notes that these findings have typically been interpreted as evidence of greater sex-role confusion in girls. However, Zammuner challenges this conclusion, arguing instead that the tendency of girls to 'prefer' toys and games more traditionally associated with boys is an attempt to redefine sex-role boundaries to allow them more freedom.

In summary, the sex role paradigm has been subjected to a great deal of criticism, much of which strikes at its very foundations. First, its status as a genuinely social theory of gender socialisation has been called into question by those who see it as resting ultimately upon the male/female biological dichotomy. Second, it is also accused of being internally incoherent insofar as it frequently embraces a concept of self (the real, inner self) for which role theory can offer no explanation. Third, the sex-role literature is accused of consistently failing to distinguish between norms as a descriptive or pre-scriptive category, resulting in the marginalisation of those who engage in so-called 'deviant' forms of behaviour. Fourth, sex-role theory is seen as blind to the operation of power. In other words, it fails to understand how the negotiation of gender definitions is part and parcel of a wider struggle between different groups in society. Finally, in failing to recognise the fact that definitions of sexuality and gender are contested grounds, sex-role theory cannot appreciate changes to definitions such as history.

Such a comprehensive list of faults has led a number of writers to dismiss completely the entire sex-role paradigm. According to Joseph Pleck (1987a), not only has it fallen from its position as the dominant paradigm in American psychology, but it currently represents little more than an interesting episode in the history of the social sciences. Carrigan *et al.* (1987) are scarcely more encouraging. As far as they are concerned, role theory is 'neither a concep-tually stable nor a practically and empirically adequate basis for the analysis of masculinity' (p. 168). Let us be blunt about it, they conclude: the 'male sex-role' does not exist.

Yet in spite of these claims, the concept of the male sex-role refuses to disappear. In fact, to some extent it has experienced a new lease of life since the resurgence of men's movements during the 1980s. Without doubt much of this literature contains many, if not all, of the theoretical weaknesses outlined above. However, in certain places there would seem to be evidence of a different, more sophisticated version of the theory. In the final section of this chapter we will examine briefly some of this work in order to ascertain whether or not it is possible to have a reformulated sex-role paradigm which goes at least some of the way to satisfying its critics.

Sex-roles revived?

While Carrigan *et al.* (1987) are undoubtedly correct in arguing that it is impossible to isolate a single coherent definition of masculinity (i.e. the 'standard normative case') which captures the full range of men's activities, it is equally clear that there are those working within the paradigm for whom the idea of multiple male roles is quite acceptable. For instance, a number of people have described men's lives as being fragmented into a number of different roles – such as husband, father and lover – where the associated norms and expectations in each case are quite different. In addition, other writers have recognised the fact that cultures very often contain more than one version of a particular role. For example, Pleck (1987b) has described how contemporary American culture contains at least two quite different models of fatherhood. It has also been suggested that the various ethnic, sexual and social class groupings may have their own particular definitions of the male sex-role (i.e. the black male role, the gay male role and the working-class male role).

Some of these writers go much further than merely acknowledging the existence of a multiplicity of male roles. For example, in Pleck's historical analysis of fatherhood, he makes it quite plain that the different conceptions exist in a state of tension rather than harmony. That is, they are in competition with each other to define reality.

> There is no question that the father-breadwinner model established in the nineteenth and early twentieth centuries remains culturally dominant today, both in fathers' actual behaviour and in its media representation. It is important to recognize that this model has a specific history. *To become dominant, it has to supplant an earlier view* in which fathers had the ultimate responsibility for, and influence on, their children. (Pleck, 1987b, p. 93 – emphasis added)

In describing the history of this struggle, Pleck provides at least a glimpse of the power relationships which, in a sense, drive the competition for cultural dominance. For example, in explaining the recent emergence of a new conception of fatherhood – one who is present at the birth of his children and participates fully in the day-to-day work of childcare – Pleck identifies the rise in the percentage of women in paid employment and the post-war feminist movement as the two most significant causal factors. Both, he suggests, 'led mothers to demand that fathers become more involved' in domestic activities. However, Pleck points out, this 'new father' role is by no means the most dominant concept available. Rather, it struggles against a number of more established alternatives, some of which are, in part at least, driven or sustained by an 'antifeminist backlash'.

Such analyses go a long way towards countering the accusations listed above. Pleck's study of fatherhood dispenses with the idea of a single, standard masculinity and, in so doing, avoids the need to rely so heavily upon the notion of deviant behaviour. His study is both genuinely historical as well as sensitive to the operations of power; for he clearly illustrates how various conceptions of fatherhood are intimately bound up with the interests of different sections of society. The question that remains, however, is whether these much more sophisticated analyses can still be realistically thought of as belonging to the sex-role perspective. It could easily be argued that they have been transformed into something quite different.

In the next two chapters we will review two more perspectives on men and masculinity which, in their own way, build upon and refine some of the key elements outlined above. In Chapter 4 we will look at some more robust theories of the relationships between men and society. Here masculine identities are not simply encouraged or reinforced. Neither are they instilled in people's minds in the form of particular patterns or configuration of mental concepts. Rather, they are seen as emerging out of the material realities of men's lives. In Chapter 5 we present a much more sophisticated analysis of masculine scripts. No longer are they seen as mere descriptions of how men are or ought to be. Instead, they are viewed as part of the cut and thrust in an often fierce and uncompromising ideological battle for social, political and economic power.

Chapter 4

Masculinity and social relations

At the heart of role theory is a relatively simple idea – a man's substance, his identity, his personality, his experience, his masculinity – derive from his place in society. As we saw in Chapter 3, role theorists try to describe the effects of this 'place in society' through the concepts of social expectations, norms and scripts; we saw, too, some of the problems with these descriptions. In this chapter we return to the basic underlying principle, the notion of the social determination of masculinity, and look at it again from other viewpoints.

According to the social determination argument, masculinity emerges from men's social activities. Masculinity is the sum of men's characteristic 'practices' at work, with their families, in their communities, and in the groups and institutions to which they belong. In many ways it is obvious that this must be so – miners, for example, and men engaged in similar occupation, are likely to have very different senses of masculinity, different forms of fraternity, ways of behaving with other men and with women, compared with professional intellectuals paid for activities such as teaching, writing, research and study. Yet, as we will see, making sense of men's various social activities raises some difficult theoretical dilemmas for social scientists.

In this chapter we will focus on the work of several sociologists and social theorists of masculinity – Andrew Tolson (1977), Robert Connell (1987), Jeff Hearn (1987), Arthur Brittan (1989), David Morgan (1992), Kenneth Clatterbaugh (1990) and Victor Seidler (1989; 1991a). In their different ways these writers draw upon two central traditions of thought – Marxist analyses of capitalism and feminist analyses of patriarchy. These two traditions differ from role theory in their emphasis on the close connections between expressions of masculinity and power relations within broader society. Each tradition represents an attempt to understand divisions, antagonisms and conflicts in contemporary social relations, whether these be between different social classes, or between men and women. Some of the authors we shall review, such as Andrew Tolson and Victor Seidler, develop a socialist critique of capitalism, and emphasise the way men are 'victimised' by their working conditions and by class divisions. Although somewhat dated now, Tolson's work on class provides a classic example of the application of socialist theory to masculinity. Other authors such as Jeff Hearn and Robert Connell focus on masculinity as an effect of men's privileges and advantages in relation to women. Here patriarchy is the object of criticism. When we combine these analyses men emerge simultaneously as victims and oppressors.

At the core of all these writings there is a set of distinctive 'materialist' assumptions about masculinity. Materialism as a philosophy derives originally from Marx but is central to a great deal of sociological research, whether Marxist-based or otherwise. The main tenet can be summed up as the claim that people's experience and sense of themselves will reflect their economic position, or, to put it another way, forms of consciousness will reflect the currently dominant human solutions to the material problems of life (Leonard, 1984). As Jean-Paul Sartre argued, a man can think only as far as the stage his group or social class has reached. The group's form of self-consciousness will structure the individual's capacity for such consciousness (cf. Barnes, 1974, p. 110). What is possible collectively will determine individual limits.

Human solutions to the material problems of life and thus the collective practices of a society vary historically. The feudalism of medieval times is an example of one set of solutions to the problem of how to survive, live, organise work and society. Modern capitalism is another solution. These contrasting 'modes of economic production' represent a set of strategies for dealing with basic economic questions: the production of goods and services, the exchange of those goods, the organisation of labour, the distribution of property, family life, and so on. This perspective assumes, therefore, that a man's identity and his sense of self will reflect his particular position within these economic and social arrangements. Masculinity is historically variable and is socially, rather than biologically or naturally, produced.

To make this more concrete, think again of the example of the male miner compared with the male teacher. The materialist argument is that to understand one individual we need to understand the social groups to which this individual belongs, the history of those groups, and their economic and social position *vis à vis* other social groups. It is assumed that to a large extent we can predict a man's mode of being from our knowledge of the activities of his groups. For the miner and the teacher, therefore, we could begin with their occupations. Our inquiry would then lead to the relationship between social class and masculinity, and how the fact of their both working within a capitalist economic system structures their options.

Is occupation the only indicator of their material circumstances? What about race? Let us assume that the miner is black and the teacher is white. Although there is no inherently biological reason why this should be so (cf.

Miles, 1989), race, like class and occupation, is an important social division. To be born black rather than white in the UK or the USA has important material consequences, both in terms of economic well-being, the exercise of power, and in terms of opportunities for self-definition. From a materialist perspective, race must be another thread in analyses of masculinity.

Finally, let us say that the miner is married with three children at school and that, although his wife works part-time, she is responsible for the majority of the unpaid work required in the home. The miner's wife is not only responsible, now and in the past, for the bulk of the child-rearing, she also does most of the cooking and cleaning, and cares for the couple's surviving elderly relative. Let us give the teacher, on the other hand, a more unusual domestic situation: he is gay with no children, currently largely celibate and living alone, but, in the past, when he was working part-time, he lived as part of an extended household and shared with their biological parents the care of the children living in the household.

These descriptions concern private life – sexuality, romance, and intimate relationships with others – but, as feminist theorists have argued, private life also has a strongly material dimension. It is also about work, paid or unpaid, a division of labour and responsibilities, and divisions in opportunities and power in both the public and private spheres. To follow up this theme, therefore, is to begin to inquire about patriarchy, the organisation of men's relationships with women within the home and the way these influence relationships between women and men outside the home.

Some of the complexities involved in developing a materialist analysis of masculinity are becoming clear. The strategy of all the researchers we will consider in this chapter is to think in terms of broad patterns and regularities across society – regularities, for example, in social class, patterns in the differential opportunities of ethnic groups, patterns in the division of labour according to gender and regularities in gender inequalities. This kind of sociological analysis depends on a process of generalising. Indeed, the very terms race, class and gender are an attempt to summarise individual experiences in terms of general categories. Yet when we look at any particular individual, such as our black married miner and unmarried white teacher, it is apparent that gender, class and race interact, and combine, too, with other important social divisions such as between the able-bodied and those with disabilities, and between heterosexual and homosexual men. The diversity and the complexity of material circumstances must somehow be balanced with regularity and pattern. In practice, most sociological accounts of masculinity tend to focus on just one dimension, and, historically within sociology, the main materialist topic has been class. Only recently has gender been explored to the same extent, while race remains largely ignored.

Our review will follow this tendency to take up one set of material circumstances after another. We will focus, first, on class, then on the much more truncated literature on race, finally moving to work on patriarchy and masculinity. In the process we will try to explain what is meant by the terms capitalism and patriarchy, and we will look at some of the distinctive syntheses attempted by various writers on masculinity. It is important to remember, however, that to understand any particular expression of masculinity from a materialist standpoint we must work across our categories. There is considerable dispute about not only how best to describe material conditions and their accompanying social relations, but also about the importance of class in relation to race in relation to gender.

Capitalism and masculinity

Socialist analysts of capitalist working practices argue that if men are competitive, aggressive, emotionally inarticulate, detached, and oppressive in their dealings with others, then many of these characteristics can be explained as a consequence of the structure of our current mode of economic production. Contradictions and tensions in the way paid work is organised will condition what Tolson (1977) calls the 'deep structure' of masculinity – self-esteem, sense of creativity, camaraderie, bodies in space and the smaller details of self-presentation. The social conflicts of capitalism become embodied in the nervous systems and energies of men, producing distinctive and entirely habitual sets of gestures, even tones of voice and personalities. Marx argued that what distinguishes capitalism from other modes of production is its basis in the private ownership of goods and resources, its ideal of a free competitive market for trade, and the fundamental division it generates between those who own the means of production, the capital and equipment required to produce goods for sale, the means for making profits, and those who simply have their labour power to sell.

Capitalism creates an inevitable conflict of interest between owners and workers, or, as Box 4.1 illustrates, between workers and the managers who act as the representatives of owners. Owners, according to Marx, rely on being able to create 'surplus value' from their workers and, in a crude sense, their main motive must be to maximise profits and this surplus value. On a typical factory production line, for example, a worker is involved in the collective creation of a new commodity. This commodity such as a car, however, is not his or her possession, or the possession of the other workers who produced it. It is usually or ideally sold by the factory owners for a profit – profit being money acquired above and beyond what is required to pay for the materials of production, the plant equipment, and the wages of the production workers. Surplus value is thus extracted for the benefit of owners from the labour and creative activity of workers. The main interest of workers within this system, therefore, lies in trying to improve their working conditions and pay, and in this sense to redistribute some of the wealth gained from their activity.

Box 4.1: Warehouse work

'In the last two years I have done a variety of temporary jobs to earn some money. One of them was working as a machine handler in a warehouse for large electrical equipment.

'The machines, from small typewriters to processors weighing a ton or more, were stored on shelving in 40-foot-high racks or on the floor. Very often the floor space was covered with machines as yet unsorted – crowded, frustrating, dangerous.

'My work included sweeping up, loading or unloading lorries, building shelves, searching for machines which had been lost, making tea. Most of the time, though, I was pushing heavy machines around or packing up and stacking smaller but also heavy video screens, typewriters and keyboards.

'As I write I feel the boredom and sloth coming back to me ... This is what hurt me most when I was there – the lack of control I had over how I spent nearly 8 hours of my day. This hurt everyone who worked there. One, the eldest man, was thin, grey and ill. He would spend the day rushing around on his fork truck trying to get everything he was asked to do exactly right. He ended up dropping machines in his hurry and making a mess of his work because he was so anxious and competitive. He would moan to everyone he worked with and fawn to management....

'I got increasingly angry with the managers. They never said please or thank you. The senior of the two had ginger hair, a face like a ploughed field, talked about the simple traditions of British industry and behaved like a pig. He had worked for the company for 30 years.

'I felt sorry for Peter, the floor manager – he was set to give himself a heart attack, he seemed to have nothing in his life but his work and even that was failing. I sometimes saw him as being very small and vulnerable and frightened. A lot of the time though, I would forget this insight because I resented the jobs I was asked to do – hated the work and it was his fault! I lost sight of of the roots of my anger in the whole environment around me and blamed Peter.'

(Nicholay, 1991, pp. 160–2)

Capitalism, as Marx and Engels argued, is a system based on competition and the struggle for comparative advantage. There is competition between producers to sell goods and make profit, and there is competition among workers within the employment market to sell their skills and labour. As sociologists have noted, competition is evident, too, in modern corporations within the hierarchical structure of the organisation as the workforce struggles to gain qualifications and promotions. 'At work, the "best" men get promoted, get recognised, get the highest bonus, get the cushiest jobs. To be in favour, we are on test as individuals, and if we fail the test, we have failed as people.' (Notes from the Collective, 1991, p. 133).

There is competition, too, to acquire and hold private property, capital, and other scarce resources, but there are also different forms of solidarity created as a by-product of this economic organisation. Owners have some interests in common and different groups of workers, too, have collective interests and common goals frequently expressed through resistance, strikes and collective bargaining. Capitalism in this sense creates patterns and possibilities of social relations and certain ways of being with others.

If this is the broad picture, what are some of the specific and immediate consequences of working within a capitalist system? Tolson (1977) and Seidler (1989; 1991a) identify a complex of experiences based on the splits, divisions, specialisations and alienation which they see as intrinsic to modern industrial life. Capitalist production is organised around a series of divisions between home and work, between work and leisure, private life and public life. Experience is thus compartmentalised as people move between these different spheres. Capitalist practices create basic divisions between people, between those on the shop floor and those in management, between those who specialise in mental skills and those who become predominantly defined by their physical capacities. Under capitalism, the broad stream of human potential becomes broken up. Most workers, in Tolson's view, are 'alienated' as a consequence; most become internally divided, fixed into patterns of conformity against their best interests, and forced to fragment their potential and talents to fit the niches available.

Victor Seidler (1991a) argues, for example, that these working practices encourage men, in particular, since traditionally they have been most involved in paid work, to split their sense of identity between a 'real me' of private life and a work personality. Men become emotionally inarticulate, not just because the capitalist ethos tends to favour self-control, stoicism and self-discipline but because, in Seidler's view, divisions in experience between the private and the public, and the institutionalisation of competitiveness cause a process of 'depersonalisation'. Men have little alternative within these sets of social relations but to become 'working machines', closed and separate from others, fearful of intimacy and vulnerability, regulated, controlled and disciplined. Men become focused on maintaining an increasingly precarious masculine authority, and familiar with violence both as a strategy, and as the potential object of the violence of others. Seidler talks of a pervasive sense of 'unreality' that he claims many men feel as a consequence of the structure and organisation of their working lives.

In these socialist critiques, men are said to suffer from a basic alienation which is seen as a central psychological consequence of capitalism. Alienation refers to the 'distance' which arises between workers and their labour or creative activity. This distance is inevitable in any act of creation – a student writing an essay, a carpenter making a table – both produce an object which comes to have an independent life. Inevitably, the creator loses control of his or her creation as it becomes an object for other people and subject to their independent evaluations and uses: alienation is intensified when the results of one's labour are actually appropriated by others. Alienation is intensified, too, Marx argued, when a person's creative power and his or her capacity for work become a commodity to be bought or sold among employers. Production line work can then magnify the experience of alienation even further. Since the worker typically makes only one component, the connection between work on this particular component and the final product may feel mysterious and even more distant.

According to these arguments, capitalism draws men into a network of social relations which encourage sets of behaviours which we recognise as typically masculine, and which, further, Seidler and Tolson see as actively harmful for men. These social relations are seen as harmful for women, too, since, as Clatterbaugh (1990) argues, men become the main agents of alienation within the home because of their own experience of alienation outside of it. Men come to control women's labour and their bodies, dehumanising and stifling their creative power, and, of course, as women also work outside the home, they are equally subject to the alienating pressures of public life.

Why then do men work? Or since it seems obvious that men must work to support themselves, why do men seem actively to want to work within this system? Some jobs are clearly more rewarding than others and we will discuss these differences shortly, but Tolson argues that, despite the obvious negative consequences of capitalist practices, especially for working-class men, most men have a mixed or an ambivalent attitude to work. Male unemployment thus has a particular poignancy and salience (cf. Morgan, 1992) – unemployment is not just a matter of adjusting to poverty, it seems to strike at the heart of masculinity, but why is this the case?

Tolson argues that men's experiences of work are in fact fed by two diverse sources. First, they are determined by the general types of behaviour which are possible in the different workplaces found in capitalist societies, and these have their own rewards and costs, but, second, they are influenced by what Tolson sees as the older, vestigial traditions of patriarchy or male domination within the home. These two sources, in his view, are often contradictory, resulting in a 'dual experience' for men. By patriarchy Tolson means a set of ideas, customs and traditions which men inherit from their fathers and through their families. For Tolson, patriarchy is not a set of material forces but a matter of people's beliefs and opinions, a set of habits and traditions modified by capitalism but distinct from it. This definition of patriarchy is at odds with more recent feminist accounts which do see a material basis to patriarchy. We will consider these accounts shortly, but for the moment we will go along with Tolson's definition. His main claim is that men experience, not just modern capitalist working arrangements but another, older, practice of male pre-eminence within the family, captured in the ideal of the male breadwinner and represented in the duties and privileges of that position. Notions of a patriarchal masculinity emerge from male inheritance of property and the concept of a male line, from paternal authority, or the authority which accrues to the male head of the house, and older craft traditions of work which depend on customs and rituals passed from father to son.

Tolson paints a vivid picture of the way patriarchal notions of what it means to be a man are passed down from father to son. The young boy first learns that being a man like one's father involves being centred outside the home in the world of work. Fathers, unlike most mothers, are mainly elsewhere in a little-known and mysterious world outside the home. Boys, says Tolson, quickly learn to associate work with masculinity such that the transition to earning becomes an important sign of manhood. The small boy learns to respect, and hopes to duplicate, the alienness and distance of his father, preoccupied with a world outside the home. Work thus becomes seen as a privilege, an instantiation of masculinity and, as Tolson notes, part of a man's birth-right, but men, he says, also become caught in a trap through this association. On the one hand men look to paid work to validate and affirm their masculinity, work is actively anticipated for this reason. Men want to work, and find it difficult to imagine not structuring their life in this way. On the other hand, their sense of masculinity and their 'birth-right' derived from patriarchal sources must be played out in ways which mesh with capitalist structures. These capitalist structures, Tolson argues, both reinforce and seriously undermine patriarchal notions of masculinity.

Patriarchal ideology can help oil the wheels of capitalism; it helps keep men in line for, as Tolson notes, to protest too much is to threaten the manly authority which comes from being in employment and from conformity to the demands of work. Work can also be a place where men can act out a macho sense of being 'proper men', validating this identity through various male fraternities. Yet for many working-class men, work can become an experience of powerlessness, of interchangeability with others, of redundancy, an experience of humiliation through subordination to authority. Many men, then, are in a situation where what Tolson would see as their *real* experience of work is one of powerlessness, yet this may be disguised and concealed through the macho relations of the shop floor. In any case, even if this powerlessness were perceived, men could not rebel, because to rebel is to endanger another crucial patriarchal masculine identity of the breadwinner.

Tolson suggests, then, that patriarchal ideologies and capitalist social structures lock together for the benefit of capitalism. Patriarchal notions of masculinity help to perpetuate the social structures of capitalism and thus class divisions. In this sense we could talk about patriarchy, and the masculinity emerging from it, as functional for capitalist modes of economic production, but, for Tolson, what is most evident is the way this locking together devastates the lives of ordinary men and women. All the traits which make men's (and women's) lives a misery of competitive individualism and macho posturing derive, in his view, from this particular current historical juncture of new social structures and older ideologies.

Masculinity and class divisions

So far we have discussed the effects of capitalist practices on men and masculinity in general terms. Yet it is clear, as the sociologist Max Weber noted, that one of the main features of capitalist modes of production is the creation of divisions between groups of workers. How do these class divisions structure masculinity? Are there different combinations of capitalist and patriarchal expectations for men in different economic positions?

The sociological language of class and distinctions between, for instance, middle-class and working-class, professionals, manual labourers, the self-employed, skilled tradesmen, etc., is an attempt to try to capture some of the differences between people in pay, status, level of autonomy, and so on. Class is a method for summarising the regularities in what is often called the 'division of labour' in a given society. Potentially, we could discuss how the expression of masculinity varies across a number of these divisions. In practice, however, masculinity researchers such as Seidler, Tolson and Clatterbaugh have tended to focus on one broad distinction – between working-class and middle-class masculinity. Their strategy has been to try to describe representative individuals, or representative characteristics which are not necessarily found in all middle-class or working-class men, but are *typically* found among these groups. As Clatterbaugh notes, middle-class men engaged in management or in the professions have a higher profile than working-class men, but working-class men tend to be the larger group, depending on how class is defined. Working-class and middle-class men have substantially different interests within capitalism. They are antagonistic groups, and, as Clatterbaugh points out, what has been distinctive about the 1980s, in both the USA and the UK, is the massive increase in the transfer of resources from the working class to the middle class, as the gap between the well-off and the poor has widened.

The difference between working-class and middle-class men is essentially the difference between the kinds of masculinity which are possible when a man has a wage versus a salary, works by the clock versus by appointment, has job security and a career structure versus job insecurity and fear of personal injury. There is, in Tolson's view, a major difference between the type of masculinity which can emerge in corridors with personal offices, meetings, telephones, and names on doors, and which ranges across a global territory, compared with the masculinity which emerges through the fraternity of the factory floor and through confinement to local spaces and local communities.

Tolson argues that working-class men have a more instrumental and, from a socialist perspective, a less deluded attitude to work. Work becomes more obviously a matter of getting by, of making money. Middle-class men, on the other hand, are required to invest themselves, to identify with their job, and, crucially, are required to discipline themselves. For working-class men the structures of discipline within the workplace are usually imposed more externally. As a consequence, working-class men are more directly humiliated by capitalist practices, and more directly subordinated. In Tolson's view, working-class men are more likely to adopt, as compensation, an exaggerated masculine culture within the workplace, a language of brotherhood, a chauvinistic sexuality, blatant machismo, and to invest in forms of resistance which involve direct confrontations with authority. Tolson talks about the drama of group interaction and self-presentation involved, and the development of defensive masculine displays which, through talk of sport, sex, and practical joking, achieve what he describes as a highly stylised symbolic exchange of masculinity (cf. also Willis, 1977).

Autobiographical accounts of men involved in these forms of camaraderie (see Box 4.2), however, make it clear that working-class fraternities of this kind can also become a central source of meaning, of affection, friendship and male bonding, and thus a powerful source of self-affirmation and validation. Middle-class men, of course, have their fraternities too, as Barbara Rogers (1988) points out in her studies of groups such as freemasons, Rotary clubs, and men's clubs, but these are not a form of compensation for a masculinity undermined by systems of authority at work. Indeed, they are institutions which effectively co-ordinate and coalesce that authority.

Seidler suggests that contrasting forms of self-estrangement result from working-class and middle-class men's differential placement within capitalism. For some working-class men, it becomes the case that the distinction, created by capitalist practices, between home and work, between public life and private life, becomes even sharper, as home and leisure have to carry more of the weight of a working-class man's sense of who he is. If work is mainly instrumental, detached from oneself, then home, consumption and hobbies have to become the principal way of defining a sense of personal identity, particularly in the absence of the kind of male fraternities described in Box 4.2. Working-class men are more directly objectified, their labour is more directly channelled and controlled. Their alienation is thus clear and evident.

The self-estrangement and costs for middle-class men are more subtle but, as Seidler argues, and as Box 4.3 indicates, can be equally profound. Middle-class men are more isolated, engaged in an individual struggle with themselves for success. Work is less containable and more engulfing of both time and identity. The development of a successful middle-class career, argues Seidler, demands deeper self-alienation as personality, character and social skills become a commodity to be sold on the labour market, along with knowledge and expertise.

The working lives of middle-class and working-class men are also thought to structure in profound but different ways their relations with women within the family. Tolson and Seidler argue that working-class men

---

Box 4.2: The mining fraternity

'Men relate to each other through objects and object-centered activity. With miners this is further mediated through an admixture of aggression and humour. In 14 years in the pit I have only seen one blow "struck in anger" – I saw more at college and university! Yet there is constant reference to violence – "pass that shovel before I smack you in the mouth" – all of it in humour. Indeed saying nasty or violent things is a sign of affection, they can only be said to a mate. Likewise with greetings: "How are you going on you old nobbly-backed bastard?" On the other hand there are no words of tenderness and affection for each other. I remember carrying on a stretcher a workmate who had injured his leg. There were six of us carrying him the couple of miles to the man-rider. The man was very popular being a very good worker with a zany sense of fun. The men were obviously concerned at his injuries – at first thought serious – but they didn't say so. Instead they just "took the piss out of him", referring to his notorious antics as a Romeo – he had been due to take his ex-wife and girlfriend out that night. The whole journey of six miles was a great deal of fun for all concerned. Talking later to a member of the party – an Estonian miner – he agreed that the humour was partly to cover up the embarrassment of not being able to express their true feelings and to keep an emotional situation under control. In fact, the humour was better for the injured man than hand-wringing and tears – it took his mind off it.

'Physical contact between miners is also a mixture of aggression and humour, the friendly punching and wrestling that is common amongst males. However, miners do not avoid touching genitals. At one pit I worked at there was a fashion for a man to walk up to another one and touch him, gently under the balls and greet him. I soon realised that the object was to get you to react to this treatment and get a laugh. Fortunately, I was not freaked by these ball-lifting activities and replied in kind. I was aware that, in the pit, there were no such thing as "privates". At another pit on nightshift I saw a man – the one who injured his leg – grab a young married miner and give him a lovebite, knowing that it would be difficult to explain to his wife in the morning! On another occasion I watched two 17 stone youths wrestle as one was trying to kiss the other. Talking to shop stewards in other industries I've found that this type of activity would be regarded as strange.'

(Devaney, 1991, pp. 156–7)

---

inevitably become more 'patriarchal' in the sense that, as subordination increases in the workplace, the desire to dominate and gain recognition at home becomes more pressing. Similarly if work is instrumental, just a matter of bread-winning, then family life becomes more important since the financial support of family life becomes the main motive for men to continue their working lives.

Middle-class men are more powerful outside the family, they can thus

---

Box 4.3: Work, body and soul

'Historically, I've often disregarded the needs of my body to fit in to the goals, targets and deadlines of work, particularly paid work. In this way I've approached my body as a mechanical container that carries out the pressing instructions coming from my head... My emotional investment in my work identity, through compulsively straining for stardom and success, has partly fitted me into the capitalist logic of individually and competitively pursuing goals. Sometimes the goals might have been progressive ones but the methods used to achieve them were often estranging... Compulsive activity at work seemed to offer a controlling sense of purpose and direction when other parts of my life were breaking apart... My first wife gave me unpaid, invisible support and servicing that allowed me to keep going at such a frenzied pace in the public sphere. My ability to go on giving an obsessive, driving, physical energy to my work was dependent on being looked after in the home... Of course it's never as straightforward as that. As I piled more and more pressure on myself at work, my body started to give me warnings that it couldn't stand that alienating rhythm any more... Over the years I developed habits of pushing my body so hard that I lost touch with any ability to know when I had gone too far. I was unable to set any physical limits to my life... [A]fter reaching the age of 20 and through the years of experiencing academic achievement at university I started to identify myself through my mind. That was also tied in to my daily working relations of being a comprehensive-school English teacher and beginning to see myself as a Hero Innovator through my intellectual achievements... After 30, as my marriage broke up, I began to be seized by a buried grief... Unable to deal with this pain, I started to seek refuge in a workaholic obsessiveness. A massive emotional investment in the work identity of a rational intellectual helped fill up the wounding gaps in my life left by the loss of my children and the loss of another family home. So as the years went by, I learned to avoid my pain and distress by a single-minded concentration on intellectual work. In this way, my sense of myself as a worker gave me the stability and reassurance I needed at a time of shocking disorientation.'

(Jackson, 1990, pp. 57–9)

---

afford, these commentators argue, to be more superficially egalitarian within the family, more involved in 'partnership'. Middle-class men's concepts of partnership and the 'companionate marriage' (cf. Brannen and Collard, 1982), however, are dependent on female partners acting as good 'career wives'. They are dependent upon female identification with male goals and ambitions, rather than the reverse, and highly dependent, too, on women's domestic labour which makes a male career feasible in the first place. In this way capitalism reaches deep into family life, organising the possibilities for and attitudes to private life just as surely as capitalist economics structure public life.

As Hearn and Parkin (1987) have argued, capitalist practices and organisational culture come to organise the expression of sexuality within the workplace as well as other aspects of relationships between working men and women. To the extent that corporate organisations and workplaces recognise sexuality, it is male sexuality that tends to be privileged. Tolson's example of the butcher's shop in Box 4.4 (cf. also Collinson and Collinson, 1989) suggests how this privileging can occur for working-class men through the establishment of male fraternities. Ways of making the time pass in a more interesting fashion become highly reliant on overt sexism and the explicit denigration of women. Many middle-class men, however, have more power over women in the sense that they can directly control and regulate their labour. Here issues of sexual harassment become linked to the power to hire and fire. Sexual relationships at work tend to fall into a pattern of higher status men's intimacy with lower status women within the organisation (Collinson and Collinson, 1989). As Rosemary Pringle (1989) points out, the relationship between male managers and female secretaries or receptionists, although not necessarily overtly sexualised, is nonetheless a reflection of this kind of sexual politics. Secretaries and receptionists in corporate organisations become an indicator of a man's status and an embodiment of his power to require others to service his needs.

Again it becomes clear how what are usually seen as private and personal matters of sexuality, romance and intimacy are regulated through the class and working practices which structure patterns of proximity and opportunity. For gay men the issue becomes more complex, as patterns of fraternity established through heterosexuality are also often strongly dependent on homophobia and gay bashing. For example, in his account of his working life at Unigate, David Secrett (1991) describes the tensions he experienced when participating in and observing the ways his heterosexual female and male workmates regulated their relationships with each other. Not surprisingly, it made his 'coming out' at work an extremely difficult project.

Although the portraits of middle-class and working-class masculinity painted by the likes of Tolson are persuasive and, indeed, supported by a tradition of sociological studies of the workplace going back to the 1950s, there are also some problems with the technique of focusing on the representative characteristics of a group. David Morgan (1992) argues that the main danger here is of stereotyping, particularly, perhaps, working-class forms of masculinity which may be less familiar to academic researchers from mainly middle-class backgrounds. Morgan wonders if some male intellectuals and academics who study men are not overly intrigued by 'brutish' masculinity, tending to idealise 'gritty' ways of 'being a man'. Because it is assumed to be there, this 'grittiness' can be perceived in an overemphasised and too categorical way, ignoring other aspects of men's lives. It is certainly the case that many sociologists studying the lives of working-class boys and men sometimes seem to be caught up in the admiration and romanticising of

---

Box 4.4: Fraternal sexualities

'All butchers are the same. You get them in the same crowd, the usual subjects – sex, women, you know. We talk in back-slang all day long. I mean I could talk to you in back-slang and you wouldn't be able to understand a word I'm saying . . . A girl might possibly walk past, around twenty-two, twenty-three. She's wearing a big pair of breasts on her. Well what we say is (in back-slang) "look at the girl with the big breasts" . . . I mean to say if I get an awkward customer, and you'll be serving her, she starts mucking about with you – this doesn't satisfy her, that doesn't satisfy her. You turn around to your mate and say, "She's a right old deelowoc that one." Well, "deelowoc" is an old cow. DLO = OLD; WOC = COW. You can rattle away all day and call 'em what the hell you like . . . Sometimes the carters will come around the shop like with the meat, and they'll come up with a really filthy book. And I'll read one of them – but if you've read one of them you've read the lot like, they're all the same damn story in any case. Some of the bloody things they bring, they're terrible they are . . . They'll bring them and say, "Right, I'll see you in a couple of day's time when I bring the next load, and let's have them back." We look at them in the shop you know; really filthy bloody photographs. *"You don't bring those home with you do you?'* "Good God, not bloody likely! No I just look at them in the shop for a laugh, and stick them in the mess-room" . . . These are the sort of things that go with the butchering. I mean if you haven't worked in a butcher's shop you don't know what it is. As I say, half the time we spend looking at the women walking past, and talking about them. The other half we're serving the rest of the customers like, you know. Sex comes into it all day long. It's just one of those things butchers are well-known for. I don't know why. Whether it's the smell of meat, or handling the meat or not, I couldn't tell you. But they're well-known for chatting the birds up and one thing or another.'

(Butcher, quoted in Tolson, 1977, pp. 61–2)

'laddish' masculinity. This idealising, of course, reflects the ambivalent status of this form of masculinity – valorised and criticised at the same time.

It is also the case that some class analyses of masculinity have often not kept up with transformations within capitalism. What is striking, for example, about the 1980s is not simply the prevalence of mass male unemployment, but the 'feminisation' of the workforce. Not only are a great many more wives and mothers working, but the structure of occupations has changed increasingly in the UK from manufacturing to service industries, and from full-time to part-time employment. Working at and from home is also increasingly common. These changes are likely to be profound, and the effects for masculinity are only beginning to be worked through. As Carrigan, Connell and Lee (1985) argue, perhaps the notion of the 'new man' and the current popularity of writings on masculinity simply reflect the most recent attempts to 'modernise' men, producing new types of masculine identity more in tune with the contemporary demands of capitalism.

Similarly, as theorists of post-modernity (Baudrillard, 1992; Haraway, 1990) have noted, with the rise of new technologies dependent on the computer-human interface, human 'character' is being re-constructed in new ways. Perhaps, says Baudrillard, it is no longer meaningful in such circumstances to talk of 'alienation' as the chief psychological characteristic of capitalism. Working on computers, within information networks, tends to remove the 'distancing' effects of the appropriation of creativity considered characteristic of older modes of industrial production. In Baudrillard's view, computers are more like prosthetic devices, such as contact lenses, which provide mechanical extensions of humanity. As it is increasingly through these new computer-human interfaces that work is done, he suggests, so it is also through them that the self and identity of relevant groups of workers will be defined. Although from a Marxist perspective it could still be argued that, although the capitalist mode may be continually transforming, the fact of exploitation and division remains – albeit in new guises.

Race, class and masculinity

As we have noted before, detailed analyses of the lives of black men and forms of black masculinity are one of the most striking absences in the masculinity literature. With some exceptions, writings on the social determination of masculinity share this omission. Class, as we pointed out in the introduction to this chapter, has been discussed extensively, but rarely questions of race and ethnicity. Yet, as Box 4.5 illustrates, race has strongly material dimensions which will interact with a man's class position (Miles, 1989; Marable, 1983). The findings on middle-class and working-class masculinity thus need to be re-worked. To be a black middle-class man in a racist society clearly introduces new dimensions which come from the experience of this racism. Racism is a cultural phenomenon – a matter of stereotypes and name-calling – but it is also a material phenomenon. To be black in the UK or USA is to be more likely to experience a particular set of social and economic conditions. If consciousness of masculinity reflects men's material circumstances, then the effects of racial divisions should be a major topic of investigation.

Some of the material consequences are evident in Box 4.5. The speaker reminds us that he is an exception. As Clatterbaugh (1990) notes, black men in general constitute the 'underclass' of the male working class. As an

---

Box 4.5: Race and professional identity – one man's experience

'The phone rings. I answer it in my usual confident manner before three European gentlemen are ushered into my office. They are brought in by my secretary. It is very strange that here am I, a black West Indian, speaking about my office and my secretary in this predominantly white society. By all accounts they are symbols of status and reflect to some degree that I, a black man, have made it in white society . . . By all accounts my present position would indicate a degree of success in a white man's world. I had the privilege, or more correctly, the right to attend decent schools and colleges and by many whites' standards I must be remarkable in that of the limited blacks at universities, I am currently doing post-graduate work at a second university. The passage between stepping off at Southampton into a grey, dismal-looking English south coast and now sitting in a centrally heated, beautifully furnished, artistically decorated office surrounded by the symbols of the black man's world, possibly reflects to many an observer, both black and white – success. The mental torture, the psychic scars are not visible and the sleepless nights and crying days of the white man's pressure seems like a distant dream. The trappings of modern society are only symbols. The torture and pain that white society inflicts upon its black individuals can never be compensated for, in spite of those few black faces one tends to see in so-called positions of authority . . . Professional blacks are treated as rare specimens by most of their white colleagues. I am no exception. Generally speaking, racist humour is used to make simple conversation and reactions to these generally leaves us, the black individuals, guilty that we have challenged them. It is a continuous process that those blacks like myself, who have moved up (in a manner of speaking) in society, have very often to contend with the labels that not only do we carry "chips on our shoulders", but we are over-sensitive to racial issues. No one cares if after a hard day's graft the extent of my social pleasures are limited simply because blacks are not allowed; no one cares if I am a professional when I go to the shops and a white employee has no desire to serve me; no one cares if as a black professional, I wish to buy a house in a particular area of the city, when the estate agents would suggest alternatives; and no one cares if as a black professional I question the educational output that is being given to my children and the young people I work with. To white society all that is irrelevant for if I have made it then everyone else can . . . My colleagues leave my office after sipping cups of tea. They are greatly impressed about both my position and knowledge and this is said quite openly. I get the sneaking impression that they are mildly shocked by my performance. This happens almost every day and thus like me, many blacks are contained in a society which sees and hears only what it wants and when it wants.'

(Quoted in Husband, 1982, pp. 180–1)

instance, Clatterbaugh cites Robert Staples' estimate that in North America as many as 46 per cent of black men between the ages of 16 and 62 are not in the labour force. Racism is similarly built into the division of labour found in the UK, with systematic differences for white and black British citizens in terms of rates of pay and unemployment (Braham, Rattansi and Skellington, 1992). The position of black men and women within the relations of economic production is more precarious than other members of the British and American working classes due to contemporary discrimination, conditions of immigration, the history of slavery and colonialism, and the strategies white populations have developed for containing black mobility. Discrimination is manifest, not just in employment practices but in housing, leisure pursuits and in schooling.

The research, principally North American, which has focused on black masculinity (cf. Angela Davis, 1982; Clyde Franklin, 1984; Manning Marable, 1983; Robert Staples, 1985; Michelle Wallace, 1979) has pointed to a distinctive contradiction that black men face between patriarchal expectations of masculinity, and the possibilities offered by capitalism. 'The message to black men from patriarchy is to "be a man"; the message from capitalism is "no chance" ' (Clatterbaugh, 1990, p. 143). Chapter 5 will consider further some of the cultural dimensions of black male experience which emerge from this tension.

In this chapter we wish to follow up Sallie Westwood's (1990) study of the practices of one group of young, black, working-class, British men in response to their social situation. Westwood is not arguing that her findings are representative of all black men in the UK, but her work does suggest some of the ways racism, economics, and masculinity might interact and the way aspects of black masculine expression in one case come to reflect material conditions and the organisation of social relations.

Masculinity for the men Westwood interviewed was defined through being 'streetwise'. North American writers talk about the importance for black men there of what is known as the 'cool pose' which has some aspects in common with a streetwise attitude (Clatterbaugh, 1990). As Box 4.6 demonstrates, being streetwise addresses several pressures. It is a way of acting out conventional masculine expectations for emotional control and independence while developing strategies for coping with racist violence and the police.

Andrew Tolson argues that one of the main characteristics of working-class men is their dependence on local territory and their local community for a sense of identity. This dependence is economic in origin and historically established. Westwood notes that this localism is even more intensely experienced by black men. When fear of racist attacks is a dominant experience then 'our streets' become even more crucial territory. This sense of territory may also be linked to a pattern of informal economic activity based on barter of goods and services. Westwood notes that, for the men she interviewed, being able to get things done, or to get things on the cheap through people they knew, was an important source of masculine self-esteem and masculine activity.

Westwood argues that home and the private/public distinction often have a contradictory meaning for black men, and this varies, too, across different ethnic groups. Among the West Indian community in the UK, many households are substantially controlled by women who act as the financial

---

Box 4.6: Streetwise strategies

'What is called up in relation to being streetwise is the ability to handle the dangers of street life, and this links masculinity, defence and manly behaviour. Contrary to the popular views, however, that being streetwise privileges physical prowess and fighting acumen, it is essentially an intellectual, cerebral attribute. What is required as a context for being streetwise and being able to operate safely on the streets is an intimate knowledge of locality which all the men shared . . . Faced with the power of the police the men would say that it was vital "to know how to handle yourself" and this meant everything but a physical response. As Dev commented, "You have to stay cool and let them heat up". Staying cool is essentially about maintaining dignity and control in a situation which very often denies both. It means remaining calm, signalled through a quiet voice and reasonableness in the face of what the men considered to be provocation. The quietness covers the necessity of staying mentally alert and agile. The men were conscious that their intimate knowledge gained from childhood of the local area was crucial to safety. All the men were wary of other parts of the city and especially the city centre late at night. It was dangerous and they did not voluntarily walk alone in the city up to and after midnight. It was not "safe", in fact it was known to be hostile. The language of safety expresses the feelings of trust and being at home only in their part of the town. "Safe" also applied to people, those who could be trusted, and to situations where the men felt at home. An intimate knowledge of locality allowed the men to disappear quickly if there was trouble on the streets and to reappear at some distance, usually, from the police. The speed of disappearance meant an ability to run and this was marked by the tracksuits and trainers that the men wore which were also a symbol of their commitment to sport. Tracksuits and trainers are not just about the whims of fashion, they express something about the nature of street life and the importance of physical fitness.'

(Westwood, 1990, pp. 64–5)

---

head of the house (Stone, 1983). Home is an arena where women have power. In this case some black men, partly because of their weak economic position within capitalism, and partly due to social and cultural history, have less opportunity to be 'patriarchal' in ways which are familiar to white British men. In many Muslim Asian families, however, cultural practices often empower not only older men but older women within the home. In this case, cultural preferences can reinforce what appears from a white perspective as patriarchal attitudes. Yet home life, too, has for many black families been an important source of resistance to racism, especially in the British context where immigration laws often divide black families (Carby, 1982; Parmar, 1982). The material structures of patriarchy and capitalism will, thus, interact in complex ways with racism and the established cultural practices of different groups, with differing consequences for the construction of black masculinity.

Masculinity and domestic life

Box 4.7: Men at home

'I think he's very good really, em, because he comes in and he's had a very brain filled day which can be much more exhausting than pick and shovels. And, er, they [children] just crawl all over him like ants, and he puts up with it, which I think is quite good.'

(Mother quoted in Backett, 1987, p. 83)

'He works six days a week so I don't want him to spend his one day off working around the house. He'd rather go out or he likes the garden. I think his one day off should be a day off, not a day doing *my* work.'

(Mother quoted in Boulton, 1983, p. 155)

'The mother will inevitably be in much closer contact with the children. And this is just because of my particular job, not just my particular job, many fellows in my position because of the demands of their job they are not in as close contact with the children as they could be or should be. So that your presence is required only in extremis.'

(Father quoted in Backett, 1987, p. 80)

'It's not that he's not willing to, I think he's just, he's one of these distractable people, he's always kind of off somewhere else. Uh, not that he's neglectful, but I think, like Leo's nappy needs changing now, and I'll go and do that whereas he'll just kind of not realise till the last minute.'

(Mother quoted in Croghan, 1991, p. 233)

'He probably could have helped a lot more than he did in fact, that's not his fault. He's a very very heavy sleeper and he didn't even hear him. He would wake up the next morning and say, "that was good, he didn't wake at all last night" and I would say, "did he hell! I was up nine times last night".'

(Mother quoted in Croghan, 1991, p. 235)

'I mean I participate when I feel like it, but if I feel like burying my head in the newspaper I do, or if I feel like ignoring the disturbances that are going on, then I can do it.'

(Father quoted in Backett, 1987, p. 83)

'I'm probably too clumsy... I suppose it goes back to the original awkward feeling... Um, I feel the way they are, how small they are... remarkably delicate... And since I know I'm not going to do it full-time I might as well let the experts get on with it and leave the amateurs out.'

(Father quoted in Lewis, 1986, p. 100)

'My wife insisted that I not leave everything to her; she fought with me to participate in the care of our son and apartment. I took the 2 am and 6 am feedings and changings, for our ideology did not allow me to just help out; I had to "share" and really participate in the whole thing. I resented that degree of involvement; it seemed to interfere terribly with the work I desperately wanted to achieve.

(Miller, 1974, p. 46)

'If Karl gives him a bath or gets his food ready, I'll tend to say, "thanks for doing that". We've talked about it a lot because Karl doesn't say thank-you to me when I do things. And I do feel if I say thank-you, maybe he'll do it more often. Praise him. It's kind of subtle ... managing men.'

(Mother quoted in Croghan, 1991, p. 238)

'I don't complain because if I complain he'll think, "she doesn't appreciate it, so I won't do it".'

(Mother quoted in Croghan, 1991, p. 237)

The extracts (*see* Box 4.7) from a range of mothers and fathers indicate the standard assumption that domestic work, particularly child-rearing is women's work. Men's domestic work is seen as optional and, thus, voluntary in a way which is just not possible for women. Women's working lives, with some differences across ethnic groups (cf. Bruegel, 1989), tend to fall into what Warrier (1988) describes as a pattern of two peaks and a trough. One peak occurs before children are born, with the other peak once children cease to be dependent. However, as Moss (1980) points out, most men often tend to work longer hours and are actually more likely to try to work full-time when they have young children. This is partly because family formation generally coincides with the time in their 20s and 30s when middle-class men are trying to establish their careers, but also because men across social class and ethnic groupings need to compensate for the loss or partial loss of their partner's income.

These differences indicate the presence of a sexual division of labour within the home which is just as pervasive and important for defining masculinity and men's experiences as class divisions in paid work. In recent decades, however, some aspects of these sexual divisions have been changing. Although women have always worked, their involvement in paid employment outside the home has varied in the last 50 years, from a high point, for example, during World War II to a low point in the 1950s. In 1951, 20 per cent of married women were economically active (Cohen, 1988). Currently, according to the most recent General Household Survey (1990), four in ten British mothers of children under five (41 per cent) go out to work. Of these mothers, 12 per cent work full-time, the rest part-time. As the age of dependent children increases, so does the proportion of women involved in the paid workforce. Thus, three in four mothers with children aged ten or over now work outside the home (31 per cent of these work full-time and 43 per cent part-time).

What has happened to the division of tasks within the home and the role of men? In some cases women's increased involvement in paid work means that their male partners have become more involved in domestic work. Consider, for example, the contrast this grandmother from a Sikh family living in the UK draws between her son's involvement compared with her husband's.

> Look at my son, he changes the baby's nappy and feeds him every day. He also cooks sometimes for his son and wife. He was even present at the birth of his son. My daughter-in-law just expects him to do all these things. I would not have dreamed of asking my husband even to fetch a glass of water or take care of the children when they were babies, not even when they were ill. My mother and sister helped then, not him. (Cited in Bhachu, 1988, p. 93)

Is this a trend? Researchers argue that while the variation in men's activities might have increased, along with their range of options for family involvement, the changes which have occurred have largely been restricted to particular areas of family life. Men in general, it seems, have not fundamentally altered their domestic activity. As a consequence there has emerged a 'double burden' for women as they have increased their paid work while maintaining similar levels of domestic work. Thus there has been an increase in paternal involvement around the time of childbirth, but little general difference in the performance of chores such as nappy changing (Lewis and O'Brien, 1987, p. 3). Charlie Lewis (1986) argues that fathers have always been involved to some extent in child-rearing, but nearly every generation assumes that their father is in some way less traditional than previous generations. Changes are thus often illusory.

On the basis of an intensive investigation of a sample of fathers, Russell (1983) argues that they seem to fall into four main types. Russell's research was conducted in Australia with 309 mainly white, English-speaking, two-parent families from a range of social backgrounds, but his findings match those of similar studies in the UK of white fathers across the social classes (Lewis, 1986). Russell describes one type as the 'uninterested and unavailable' father who is rarely at home. A second type is the 'traditional father', who spends more time at home, playing with his children, but who takes minimal responsibility for the day-to-day care. Third, there is what their female partners described as the 'good father'. These fathers would perform some basic childcare tasks, and were seen as good because they were willing to help their spouses. Russell describes the final type as the 'non-traditional highly participant father' who defines himself as sharing care with the

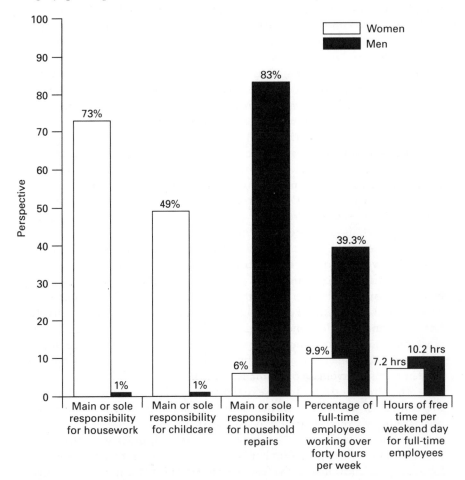

Figure 4.1 Leisure and household responsibilities
Note: Diagram shows only main responsibilities for domestic work and childcare; it does not indicate where such tasks are shared, and percentages do not therefore add up to 100. Source: Henwood, Rimmer and Wicks (eds), 1987, p. 67; data from Department of Employment/OPCS, *Women and Employment*, HMSO, 1984; Jowell and Witherspoon (eds) *British Social Attitudes, the 1985 Report*, Gower, 1985; CSO, *Social Trends 17*, HMSO, 1987.

mother. This unusual group of fathers carried out 46 per cent of childcare tasks each week, but Russell points out that even in these atypical cases mothers were seen mainly as taking overall responsibility for the child in terms of deciding the routine and organisation of the child's life.

Studies which have looked at the ways in which couples use time and at the allocation of work, leisure and parenting within marriage, have found that overall there have been only marginal increases in fathers' participation in childcare and domestic work in recent years (e.g. Land, 1983). Detailed studies of white families in the 1960s and the 1970s when women once again began to enter paid work on a large scale, note that the employment status of wives made very little difference to men's domestic contribution. The most remarkable feature of husband's domestic work-time is how little it changes, even in quite detailed activities, in response to changes in wives' working patterns, with the only notable increase in any domestic work activity being time spent cooking and/or washing up by men with full-time employed wives (Thomas and Zmroczek, 1985, p. 115).

The general pattern can be seen in Figure 4.1 which also indicates the typical consequences for the leisure time of women who work. Whereas male employees in the large sample surveyed experienced around 10.2 hours of free time per weekend day on average, and 2.6 hours during the week, for female employees the figures were 7.2 hours during weekend days and 2.1 hours for week days (Henwood, 1987).

As Russell (1983) notes, few fathers, even those most involved in child-care, take over the role of the absent working mother completely. Few, for example, carry out domestic chores in addition to childcare, and much of the domestic work is still left to the mother to complete on her return from work. Men tend to choose those parenting tasks which are highly visible, involve less engagement of time and attention, and fall towards the play end of the work/play childcare continuum (La Rossa and La Rossa, 1981). Increasingly, both men and women are earning but, within the home, men remain privileged in terms of avoidance of domestic work.

What are the effects of this sexual division of labour within the home on the control of resources? Most white mothers and fathers living within nuclear family structures generally assume that both incomes should be seen as contributions to the maintenance of the household, and that money should be shared either through a joint bank account or through the assignment of a housekeeping allowance to the female partner. This pattern, however, needs to be seen within the context of the equally prevalent assumption that it is appropriate for the main breadwinner (usually male) to decide the overall allocation of resources. Shared bank accounts need not necessarily imply equal access.

Jan Pahl (1980) has demonstrated, for example, that less than 50 per cent of couples investigated in a large study had a genuinely egalitarian 'pooling system' in which both partners had equivalent access to resources. In the

majority of couples, men either retained control of the family finances, or retained control of their own larger income and decided on its expenditure. Hilary Land (1983) argues that, as a consequence, conventional indices of poverty can be misleading, since they do not take account of the distribution of wealth *within* families. Mothers in families in quite comfortable circumstances may still be relatively badly off, even if they work. One survey conducted in 1984 suggested, for example, that married women earn only about half of their husband's earnings, with only 7 per cent of married women earning the same as or more than their husband (Martin and Roberts, 1984). These differences become even more salient when women are lone parents. According to Hearn (1987), female lone parents are four and a half times more likely to be in poverty than male lone parents.

Recent studies by Wilson (1987) and Brannen and Moss (1987) have found that whereas mothers, particularly in low income families, were often assigned the task of managing family finances, men were more likely to control access to resources and to decide on the relative distribution of family income. Thus fathers decided what proportion of family finances should be allocated to food and household expenses, while mothers ensured that those resources, however limited, provided for the family's needs. When men retain financial control, they can decide who is to benefit from expenditure and can, if they wish, distribute resources in ways which will benefit them in preference to other family members. When money becomes scarce, women

and children may well receive a smaller proportion. The importance of male control over financial resources is underlined by Graham's (1987) study of lone mothers in which she found that some were objectively better off, in financial terms, as single parents, although their household income had fallen, precisely because they now had control over their income.

> Ronald didn't like me buying anything for the children. If I went out and bought them a pair of shoes and he wasn't with me, there was hell to pay when I got home. He just didn't like me spending money without his consent. If he wanted to go out and buy things that was different. He was very keen on photography and he bought a lot of photographic equipment. What things he wanted to buy was O.K. but the basics and things I needed to get for the children, he thought was unreasonable. (Graham, 1987, p. 63)

These patterns, which suggest that the sexual division of labour within the home differentially empowers men, need to be qualified for race and ethnicity. It is important to remember that this domestic division of labour will intersect, not just with class but also race. Karen Stone (1983) argues on the basis of her studies with British West Indian mothers, for example, that quite a different ethos and distribution of resources occur in their case. The West Indian women she interviewed, unlike the white British mothers in her study, stressed the value of separate incomes and financial independence for women, and the importance of earning their own money so that they could regulate their income and choices apart from their male partners. The majority of Stone's West Indian respondents had not told their partners how much they earned and did not know their partner's earnings. This pattern is commensurate with the fact, as we noted earlier, that many West Indian mothers may well be the financial head of their household. Similarly, in the United States, Bell Hooks (1982) points out that, although family life may be exploitive for white women, we should not conclude that the family is the major source of oppression for women generally. Family life takes very different forms across ethnic groups, and often has a very different significance for black women and their role in determining the pattern of their lives.

Power within families is a complex matter, and women clearly can be powerful in certain respects through their mothering activities, but to the extent that power within the family and in society more generally depends on financial resources and freedom for paid work, then most men are in a more favourable position than most women. This unequal power relationship, from a social determinist perspective, is also likely to be an important contributor to phenomena such as male domestic violence and child abuse, along with prostitution and rape.

Patriarchy and masculinity

The inequalities between women and men and the pattern of social relations we have just described, combined with men's dominance in the world of work, in the public sphere, in politics, and culture, are what is usually meant by the term patriarchy. Originally this term had a much more specific meaning – referring to the rule of the patriarch or 'head of the family'. Today, however, while some writers retain this original sense (e.g. Andrew Tolson), it is more generally used to denote all the powers and privileges men enjoy as a group in relation to women. Feminist theorists and scholars have argued that men are as they are because of these systematic and structured differences in the social and economic position of men and women, along with the relationships and processes which sustain these differences (cf. Walby, 1990).

We will return to the concept of patriarchy in Chapter 6, giving a broader and more detailed picture of the feminist perspective on men and masculinity. For the moment, we will be concerned with understanding the material and economic basis of patriarchy and the effects of men's activities within the home. In terms of the perspective developed in this chapter the important claim is as follows – men's experiences and forms of masculinity will be strongly structured by their domestic practices and by their non-participation in domestic work. Masculinity is defined just as powerfully by what men do *not* do, as it is through the ways they *do* labour.

Feminist researchers have argued that there is a form of identity with both positive and negative dimensions which goes with female activities (cf. Oakley, 1979). Most men do not acquire the social skills that caring for others demands. This is their loss, but they also miss the experience of powerlessness, and the psychological consequences such as depression and higher rates of mental illness, which emerge from engaging in mothering and domestic work within a patriarchal context. The psychology of men in this view is structured by the fact that, in our society, men's contribution to domestic work is seen as largely optional. In an attempt to make sense of these patterns Jeff Hearn (1987) has developed an analysis of what he calls the 'reproductive activities' of society. His work builds on and, indeed, is immersed in the theoretical base established by feminist writers during the 1970s and 1980s, most notably the arguments of Juliet Mitchell (1971; 1975), Christine Delphy (1984) and Heidi Hartmann (1979). One of the aims of this feminist research was to initiate a dialogue with the categories and concepts of Marxist theory and, thus, extend Marxist analysis into new realms, while trying to make sense of the material and economic basis of male power. Following this path, Hearn describes his own research on masculinity as an attempt to develop a 'political economy' of patriarchy.

To understand Hearn's political economy of patriarchy, let us remind ourselves first of some of the main elements of Marxist theory. As we saw, Marx emphasised the antagonistic aspects of capitalism, and the way the interests of one class (the owners and their representatives) became pitted against the interests of workers. He also emphasised that capitalism had a historical basis. Modes of economic production are continually transforming, and a long-term historical perspective demonstrates these changes.

Finally, Marx developed concepts such as the notion of surplus value to try to explain the mechanism of exploitation within capitalist divisions of labour, and the concept of alienation to explain some of the psychological consequences of this pattern of social organisation.

How can this broad way of thinking about the social relations of production be applied to relations between men and women? Hearn and many feminist theorists argue that, while Marx quite brilliantly captured the essence of capitalist economic production, he underestimated the significance of a whole set of other practical human activities such as sexuality, child-rearing, nurturance and care for others, and the education and socialisation of young children. Marx perceived the exploitation of the working class, but quite failed to make sense of the way in which the economic organisation of society depended on the systematic exploitation of women to men's advantage. Women's domestic activities are not part of the mode of economic production as it is usually understood; they are concerned instead with the *reproduction* of society; that is, with the creation of new generations of workers which makes economic production possible in the first place.

In our society we tend to think of sexuality and motherhood, for example, as private and asocial experiences, usually involving love rather than money. As the previous two sections have demonstrated, however, these experiences do have a strongly material dimension, meaning that they are bound up with highly regulated social and economic patterns. These experiences also have material consequences for women and men, and it can be argued that these consequences influence the conditions for the expression of masculine and feminine identity. Further than this, Hearn argues that women and men within patriarchal societies can be seen as operating rather like the owners and workers in capitalist societies. Men, like owners to workers, stand in an exploitive relation to women. In this view men and women have become antagonistic 'gender classes'. Patriarchal societies are largely organised around the interests of men, just as capitalist societies are largely organised around the interests of the owners of capital, private property, and the means of production. Owners within capitalism control the labour of workers. Men, within patriarchy, control the reproductive activities of women, whether that be through abortion legislation, through male avoidance of childcare work, through the activities of mainly male medical experts, or through the threat of sexual violence.

Some women would argue that they do not feel controlled in that way. But, as Marxist theory points out, many workers do not perceive the real nature of their relationship with employers. Indeed, it is in the interest of owners and men to present their control of others as natural and reasonable, and to obscure this control – mystifying, for example, the process of the extraction of surplus value. Hearn and feminist theorists argue that they are describing a general pattern of male rule, and this pattern will, of course, contain many exceptions. The direct rule of patriarchs (fathers) within families is no longer so common, but it is still the case that men in general dominate women. Men as a gender class can also be divided into different class fractions, where, as we saw with our initial example of the married black miner and the gay white teacher, some men are more implicated in patriarchy than others. Men and women within patriarchal societies are thus seen as locked into a type of class struggle, with women, particularly child-workers, as an exploited group. One implication is that middle-class and working-class men, although divided within productive relations, will have vested interests in common when it comes to reproductive activities, but what are the mechanisms of male control?

Hearn points out that, unlike relations of production, reproductive activities do not involve producing commodities and goods for sale which have an 'exchange value'. The domestic work women do within families is not a form of labour, either, which could be sold to the highest bidder on an employment market. Women are not paid for their reproductive 'products'. Exploitation is not a matter of appropriating the surplus value from some-one's work. Instead, men appropriate what Hearn calls the human values that women produce. In Hearn's description, men extract 'human tithes' from women, and these tithes can extend from trivial favours, to major domestic commitments. As husbands and fathers, men routinely receive privileges from women without recompense for them (1987, p. 69).

Like capitalism, patriarchy is shored up by a series of institutions where male power is consolidated and developed. Following the work of the femin-ist theorist Mary O'Brien (1981), Hearn describes fatherhood as one of these key institutions. As O'Brien (1981) notes, fatherhood, unlike motherhood, is an uncertain state. Men cannot be totally confident that a child is theirs unless they are totally confident of their control over the women's sexuality. O'Brien argues that men are, in this way, 'alienated' from the birth process, and from the products of their semen. Once men began to understand their role in procreation – that there was some connection between their sexual activities and the birth of babies – then it became in their interests to regulate women's sexuality to overcome their alienation. Monogamy and marriage can be seen as male strategies which underpin the institution of fatherhood. As Arthur Brittan (1989) points out, marriage is a kind of collective bargaining among men to legitimate their control over their female partner's sexuality and children. As Hearn argues, powerful male fraternities based around the law, the Church and the State also underwrite this matrimonial control through legislation and economic practices, with domestic violence as an additional level of threat.

A second institution of patriarchy is one Hearn calls 'hierarchic hetero-sexuality' which can be seen similarly as a form of collective bargaining among men about the expression of sexuality. As Brittan notes, this insti-tution involves the transformation of biology, or all the possible ways in which sexuality can be expressed, into politics, or a set of laws, prohibitions, and habitual practices. Some forms of heterosexuality become seen as normal and permissable, along with patterns of flirtation, male advances and court-ship, while other patterns such as sexuality based on non-penetration, or cases where women initiate sexual contact, become seen as unusual and unexpected. Some of the most rigorous policing, however, concerns male homosexuality which becomes seen as a transgression. Jarman's account (*see* Box 4.8) reminds us of the extent to which male and female sexuality is legislated and controlled by patriarchal procedures of inheritance, marriage, and the registration of fatherhood.

Box 4.8: Hierarchic heterosexuality

'I was born on the 31 January 1942 at seven thirty in the morning at Royal Victoria Nursing Home in Northwood.

For the first twenty-five years of my life I lived as a criminal, and the next twenty-five were spent as a second-class citizen, deprived of equality and human rights. No right to adopt children and if I had children, I could be declared an unfit parent; illegal in the military; and age of consent of twenty-one; no right of inheritance; no right of access to a loved one; no right to public affection; no right to an unbiased education; no legal sanction of my relation-ships and no right to marry. These restrictions subtly deprived me of my freedom. It seemed unthinkable that it could be any other way, so we all accepted this.

In ancient Rome, I could have married a boy; but in the way that ideals seem to become their shadows, love came only to be accepted within marriage. Since we could not be married, we could not fall in love. Since we could not fall in love we were not loved.'

(Derek Jarman, 1992, p. 4)

Feminist social policy researchers have suggested that other key patri-archal institutions are the 'caring and medical professions' which are often staffed by women, but managed by men (Wilson, 1977). Increasingly, male experts are taking over from individual fathers in regulating the shape of family life. This regulation is connected, too, to government and the State, again largely male enclaves. Through social policy, the law, and the eco-nomics of the welfare state, governments can exert considerable control over the family lives of men and women. As feminist researchers have pointed out, these arrangements, whether it be in terms of pensions or the structure of benefits, typically reinforce female economic dependence on men.

Are men deliberately choosing, therefore, to oppress women? Hearn argues that men do have a considerable degree of choice. They can choose not to exploit women's domestic work; they can choose to turn fatherhood from a symbolic activity into a real commitment of energy and time; and they can choose to degrade women sexually or to look for alternative types of hetero-sexual relationships. However, he says men's choices also depend on perceiving and undercutting what he calls the process of 'self-oppression'. 'We men are formed and broken by our own power' (p. 98).

To choose alternatives, in Hearn's view, depends on being socialised and constructed differently, and radical change depends on drastically changing the material conditions of patriarchy. Patriarchy is not, in the final analysis, simply a matter of choice, or a male conspiracy, since masculinity is constructed from these structured social relations. According to the general perspective on masculinity outlined in this chapter, to be a man is to enter into relations with women through a social structure, and that structure exists over and above the individual actions of any particular man.

Patriarchy and capitalism

One of the dangers involved in studying men's paid work outside the home, then patterns of work within the home, is that patriarchy and capitalism come to be seen as separate systems. Patriarchy becomes applied to understand the world of women and the private sphere of the home, while capitalism becomes synonymous with the public sphere of production outside the home, but this is to misrepresent the complexity of the material and economic relationships between the two. As a number of feminist scholars have argued, patriarchy and capitalism are best seen as 'dual systems', working in combination, or with such a degree of inter-connection that the two have become fused (Eisenstein, 1979; Hartmann, 1979; Mitchell, 1971; 1975). Race, of course, interacts here, too, as a third inter-locking system producing economic and material patterns.

As Arthur Brittan (1989) notes, there is no reason why capitalism could not be gender-blind (or race-blind, for that matter). It is possible to imagine, for example, all our current economic practices occurring with a hermaph-roditic population, or in societies where there are no notions of sex differences. Someone needs to raise the next generation of workers, someone must iron shirts and buy soap powder, someone must work as typists, receptionists and serve in shops, someone must be available to work part-time when the economic climate favours this mode of extracting surplus value. However, there is no reason at all, intrinsic to capitalism, why it should be women who mainly do these things, or why black people should also be concentrated in certain economic areas. The fact that it *is* women suggests the way patriarchy has come to intersect with capitalism as the kind of 'dual system' proposed by feminist theorists. Although millions of women have entered the paid work-force, they have largely had to do so on men's terms, and so women's power and influence in society have not increased accordingly. Susan Faludi (1992) notes, for example, that it is still the case that the average working woman, in both the UK and USA, earns only just over two-thirds of a man's wage for the same work. Part-time female workers (and in the UK 86 per cent of part-time workers are women) are particularly poorly placed, with an average hourly rate in 1990 which is little more than half that of male full-time earnings.

Feminist theorists (Walby, 1990) argue on the basis of empirical research into the workplace that this pattern is not due to lower skills or qualifications and is not entirely due either to the way childcare is assigned to women. Rather, this inequality arises because women are concentrated in low-paying industries. There is a complex process of job segregation which occurs to the advantage of men and the disadvantage of women, resulting in a class of 'women's occupations' and a (higher) class of 'men's occupations'. Women become nurses, men doctors. In factories, women frequently end up in jobs which are more arduous than some men's jobs, for which they receive half the pay because the male jobs, through a complex process of negotiation, have been defined as more skilled. In modern computing industries women are hired as data entry key-punchers; men predominate as operators, salesmen, system analysts and managers (Connell, 1987). The social processes which produce this occupational segregation are complex, subtle, and probably to some extent vary, Walby argues, from workplace to workplace. The design of technology combines with the definition of skills and with training

---

Box 4.9: The old boy network

'Many old boys will deny the very idea. Lieutenant Colonel John Stephenson, the MCC secretary, for one. Interviewed on radio yesterday he denied the existence of an old boys' network. All that happened was that men who knew each other talked to each other. On the other side of the gender barrier it all looks very different. Not many women want to play cricket for England, but many would like promotion at work. Most will fail to reach the level that their competence deserves: only three out of 100 senior managers, for example, are women. Yet according to a survey of 1,500 women managers published yesterday, the cause of this shortfall is old and familiar. What concerned them most was not the lack of childcare facilities or the prejudice of colleagues. Top of their list by far came the men's club culture . . . Discrimination has always come in three forms: overt and intentional, disguised but deliberate, and unintentional but adverse. The last two categories – which cover the old boys' network – are by far the most difficult to tackle. There is nothing organised about the men's club culture. There are no rules, formal meetings or leaders. Membership is unregistered. Meetings are spontaneous. The people meet – in pub, wine bar, or canteen – to talk over common interests: last Saturday's football results or next week's boxing. Conversations on sport flow naturally into business contract talk. Yet the culture is shutting out 51% of the nation's brainpower.'

(Editorial in the *Guardian*, Nov 3 1992)

practices. Male closure against women in key industries, covert acts of sexism, and mass male avoidance of childcare work are other strategies by which men have historically consolidated their economic position.

The processes through which men come to dominate the public sphere of paid work include, as Box 4.9 indicates, the construction of fratriarchies (Remy, 1990) and male closed shops. Women managers thus complain of meeting 'glass ceilings', or invisible barriers to promotion. As Cynthia Cockburn (1981; 1983) shows in her studies of print workers, other strategies include the design of machines so their use depends on certain levels of physical strength, despite the availability of alternative technologies. Access to training is also controlled, along with the definition of what counts as skilled labour. 'The compositor sitting at a keyboard setting type is represented as doing skilled work. A girl typist sitting at a desk typing a letter is not – though the practical difference today is slight' (1981, p. 49).

Robert Connell (1983; 1987) points out that, as a consequence of these lines of feminist research, it is now difficult to argue that gender divisions represent simply an addition to capitalism. Connell disagrees, therefore, with other theorists of masculinity such as Tolson who, as we noted, seems to suggest that patriarchy supplies an ideology merely working 'on top' of the basic determinants of male behaviour which lie in capitalism. Gender inequality is a profound feature of the organisation of economic production in itself. It is not meaningful to talk of patriarchy plus capitalism. Instead, we should be identifying a whole series of inter-connected social processes which produce male dominance across the board. Men, Connell points out, are in a position where they can systematically accumulate the profits from women's labour, whether that is in the home or through male control of women's activities in the paid workforce. 'Socialist theory can no longer evade the fact that capitalism is run by, and mainly to the advantage of, men' (1987, p. 104). In considering the social practices which produce masculinity, we have to look not just at the organisation of capitalism, but also at work in the home, and at how capitalism and patriarchal structures interact, along with the further dimension of race neglected by many researchers.

Hegemonic masculinity

These arguments about the intertwining of capitalism and gender divisions chime with other recent trends in feminist and social theory, and the general move away from 'categorical theories' (Connell, 1987; cf. also Nicholson, 1990). Categorical theories are those which seek to find a single systematic cause for men's social position, whether that is in biology, in the organisation of sexual reproduction, in capitalism, or in the organisation of family life. These theories also assume that men and women can be treated as homogeneous groups, acting jointly as social categories with the same interests. A prime example of this assumption can be found in Hearn's argument, reviewed earlier, that men act as a 'gender class' pitted against women who form the antagonistic 'gender class'.

Are men this kind of group? Arthur Brittan (1989) argues that, although men clearly have some interests in common, they cannot be described as a class in the sense of being united by their material interests, their common identity, community and social position. What we seem to be dealing with, as Hearn acknowledges, is a regularity with major anomalies. In other words, there is a pattern to men's behaviour, but men are positioned in relation to this pattern in very different ways. As Connell points out, the advantages and disadvantages of gender divisions are not distributed evenly between men, let alone between women or between men and women.

> The printing tradesmen studied by Cynthia Cockburn are minor beneficiaries; the media capitalists who employ them are major beneficiaries. Not all women are major losers, a fact of strategic importance to feminism. Overall the benefits, opportunities and costs are large enough to be worth fighting for, and motivate the practice of demarcation and exclusion by many groups of men. (Connell, 1987, p. 105)

Similarly, it is clear that many black or gay men are the recipients of the violence of other homophobic and racist men. In this case, some men are acting to oppress and control the masculinity expressed by other men.

Connell and his colleagues (Carrigan, Connell, and Lee, 1985) suggest that many analyses of the social basis of gender relations tend to be too schematic. They work with too broad a brush, beginning their studies with two groups, 'men' and 'women' as absolutes, developing case-studies of representative individuals, and thus neglecting differences and finer gradations. Connell's solution has been to focus his attention, not on men and women as pre-given categories, but on what Carrigan, Connell and Lee (1985) call, following the feminist anthropologist Gayle Rubin (1975), the workings of the sex/gender system. We can think of the sex/gender system as covering a set of social processes, activities and practices which are continually changing through history. This system throws up certain social structures or constraints on people's actions, interacting with social systems of class and race. Certain practices and activities become dominant and habitual in certain areas of society as a result of prevailing material pressures. As a consequence, different types of men and women emerge, and different types of masculinity and femininity. There is the possibility of considerable variation depending on people's local circumstances and the way these interact with national and global movements.

Connell argues that the continuation of this system is not automatic; the entire structure is heaving with local struggles as women workers, for example, fight for equal pay, or better childcare facilities. There are struggles between groups of men over the proper expression of masculinity, whether, for instance, gay men should be legally permitted to be part of the military and could count as 'proper soldiers'. Male capitalists compete with each other for the control of women's labour, but at the centre of all these developments is a series of battles for power and control. Masculinity and femininity, then, emerge through power relations which are characterised by constant contradictions, turmoil and change.

Carrigan, Connell and Lee (1985) suggest that what masculinity researchers should be investigating is what they call 'hegemonic masculinity'. In other words, the power of certain groups of men to force an interpretation of what masculinity should be and, thus, to subordinate or repress other styles of masculine expression and women more generally. Men's different positions in relation to women, in terms of class, race, and sexual expression, construct men with different personalities and ways of being men. What is striking, however, is the way some of these personal styles are accepted as more legitimate than others, becoming rewarded and powerful. This theme will be taken up in more detail in Chapter 5. Carrigan, Connell and Lee argue that many men, if not actually living up to the cultural notions of dominant masculinity themselves are, nonetheless, complicit in sustaining this hegemonic masculinity, since they have a great deal to gain from the general subordination of women by hegemonic men. The principal research question must be 'how particular groups of men inhabit positions of power and wealth, and how they legitimate and reproduce the social relationships that generate their dominance' (1985, p. 592).

This emphasis on divisions within men is useful for studies of masculinity and social relations. There are some areas of ambiguity, however, and often it is not quite clear from Carrigan et al.'s account just what counts as hegemonic masculinity. Take, for example, the case of the butcher in Box 4.4. The male strategies described here seem designed, not only to make the time pass, but also to control and dominate women. This surely must be an example of a culturally sanctioned hegemonic masculinity. Yet in many respects the butcher and his workmates cannot be described as powerful men in broad political and economic terms. At the time of writing, powerful men such as John Major, Prime Minister of the UK and Bill Clinton, President of the USA and other figures of the male establishment, frequently do not seem to possess this immediate sense of machismo. Hegemonic masculinity itself turns out to be contradictory and variable. What is most helpful, however, about the analysis offered by Connell and his colleagues is its emphasis on the dynamic properties of social practices and, thus, the scope for change.

We have covered a wide canvas in this chapter from analyses of capitalism, to theories of patriarchy, and finally, the concept of hegemonic masculinity. Along the way we have considered the neglected area of masculinity and the social structures and divisions of race and spent some time documenting the influence of feminist scholars. Yet, despite this broad sweep, one theme has recurred – to understand men one has to understand their social and economic activities. We have to understand the kind of social practices in which men are embedded, whether at home or at work, and we have to theorise the material and economic position of men. We called this claim a materialist or social determinist argument, and we have seen that, although all the theorists discussed in this chapter wish to root masculinity in men's experiences of social and economic conditions, they disagree profoundly about how best to describe those conditions. In evaluating this material, you need to be aware of the different stresses on class versus patriarchy versus race and the different means for integrating these. We have seen, too, that this body of work develops a much more complex and conflicting picture of men's social position than role theory. Chapter 5 will build on the analysis presented here, looking at the social history of various cults of masculinity and reflecting on the relationship between ideas of what men should be like and the social practices and power relations we have just considered.

Chapter 5

The cultural domination of men

Chapter 4 emphasised the material realities of men's lives. Masculinity was analysed as a response to certain economic and domestic situations, and was seen as a consequence of men's involvement in particular sets of social practices. In this chapter we will be adopting a different perspective, one which sees masculinities as a set of 'cults' or ideologies. In a way this represents a return to one of the key themes of Chapter 3. There we heard role theorists arguing that males become manly by learning to perform a set of social *scripts*. Now that we have got a more sophisticated understanding of the social practices underpinning masculinity, it is time to take a fresh look at the notion of masculine scripts, this time from the perspective of those working within cultural studies.

According to Stuart Hall (1981; 1977; Hall *et al.*, 1980) cultural studies began life as an academic discipline, sometime during the late 1950s and 1960s, with the publication of several important texts. Richard Hoggart's (1957) *The Uses of Literacy,* Raymond Williams's (1963) *Culture and Society* and E P Thompson's (1968) *The Making of the English Working Class* all broke with the previous tradition of cultural analysis (such as the literary criticism of F R Leavis and the journal *Scrutiny*) which understood culture in terms of 'high art' such as opera, theatre and classical literature. Instead, Hoggart, Williams and Thompson considerably broadened the concept of culture, defining it to include the customs, traditions and even language of a cultural community. It became seen as the 'whole way of life' of a society or group. Culture became understood as a framework, passed down from generation to generation, through which ordinary people conduct and make sense of their everyday lives. Cultural studies workers were interested in how these 'ways of life' were related to the kind of social and economic divisions described in Chapter 4. They were particularly concerned with the history of different cultural codes and the limits of human agency in the construction of cultural forms.

131

From a cultural studies perspective almost every culture in the world must embody a set of particular ideas or themes which relate to men and masculinity. Like the scripts of role theory, these 'cults' can be seen as providing members of the wider cultural community with a shared understanding of what it *means* to be a man; what one looks like, how one should behave and so forth. The first task of the cultural analyst is to identify and record these messages; to be able to read what the culture has to say about men and masculinity. But how does one 'get at' this information? In contemporary Western societies, perhaps the easiest way is to simply switch on the television or open a book or magazine and study the ways in which men are commonly talked about and portrayed. For example, Figure 5.1 shows four different photographs of men taken from various sources. If we look carefully at these images we should be able to see that each provides us with information about the meaning of masculinity. However, it is also clear that they present, not a single, consistent image of manhood, but a range of different and even contradictory representations.

The fictional figure of James Bond (Figure 5.1(*a*)) will be familiar to most readers. For several decades Bond has provided a very powerful and attractive model of (particularly British) masculinity. Bond is an archetypal hero, forever willing to risk his own life in order to defeat evil. As a man, Bond is invariably portrayed as a charming and sophisticated gentleman with impeccable style and manners. He is courageous, loyal (to Queen and country at least) and romantic. Yet perhaps the most intriguing or compelling thing about Bond is that behind all of this gloss, he remains a highly accomplished killer.

In contrast, the image of manhood captured in Figure 5.1(*b*) contains none of Bond's polish. The man represented here is far more primitive, raw and rugged. He is no gentleman, with no time for social graces and niceties. Indeed, his masculinity is, in part, signified by his complete disregard of such conventions. He is free. It is also significant that the photograph portrays the man merely in terms of his head or face (which wears a cunning, contemplative expression). This style of representation (the head and upper body shot) is most common for men, in contrast to images of women which typically feature their entire bodies. The symbolic implication of this pattern of representation is, of course, that masculinity is a state of *mind*, rather than body.

This standard practice makes the image in Figure 5.1(*c*) all the more remarkable. Here we have a man who is virtually head*less*; portrayed as just a body or torso. Furthermore, it is a very muscular body, big, shiny and full of athletic potential. As if to emphasise this impression, the body is caught in an active pose or posture (similar to those struck by body builders in competition) which shows the muscles at work. It is a masculinity defined by brawn rather than brains.

The fourth and final image (Figure 5.1(*d*)) is different again. Here we see a man portrayed very much in terms of his relationship with another person.

(a)

(b)

(c)

(d)

Figure 5.1 A Multiplicity of Masculine Identities (a) © Lex Features Limited, (b) and (c) © The Image Bank, (d) © Stock, Boston, Inc.

The scene is of an intimate moment between a man and a woman. They are surely lovers. The couple, quite literally, only have eyes for each other as they sit close together with their legs intertwined. Man, here, is portrayed as an emotional being; someone with feelings and desires and, therefore, vulnerabilities. (Bond, in contrast, is a womaniser who rarely if ever falls in love.)

These four images are united by their *positive* representation of men. They provide the reader with straightforward examples or illustrations of what a man should be like. However, the same sort of information can be conveyed through the use of *negative* images. For example, in the early 1990s there was a series of advertisements on British television promoting a range of cleaning fluids called 'Mr Muscle'. In each advert the same man is shown using the products. He is small, thin, wears glasses, and does his cleaning dressed in a vest and boxer shorts. These adverts work primarily by means of a contrast between the man and the product. Mr Muscle is strong and effective, it gets even the most difficult jobs done in next to no time (this could easily be a line taken from the advert itself). The man in the advert, on the other hand, has no 'muscle' (and because he is only semi-clothed we can see this), he appears weak, and by implication, impotent. He, unlike the product, falls short of the masculine ideal. The point is, of course, that through the use of Mr Muscle the man is able to make up for his own deficiencies. Mr Muscle, in a sense, makes a real man of him.

It should now be clear how representations of men in popular culture inform their audiences about the meanings of masculinity. In most instances, however, the meanings of such representations do not reside *solely* within the images themselves. For example, in a recent edition of *Arena* magazine (a glossy, British-based publication aimed specifically at a male readership) there appeared an advertisement for *Knickerbox* underwear. It featured a number of photographs of the same black male model, dressed in various garments, and adopting a range of different 'muscular poses' similar to that found in Figure 5.1(c). Like many adverts, this one works simply by associating the product with something of high social value – in this case a *real* man's body, signified by muscle. But the point is that unless the readers themselves make the equation of manliness with muscle (unless they bring this assumption to the advert), the commercial impact of the image is completely undermined.

Possibly the best way to understand how the images in Figure 5.1 function in relation to the wider cultural environment is to think of them as 'buying into' a set of already established ideas about men and masculinity. In the process of so doing, they help to reproduce or recycle the culture, ensuring its continuation. This is not to say that is is impossible to produce images or representations which develop, or even challenge, existing ways of under-

---

* (It is significant that black bodies seem to be frequently used to signify this form of masculine identity; a fact which indicates something of the history of white, Western representations of black men – we will return to the issues of the cultural representations of black men later on in Chapter 5.)

standing the world. Indeed, as we hope to demonstrate, the history of the concept of masculinity is a story, not of smooth consistency, but of struggle and change. Nevertheless, it is still likely that most of what one understands by the concept of masculinity has been inherited from the past, like some great family heirloom.

One of the principal aims of any cultural analysis is to reveal the system of meanings and understandings through which members of a given cultural community live. This is achieved, by and large, through the use of historical and cross-cultural comparisons. Both of these techniques function by drawing attention to the fact that our own view of the world is neither natural nor inevitable. Instead, it is merely one perspective among many others.

We will begin our review with a look at some of the historical work on men and masculinity, focusing upon the various ways in which concept has been defined at different points in the past. As well as throwing contemporary culture into 'relief', this work also allows us to see the origins of some of today's images, symbols and myths of masculinity. The section which follows presents some cross-cultural analyses of masculinity. This presentation evokes a different, but equally important, issue for the cultural analyst; namely, the relationship between culture and society. Our guiding questions are, therefore, these: how does the cultural analyst explain the historical development of the concept of masculinity, and, what is it about the conditions of a society which allow a particular definition of the concept to dominate? In the final section of this chapter, we move on to look at how cultural theorists have viewed the relationship between 'cults' of masculinity and individual men. How, in other words, are men constituted by or through a given culture? At the same time we consider the issue of cultural determination, asking to what extent men are free to intervene in the construction of their own identity.

A history of concepts of masculinity

The myth of masculinity certainly goes back to the ancient world of Greece and Rome; however, its present form is stamped indelibly by the Renaissance and by the rise of capitalism. No attempt to analyse masculinity ... can ignore the way masculinity is defined by history.

Antony Easthope (1990)

As has already been implied, the meaning of masculinity is not stable. It changes over time. What might be considered appropriate male behaviour in one historical period, in another may be thought inappropriate or even antithetical. Dover (1978) and Veyne (1985) describe, for example, how, unlike today, homosexual behaviour between males was a common and accepted part of both ancient Greek and Roman society.

So long as this homosexuality conformed to current images of the 'male' (active) role in sex play, it was entirely compatible with, in fact, supportive of, a fully masculine image in the society at large. Indeed, the Spartans, like other Greeks of the time, thought that such men made better soldiers because they had their lovers with them on the battlefield to prevent them from becoming lonely and depressed. (Gilmore, 1990, p.154)

Today, of course, the idea of a brave and skilful warrior (such as James Bond perhaps) enjoying sexual relations with adolescent boys might strike many as incongruous, for our contemporary common sense presents us with very different images of the homosexual and the warrior. The stereotypical gay man is seen as rather gentle and pacific, whereas the warrior is portrayed as someone who is (also) fiercely heterosexual.

In one of the most interesting studies of the history of masculinity, Paul Hoch (1979) argues that, not only has the concept undergone a series of changes, but also that these transformations fall into a clearly discernible pattern. Hoch suggests that the last 3000 years of Western history can be broken down into periods where either one of two opposing forms of masculine ideal has been culturally dominant (*see* Table 5.1). On the one hand, there is an identity which Hoch calls the Puritan; a 'hard-working, hard fighting hero who adheres to a production ethic of duty before pleasure'. Alternating with the Puritan is a very different form of masculinity which Hoch labels the Playboy. He is much more of an aristocratic figure, one 'who lives according to an ethic of leisure and sensual indulgence' (p.118).

Reading from Table 5.1 we can see that there have been four periods in

Table 5.1

Puritan	Playboy
Early Rome (1000–186BC) e.g. farmer-warrior	
	Roman Empire (186BC–476AD) e.g. patrician courtier
Dark and Middle Ages (476–1300) e.g. knight	
	Renaissance (1300–1519) (somewhat later in England) e.g. chivalrous courtier
Reformation (1519–1600), Cromwellian period (1640–1660) e.g. Calvinist Puritan	
	Age of Gallantry (1650–1789) e.g. Enlightenment gallant
Methodism and Victoriana (1760–1880) e.g. Victorian businessman or American frontiersman	
	Consumer society (1880–present) e.g. modern playboy

which, Hoch argues, the Puritan type of masculine ideal has held sway. In the first, manliness was equated with the life of a farmer-warrior. A man had to strive long and hard in the fields to produce enough food to feed himself and his family. At the same time he was frequently called upon to defend his property from the attacks of enemy tribes. Life as a ninth-century feudal knight was similar in many ways. Once again manliness was associated with 'the virtues of industrious farming' and courage and skill on the battlefield. Serfs were taught how to use the longbow, quarterstaff and pike, although they were not considered manly enough to wield either the longsword or mace (Hoch, 1979, p.125). The sixteenth and seventeenth centuries heralded a new age of the Puritan male associated with the rise of Protestantism. According to the pronouncement of Martin Luther and the fathers of the Calvinist churches, sloth (laziness) was one of the most terrible sins.

> The masculine archetype of Calvinism can be found in the stately black-garbed figures of Vermeer portraits: sober, almost sombre; avoiding the romanticism of the 'Romish' courtiers and cultivating instead a serious personality; what was called a decent restraint. 'His life is that of a soldier in hostile territory', writes Tawney. 'Tempered by self-examination, self-discipline, self-control, he is the practical ascetic, whose victories are won, not in the cloister, but on the battlefield, in the counting house and in the market.' (Hoch, 1979, p.134)

According to Hoch, the fourth and most recent era of the Puritan occurred around 140 years later. In both Victorian England and nineteenth-century America, the central qualities of the masculine ideal were courage, determination and an infinite capacity for vigorous activity.

In stark contrast, Hoch suggests, the Playboys of the Roman Empire, Renaissance and Enlightenment periods saw nothing manly in a life of blood and toil. Indeed, in the case of the Roman patricians, such activities were considered beneath the status of a man. For them, a real man employed slaves to do his work and allowed foreign soldiers to do his fighting. Their conception of masculinity 'tended to revolve around a consumption ethic of elegant living, cultivated prostitution, high culture and life at the Emperor's Court' (Hoch, 1979, p.122). The chivalrous courtier of the Renaissance period was similarly an identity opposed to the gritty stoicism of the Puritan male. This was the time of knights in shining armour wooing and winning the favours of fair maidens. Men were romantic beings, rather than people who repressed or denied their feelings. The third phase of the Playboy ideal emerged, Hoch argues, during the middle part of the seveeenth century. The 'court dandy' or Enlightenment 'gallant', like his predecessors, rejected the values of the previous period (in this case, of Calvinism). Instead, they busied themselves with dressing up in fancy costumes and attending high-society functions.

> The courtier class devoted much attention to the latest fashions, developed elaborate codes of manly decorum, and practised tossing their periwigs back and forth in a special swoop called the 'French wallow'. (Hoch, 1979, p.137)

As we can see from Table 5.1, Hoch's argument is that twentieth-century Western men are the latest developments in this oscillating, alternating history. Certainly around the time when Hoch was writing (mid to late 1970s) there appeared to be strong parallels between, say, the fashion-consciousness of the Enlightenment gallants, and that of the 1970s' man who, instead of ruffles, lace and periwigs, sported purple shirts, flared trousers and platform shoes. The sexual mores of society in the 1960s and 1970s also seemed more in line with the libertarian attitudes of previous Playboy periods (e.g. tolerance to extra-marital and homosexual activities) rather than the strict moral conservatism characteristic of the Puritan eras.

Hoch's historical account of the development of masculinity is undoubtedly a piece of work that is interesting and full of insight. By surveying such an extended period of time, he is able to gain a sense of the broad pattern of changes in manliness. It would seem harsh, therefore, to criticise Hoch for presenting too simplified a picture of these changes. For it would have been virtually impossible to have provided a more detailed level of analysis while maintaining such a long-term perspective. Nevertheless, as it stands, Hoch's analysis presents a somewhat misleading history, for if we look again at Table 5.1, we get the distinct impression that the history of concepts of masculinity is a story of long uninterrupted periods of stability, punctuated by dramatic moments of change. To some extent this is a product of the fact that Hoch appears able to provide very specific 'turning points' between the two ideals of manliness he identifies. Indeed, for the first two transformations. Hoch claims to be able to identify the precise year (despite suggesting that his dates are only 'rough approximations'). This impression is then further reinforced when, in reference to the change-over from Calvinist Puritan to Enlightenment gallant, he states:

> *In a matter of months* the standards of dress and decorum [of the Cavaliers at the English Restoration Court of Charles II] jumped from the sombre austerity of Cromwell's Puritans to the flamboyant frippery of the returning aristocrats. (Hoch, 1979, p.137 – emphasis added)

Hoch does not claim that there was a series of absolute changes in thinking about masculinity. By adopting the notion of cultural dominance, he obviously understands his history to be a chart of the fluctuating 'popularities' of these two discourses of masculinity. When the Playboy identity is dominant, the Puritan ideal is not culturally absent. Rather, it lurks in the background, either as an object of criticism or as a minority view (held by the old-fashioned or nostalgic). However, in portraying the transitions from one ideal to the other as relatively brief affairs, Hoch seriously understates the extent to which the meaning of manhood is culturally contested. While he implies that consensus is the historical norm, other analysts have suggested that argument and debate is the more common state of affairs. For example, whereas Hoch portrays nineteenth-century American culture as embracing a single version of the Puritan ideal, Rotundo (1987) has argued that there were three quite different ideals of manhood existing side by side: the 'Masculine Achiever', 'Christian Gentleman' and the 'Masculine Primitive'. Let us now consider these three competing nineteenth-century ideals in more detail.

Emerging at the end of the eighteenth century, the Masculine Achiever was an identity which, according to Rotundo, emphasised the importance of independent action. Influenced by John Locke's political philosophy (sections of which appear almost verbatim in both the American Constitution and the Declaration of Independence), this identity was equated with self-advancement and the unceasing pursuit of wealth, underpinned by a 'tremendous faith' in the idea that hard work, almost irrespective of ability, was the key to individual success (the basis, of course, of the 'American Dream'). For example, Rotundo quotes a lawyer called Horace Leete, who in 1846 wrote 'a man of moderate abilities, by close application may rise above those of the brightest genius' (p. 37).

In contrast, the Christian Gentleman was an identity which Rotundo sees as very much opposed to the values of the Masculine Achiever. Echoing the sentiments of Martin Luther more than 200 years beforehand, proponents of this ideal denounced the pursuit of fame and worldly fortune as neither manly nor Christian. Instead, they emphasised the importance of love, kindness and compassion. Self-sacrificing behaviour was seen as the road to salvation, self-seeking behaviour as the road to damnation. Ironically, both the Christian Gentleman and Masculine Achiever placed a heavy emphasis upon the notion of self-control. In the case of the Christian Gentleman this took the form of a check on the 'pleasures of the flesh' (i.e. sex and drink), whereas in the case of the Masculine Achiever curbs were placed on all emotions that might undermine or otherwise interfere with a man's ability to compete in the market-place.

Rotundo argues that the Masculine Primitive existed as an obvious and direct contrast to both of the above; celebrating, instead, men's 'natural passions and impulses'. According to this ideal, men harbour a primordial instinct for survival, which, if anything, could be dulled or even eradicated by excessive social restrictions. In a way which clearly resonated with Darwin's *On the Origin of Species* (published in 1859), society was likened to a jungle environment in which men had to fight for survival. The ideal of the Masculine Primitive promoted an almost obsessional interest in the physical size and strength of the male body. Historical records show that many youngsters living around that time began programmes of exercise and closely monitored their own physical development. Others abandoned the comforts of city life and headed for the wild outdoors 'hoping to cultivate their own "natural" masculine strength and aggressiveness for life's battles'. Many more became avid readers of books and magazines about such adventures.

By the 1890s the ideal image of the male body had shifted completely from lean and slim to a muscular, V-shaped build (Park, 1987), similar to the black body in Figure 5.1(c). Middle-class attitudes towards acts of physical aggression also shifted. Fist-fights between boys were greeted more often by a sense of approval rather than condemnation. On a more institutional level, intercollegiate sports became an increasingly important element of American cultural life during the second half of the nineteenth century (similar cultural develomments having also taken place on the other side of the Atlantic within the English public schools – see Box 5.1).

Clearly elements of Hoch's Puritan can be seen within each of the above identities: the industry of the Masculine Achiever, the morality of the Christian Gentleman and the physical strength and courage of the Masculine

---

Box 5.1: Hard men in history

Eric Dunning (1986) provides a wonderfully evocative account of the norms of manliness which prevailed in Britain around the mid-part of the nineteenth century. Quoting from an 1860 edition of the Rugby School magazine, an anonymous Old Boy is heard lamenting the declining standards of the game of rugby football. The parallels with Rotundo's ideal of the 'Masculine Primitive' are clear.

'You should have seen the scrummages in the Sixth Match two years ago … Fellows did not care a fig for the ball then except as it gave them a decent pretext for hacking. I remember a scrummage! … we'd been hacking for five minutes already, and hadn't had half enough, in fact, the swells had only just begun to warm to their work, when a bystander … informed us that the ball was waiting at our convenience on top of the island … And then there was Hookey Walker, the swell hack on the Sixth side; my eye! didn't he walk into the school! only shut up ten fellows for the season and sent half a dozen home for the rest of the half … [M]erely to see him come through a scrummage was a signal for all the ladies to shriek and faint. Bless you, my dear fellow, they enjoy looking on at a scrummage of all things now … more shame to us. And there was none of that underhand shuffling play with the ball then that there is now; no passing it along from one to the other; all was manly and straightforward. Why, to let the ball go after you had once got into a scrummage was considered to be a flagrant transgression of the rules of football as to take it up when you were off your side. Nor did you see any of that shrieking outside scrummages that's always going on nowadays. No one thought you worth your salt if you weren't the colour of your mother earth from head to toe ten minutes after the match had begun. But, dash my buttons! you haven't a chance of getting a decent fall in the present day; and no wonder either when you see young dandies "got up regardless of expense", mincing across Big Side, and looking just as if their delicate frames wouldn't survive any violent contact with the ball. Hang the young puppies! We shall have fellows playing in dress boots and lavender-coloured kid gloves before long … My maxim is hack the ball on when you see it near you, and when you don't, why then hack the fellow next to you.'

Primitive. However, rather than implying that they are in some way reconcil-able, Rotundo's study would suggest that, insofar as it existed, the Puritan archetype would be one which embodied a number of fundamental tensions and contradictions.

In a similar way, the presentation of twentieth-century thinking on masculinity as straightforwardly fitting into the Playboy mould appears too simplistic. To begin with, at no point did either the androgynous/glam rock style of dress or the more 'permissive' moral perspective of the 1970s become a fully accepted part of mainsteam culture. Rather, they remained predomi-nantly as part of a youth or counter-culture challenging what was, at least, perceived to be the dominant gender definitions of the day. Furthermore, while Western societies remain very much driven by consumerism, in the few years since the publication of Hoch's book, there have been tremendous cultural upheavals associated with the rise (and subsequent fall) of Thatche-rite/Reaganite politics. If anything, it could be argued that the 1980s were characterised by the reinstatement of a new form of puritanist philosophy, once again emphasising hard work and the importance of traditional family values (Levitas, 1986). Typified in the character played by Michael Douglas in the film *Wall Street*, the stereotypical or ideal 1980's man was portrayed as a hard, aggressive person, single-mindedly driven by the desire for power and status. Since the beginning of the 1990s, however, various commentators have suggested that there has been something of a movement away from these values. The ideal of the ruthlessly ambitious businessman fell somewhat into disrepute as it came under challenge from a new identity which, like the character in Figure 5.1(*d*), promoted a more caring, sensitive, and emotion-ally expressive model of masculinity. As Chapman and Rutherford (1988) point out, this cultural struggle or 'debate' between what they call the 'New Man' and the 'Retributive Man' is still very much ongoing. It is evident, they suggest, in men's magazines such as *Arena*, which lives up to its name in being a 'gladiatorial stadium' where these two contradictory representations of masculinity 'battle it out' (p. 38).

As this chapter unfolds, the history of concepts of masculinity will be further elaborated. However, for the time being we want to move on to consider the ways in which various authors have addressed the issue of cultural determination. What are the origins of these varying 'cults' of masculinity? Why does a particular definition come into existence at any given historical moment? What determines their shape and 'shelf-life'? We will examine two different types of explanation: functionalist and Marxist.

A functionalist account of masculine cults

One of the most straightforward theories of cultural production applied to an analysis of masculinity appears in a volume by David Gilmore, entitled

Manhood in the Making (Gilmore, 1990). Using the methods of comparative anthropology, Gilmore's basic argument is that cults of masculinity can be best understood as direct responses to particular social and environmental conditions. The meaning(s) of masculinity in any given culture can be seen as 'solutions' to specific social problems or needs (in precisely the same way as Talcott Parsons suggests – *see* Chapter 3). Gilmore starts with the obvious fact that every society depends for its survival on the successful propagation of future generations. Women must become pregnant and their children must be provided for and protected. These latter responsibilities, he argues, generally fall upon men's shoulders, not only because of their greater physical size and strength, but also because of their freedom from the occupations of pregnancy and childbirth. However, because these duties often require the male to engage in dangerous and potentially injurious activities, such as hunting wild animals and fighting hostile enemies, cults of masculinity have to encourage men to overcome or ignore their natural instinct to avoid danger.

> Because of the universal urge to flee from danger, we may regard 'real' manhood as an inducement for high performance in the social struggle for scarce resources, a code of conduct that advances collective interests by overcoming inner inhibitions. In fulfilling their obligations, men stand to lose ... their reputations or their lives; yet their prescribed tasks must be done if the group is to survive and prosper. (p. 223)

It is important to note that, despite its distinctly conservative overtones, this is still a thoroughly social theory. Unlike many sociobiologists, Gilmore does not argue that males are naturally aggressive, dominant and brave. Rather, he maintains that they have to be *encouraged* to exhibit these masculine qualities so that they might, almost inadvertently, act as society's guardians.

This is accomplished, Gilmore suggests, by setting up manhood as something desirable; something worth trying to become. Then, by making these qualities 'the mark of a man', adolescent males are enticed or 'prodded' into adopting masculine attitudes and behaviour. Male childhood serves as a kind of apprenticeship or training for manhood. In some societies this apprenticeship culminates in a public test or trial of masculine credentials of which Gilmore provides a number of colourful examples. Although they vary in detail, most of these rituals involve quite arduous tests of skill and endurance. For example, 12- to 15-year-old boys of the New Mexican Tewa tribe have to endure a severe whipping to secure their rite of passage to manhood.

> Each boy is stripped naked and then lashed on the back four times with a crude yucca whip that draws blood and leaves permanent scars. The adolescents are expected to bear up impassively under the beating to show their fortitude. The Tewa say that this rite makes their boys into men, that otherwise manhood is

doubtful. After the boys' ordeal the Kachina spirits (their fathers in disguise) tell them, 'You are now a man'. (p. 15)

In many other cultures there is no such neat dividing line between boyhood and manhood. Here adolescence functions as a kind of protracted period of testing throughout which a boy has to demonstrate his masculine qualities repeatedly. Again Gilmore provides a range of examples involving an assortment of brutal activities such as whipping contests, scarring the flesh with red-hot embers, and a host of other kinds of beatings, usually administered by older males of the same tribe. However, Gilmore is at pains to emphasise that such practices are not the exclusive preserve of far-away, primitive societies. Time and again he points to parallels between these 'exotic' cultures and our own, more familiar (Western) worlds. For example, at one point he compares the preparation for manhood found in East African tribes with that experienced by upper-class English boys.

> There young boys were traditionally subjected to similar trials on the road to their majority. They were torn at a tender age from mother and home ... and sent away in age sets to distant testing grounds that sorely took their measure. These were the public boarding schools, where a cruel 'trial by ordeal', including physical violence and terrorization by elder males, provided a passage to a 'social state of manhood' that their parents thought could be achieved in no other way. (p. 17)

All of these trials are similarly 'justified' in terms of their preparing the male individual for his role as protector and provider.

> To support his family, the man has to be distant, away hunting or fighting wars; to be tender, he must be tough enough to fend off enemies. To be generous, he must be selfish enough to amass goods, often by fighting other men; to be gentle, he must first be strong, even ruthless in confronting enemies; to love he must be aggressive enough to court, seduce, and 'win' a wife. (p. 230)

There can be little doubt that Gilmore's theory of cultural production is contentious. Any theory which seeks to reinterpret men's violent and insensitive behaviour as not only pro-social but actually *essential* to the evolution of society, has to be treated warily. Aside from the negative political implications of his work, however, Gilmore's argument can be seen to embody a number of other important problems and limitations. First, his claim that 'life in many places is hard and demanding' deserves some critical attention. More specifically, it seems crude, to say the least, to group together the kinds of dangers and difficulties experienced by, for example, a tribe of hunter-gathers and those felt by a typical late twentieth-century Westerner. Indeed, generally speaking, the extent to which life in these latter societies is dangerous would seem to be arguably a result of macho psychology, rather than the other way around.

Second, Gilmore's use of an evolutionary model of cultural production is, in some ways, quite misleading. Whereas the transformation of a species of living organisms (in response to changes in environmental conditions) is an unconscious and unmotivated process, this is not always true of cultural development. The meanings which we give to the world, including what it means to be a man, are not the result of some random process, neither do they crystalise out of thin air. Rather, they are the concrete products of human negotiation.

A third problem with Gilmore's analysis is that, in constructing what is, to all intents and purposes, an apology for masculine behaviour, he portrays men as the hapless victims of culture. According to him men are exploited. They are pushed into behaving in ways which, while benefiting society in general, often prove costly to the individual male (in this respect, of course, Gilmore is echoing the sentiments of both role theorists such as Pleck and Sawyer and socialist theorists such as Tolson and Seidler – *see* Chapters 3 and 4 respectively). Gilmore, however, fails to acknowledge the considerable amount of power enjoyed by men who fulfil their culture's ideal of masculinity. Across many different cultures, the passage into manhood brings with it important and exclusive privileges, such as the right to own property, the right to participate in the making of important decisions and even the right to free movement and speech. In the light of such advantages, it becomes slightly more difficult to see men as reluctant heroes. Indeed, quite the reverse, it helps to explain the extraordinary lengths to which boys will go in order to be recognised as 'men'.

Finally, in common with many applications of functionalist theory (where societies are seen as self-regulating systems pre-disposed towards integration and stability), Gilmore entertains a very consensual image of society. He assumes that societies are integrated wholes served by equally integrated cultures. However, as other more Marxist-based cultural theorists have pointed out, many modern societies are divided into fundamentally different, and opposing social groups or classes (*see* Chapter 4). It is impossible, therefore, to have a single culture which functions in the interests of all. Instead, the situation is one in which there is a multiplicity of different cultures, each representing the interests of a particular section of society. This brings us to our second broad theoretical perspective on cultural production.

Masculinity as ideology: a Marxist approach to cultural production

There have been several cultural studies of masculinity which have embraced a more fractured and antagonistic view of society. The analysis produced by Hoch (1979) is one such example. As we have noted already, Hoch sees the last 3000 years of Western history as an oscillation between two fundamentally opposed images of masculinity; the Puritan and the Playboy. In contrast to Gilmore, Hoch tries to indicate how these identities have been linked with struggles for social, political and economic power. Theoretically, Hoch's work is situated very much within the 'classical' Marxist tradition. He maintains that it is the economic conditions of society which, in the final analysis, determine all the different 'theoretical products and forms of consciousness' (Marx and Engels, 1989 – *see also* Chapter 4). Hoch suggests, for example, that the rapid spread of Christianity during the first few centuries AD was *'precipitated* by the virtual collapse of the slave-based economy' (p. 125 – emphasis added). Drawing from the work of the economist Thorstein Veblen, Hoch argues that the fluctuating history of his two masculine ideals is inextricably linked with the changing economic conditions of Western society over that time.

Veblen argues that the success of the two concepts is directly related to the state of the economy at any given historical moment. The basic pattern sees the Puritan type of masculine identity dominating during periods of economic hardship, only to be overtaken by the Playboy alternative when economic conditions improve. The production of the Puritan ideal becomes a matter of economic necessity. It is obviously essential to have an ideal which promotes the values of hard work and physical toughness in order to encourage men to increase their productive efforts, but while Hoch's Puritan can be viewed (like Gilmore's man) as a response to a serious social problem, this is clearly not the case with the Playboy. So what accounts for *his* appearance?

[A]s society's economic surplus increased, qualities of industry and martial valour eventually became of decreasing importance. For the new 'leisure class', work and welfare no longer connote manly status, but inferiority: its battles for masculinity are fought not with swords, but in terms of an ethic of wealth and conspicuous leisure, emphasising upper class etiquette and elaborate playboy rituals of extra-marital dalliance. (Hoch, 1979, p.118)

The production of the Playboy ideal appears to be motivated by the desire of the wealthiest section of society to claim for itself the exclusive right to manhood. By defining masculinity in terms of a way of life affordable only by a small fraction of society, this relatively rich group of people could not only deny men of the lower social orders the status of manhood, but they could also then justify the withholding of its associated powers and privileges. For example, if the right to vote is extended to all 'men', but manhood is defined in terms of the ownership of property (as was the case in the seventeenth century) then only the most wealthy individuals gain a political voice. The crucial issue, therefore, is how a given social group goes about trying to gain acceptance for its own definition of the concept (i.e. the version of masculinity which it finds most favourable).

At this point we arrive at the concept of ideology, frequently described as one of the most important and yet difficult concepts in the whole of the social sciences (e.g. McLellan, 1986). This is not the place for a detailed examination of concepts of ideology; our aim is merely to provide a useful 'working definition'. According to this definition, an ideology should be thought of as a special subsection or, more precisely, a condition of a culture. What kind of condition is this?

Cultures, as we stated at the outset, can be understood as particular ways of making sense of the world. They are perspectives or viewpoints upon an object or event which are linked to practices, activities and everyday modes of life. While two different cultures might 'disagree' about how the world should be interpreted, neither can be said to be 'true' or 'false' in any objective sense. The problem is that cultures invariably fail to declare their own partiality and interpretative nature. Instead, cultural norms tend to be presented as simple, straightforward descriptions of the world. As a consequence, if everybody in a given cultural community shares the same view of an object or event, there is a strong tendency for everyone to assume that what they see is a simple fact of life (in the face of no dis-confirming evidence).

This, then, is the first point about cultural and ideological understanding. Cultural ideologies operate as taken-for-granted world views which frame events in a particular and often partial way. If you are looking at an event through one frame, or set of assumptions, it is often extremely difficult to shift frames and adopt some alternative perspective. The concept of ideology refers to more, however, than this point about partiality. It also emphasises that cultural representations are not only one-sided but are also 'interested', and it is this 'interested' dimension which links to the power of various groups to control cultural meanings or understandings. The term 'interested' refers to the claim that ways of seeing the world can often function in the interests of particular sections of society. For example, the power and influence of a small number of aristocratic families were ensured for a very long time by the notion that the suitability to govern was a matter of 'good breeding'. No matter how bright or hard working a 'lower'-class person was, it was assumed that he or she simply did not 'have it in them' to take up such a position. Today, of course, there are few people who would subscribe overtly to this view. Instead, we are more likely to stand behind Locke's famous dictum that 'all men are created equal'. The idea of hereditary rule is no longer an established part of society's common sense. Yet centuries ago, people from all sections of society 'knew their place' and respected that of others. This particular cultural assumption which worked to sustain relations of domination (of the aristocracy over the working classes), can be said to have functioned *ideologically*.

The concept of ideology is important within Marxist theory because it helps to explain how one social group can dominate others, without recourse to explicit forms of coercion such as physical violence. This is especially important where, as in the example above, the subordinate groups are considerably larger than the one trying to dominate them. Through ideology, the operations of power can pass virtually unnoticed, because unwittingly, the subordinate groups come to consent to the conditions of their own exploitation.

> The dominant culture represents itself as *the* culture. It tries to define and contain all other cultures within its inclusive range. [W]hen one culture gains ascendancy over the other, and when the subordinate culture *experiences* itself in terms provided by the dominant culture, then the dominant culture has also become the basis of a dominant ideology. (Clarke *et al.*, 1981, pp.54–5)

At several points throughout his analysis Hoch draws the reader's attention to the ways in which different definitions of masculinity have been linked to systems or structures of power. He describes how the 'leisure classes' have repeatedly 'justified' their position at the apex of society through the promotion of the Playboy ideal, while the Puritan ideal has been employed to discredit them. However, to some extent at least, Hoch sees the struggle to define the meaning of masculinity as of secondary importance compared with the fight for economic superiority. Like other Marxist theorists, he maintains that the economically dominant class inevitably has an important advantage in the battle to control meaning as a consequence of their ownership, and control of the means of cultural production (educational and religious institutions and of the media) (*see* Chapter 4). Therefore, it is generally their versions of the world which, in the words of Clarke *et al.* (1981), 'command the greatest weight and influence [and] secrete the greatest legitimacy'.

Just as with the descriptive aspect of Hoch's analysis, his theory of cultural production embodies important insights as well as problems. On the positive side, Hoch acknowledges the centrality of power. Cults of masculinity are rarely innocent; invariably they work to the advantage of one group or another. At the same time his account allows us to explain the coexistence of contradictory representations of masculinity (as revealed in Table 5.1) – something that the more naïve functionalism of Gilmore was incapable of doing. More negatively, his analysis can be criticised for exaggerating the role of economic factors in shaping the cults of masculinity. This is not to suggest that there is no relationship between, say, the state of the economy and prevailing definitions of manhood. Rather, it is to question the assumption that this is a straightforward causal link (from economy to culture).

As many readers will recognise, this criticism fits into a long and established history of complaints about the rigid economic determinism of 'classical' Marxist theory. In response, Marxism has undergone a series of important developments aimed at re-evaluating the influence of economic factors. For example, Louis Althusser argues that the mode of economic production should be viewed as just one of several 'relatively autonomous' influences on the shape of society (Althusser, 1969; 1971). This view would lead us to study not just the ways in which cults of masculinity reflect changing economic interests, but also the ways in which certain styles of economic activity become possible because of already existing notions of what 'real men' do and what 'real men' should not do around the house, for example. In sticking with the more classical Marxist model, therefore, not only does Hoch appear to ignore these theoretical developments, but he also goes against the tide of most work in cultural studies, which draws from the more recent 'critical European tradition' (Bennett, 1981).

In the following section we will review a range of different studies which, while not necessarily representing Marxist-based analyses in the strictest sense of the term, nevertheless pay specific attention to the ideological functions performed by some of the different cults of masculinity we have considered already. We will see how efforts to control the meaning of masculinity have played a central part in power struggles between different social classes, nations, races, as well as gender and sexual groupings.

Defining masculinities through struggle

Most investigations of the ideological impact of cults of masculinity take class struggle as their main organising principle. For example, Catherine Hall (1992) has examined the way in which, during the early part of the nineteenth century, the political strength of the old landed aristocracy was seriously undermined by the middle classes through the successful manipulation of the masculine ideal. She notes that the new bourgeoisie, having identified themselves closely with Evangelical preachers such as William Wilberforce, argued that religious belief was the mark of a man rather than, as had previously been thought, land and wealth. Under this new definition, the same rich and leisurely lifestyle which had once confirmed the manliness of the aristocracy, now became contemptible for its 'softness, sensuousness, indolence, luxuriousness, and lack of a proper sense of purpose and direction' (Hall, 1992, p. 257).

Other class-based analyses of masculinity appear in Mangan and Walvin's edited volume *Manliness and Morality* (Mangan and Walvin, 1987). With a general focus upon the ways in which middle-class notions of masculinity rose to dominance in Britain and America between 1800 and 1940, several contributing authors point to the roles of English public schools and the American collegiate system in spreading middle-class notions of manly virtue. Others, such as John Springhall, look at how organisations such as the Boys' Brigade and Scouts tried, often in vain, to instill the same values into boys from more working-class backgrounds (*see also* Hantover, 1978). Similarly, chapters by MacKenzie and Mangan analyse the part played by popular juvenile literature, such as the *Boys Own Paper* and Thomas Hughes' tales of *Tom Brown's Schooldays*, in promoting a middle-class cult of masculinity (*see* Box 5.2).

Box 5.2: Robert Baden-Powell (1908) *Scouting For Boys*

'There are the frontiersmen of all parts of our Empire. The "trappers" of North America, hunters of Central Africa, the British pioneers, explorers, and missionaries over Asia and all the wild parts of the world, the bushmen and drovers of Australia, the constabulary of North-West Canada and of South Africa – all are peace scouts, real *men* in every sense of the word, and thoroughly up on scout craft, i.e. they understand living out in the jungles, and they can find their way anywhere, are able to read meaning from the smallest signs and foot-tracks; they know how to look after their health when far away from any doctors, are strong and plucky, and ready to face any danger, and always keen to help each other. They are accustomed to take their lives in their hands, and to fling them down without hesitation if they can help their country by doing so.'

(quoted in MacKenzie, 1987, p.177)

Thomas Hughes (1857) *Tom Brown's Schooldays*

'From 1857 the copper-bottomed mould for the public schoolboy was Tom Brown, and young Brown, as the *Spectator* reported admiringly in May of the same year: "is a thoroughly English boy. Full of kindness, courage, vigour and fun – no great adept at Greek or Latin, but a first rate cricketer, climber and swimmer, fearless and skilful at football, and by no means adverse to a good stand-up fight in a good cause … [his] piety is that of manly order, that not even in an ordinary schoolboy of the present day will find himself wearied of it."'

(Mangan, 1987, p.137)

Mangan and Walvin's collection of articles is not only concerned with the ways in which the masculine ideal has been adapted for the purposes of class struggle. One of the most interesting aspects of the book concerns the influence of religion in changing ideologies of masculinity. As we have already noted, Christian philosophy was an important cultural resource for the middle classes during this period, as a point of critique for the lifestyle of the aristocracy or leisure classes. Religious virtue was at the heart of middle-class thinking about manliness until around 1850. Dr Thomas Arnold (headmaster of Rugby school from 1827–39), for example, understood manliness to be the pursuit and practice of 'first, religious and moral principle; second, gentlemanly conduct; and third, intellectual ability' (Richards, 1987). During the second half of the nineteenth century, with the middle classes now taking up most of the dominant positions in society, the centrality of Christian values was gradually overtaken by a new emphasis on man as a source of strong and aggressive action. Initially a kind of hybrid identity emerged. 'Muscular Christianity', as it became known, promoted the values of 'physical strength, courage and health [and] the importance of family life and married love' (Richards, 1987, p.103). One of the major proponents of this ideal was Thomas Hughes (*see* Box 5.2) who not only argued that a fit and healthy body was important for the leading of a properly Christian lifestyle, but also claimed (in a book entitled *The Manliness of Christ*, published in 1890) that Jesus himself was a physically strong and courageous leader (Springhall, 1987, p.66). By the end of the nineteenth century the emphasis upon the physical basis of masculinity had all but eclipsed the religious aspect of the ideal. The Christian gentleman had served his ideological purpose. On both sides of the Atlantic, manliness now came to mean being an able sportsman, particularly in team games such as cricket, rugby and American football. This new 'cult of athleticism' (what Rotundo called the Masculine Primitive) functioned, not in the interests of a particular social class, but in the interests of entire nations battling it out on an international stage.

> 'Fair play' became the motto of a nation whose ideology and religious faith were subsumed under Imperialism, with its belief in the British as the elect who had a God-given duty to govern and civilise the world. (Richards, 1987, p.104)

In portraying foreign nations as being somehow lower on the evolutionary ladder, Britain, in particular, sought to justify its imperialist project. Like the harsh and often violent control of the working class, the conquest of the 'darker' peoples of Africa, Asia and the Americas was typically pursued in the name of civilisation. For the more liberal minded, the black man represented a thoroughly uneducated fellow who, with the aid of intensive schooling, might rise to be as civilised as a white gentleman. As far as others were concerned, the black man was little more than an animal (*see* Box 5.3), and as such, there seemed to be little wrong in rounding them up and selling them to American plantation owners in return for supplies of cotton and sugar.

Significantly, the beginning of the slave trade coincided with the development of the new, essentially middle-class, definitions of masculinity. Thomas Hobbes and John Locke, both major philosophical figures of the seventeenth century, declared that 'man was fully human insofar as he was free, and free insofar as he was in full and sole "proprietorship" of his own person' (Hoch, 1979, p.135). Clearly, under this definition, the black male slave was the very antipathy of manhood; far from being his own person, he was seen as a commodity that could be bought, sold or otherwise disposed of (Franklin, 1993).

The fact that black men were never really accepted as *men* was indicated by the tendency of whites to refer to them as 'boys' (Wallace, 1979). This mirrors the findings of Dyck (1980) who, in studying the relationship between masculinity and brawling in parts of rural Canada, found in these situations, too, the distinction between 'man' and 'boy' was a highly salient one.

> ... men engaged in a form of ritualised 'scrapping' by which they demonstrate that they are real men ... Their working assumption is that the measure of a

---

Box 5.3: The myth of the black super-stud

'[In the seventeenth century] Black male slaves were considered subhuman and expected to behave only marginally human. Most of the rights and privileges accorded "men" in America were denied this subhuman male. But, the Black slave *was* expected to be healthy, strong, work hard, and to be a good breeder. Ironically, the very system which mandated nonbinding, intensive, and frequent sexual relationships between Black males and Black females (for breeding purposes), also defined Black males as hypersexual subhumans. A plethora of sexual myths surrounded the Black male slave. The myths ranged from the unusual enormity of the Black male slave's penis to his spectacular feats and endeavours in the sexual arena. Indeed, the Black male slave *was* an animal ... a subhuman who was only fit for working and breeding. This perception of Black male slaves as studs supreme meant that white women had to be protected from the potentially sexually aggressive subhumans. This perception of Black male slave as stud supreme along with the resulting paranoia that Black male slaves would rape white women led to numerous lynchings of and other heinous crimes against Black male slaves.'

(Clyde Franklin II, 1993, p.5 – emphasis in original)

---

man's masculinity and worth is his willingness and ability to 'look after himself' in a fight ... A brave scrapper is praised as a man 'who can take care of himself', while a failure is ridiculed as a 'chicken-shit bastard', a 'mark', and a 'boy'.
(quoted in Gilmore, 1990, p.75)

The process of becoming a man is almost universally understood in symbolic terms as a passage from childhood (Gilmore, 1990). A 'man' has left childish things behind him; he no longer needs to be cared for and supported. Instead, he is strong, resourceful and independent. Hence, to call a man a 'boy' is to de-mean him.

By the time most American states had abolished slavery, the 'goalposts' of masculinity had shifted once again. No longer was the freedom to compete sufficient in itself to warrant the status of manhood: now it was *success* in competition that mattered. Masculinity meant being rich and powerful; beating the opposition in a kind of Darwinian struggle for supremacy. However, because most routes to self-advancement for black men were blocked by prejudicial attitudes and discriminatory practices, societies such as Britain and the USA continued effectively to deny black men membership of this exclusive club. Most black men, as well as many working-class whites, were therefore caught in a painful 'double bind'. On the one hand society urged them to make men of themselves; to go out and conquer the world. This, they were told, was just a matter of hard, honest endeavour (*see* reference to Rotundo's 'Masculine Achiever' earlier in this chapter). Yet, on the other hand, the few opportunities available for self-advancement were invariably denied them (*see* Chapter 4). In Box 5.4 we see Franklin drawing upon the work of sociologist Robert K Merton in outlining a number of ways in which black men have responded to this dilemma, with each 'solution' representing a different type or form of black masculinity.

Franklin (1984) maintains that in the USA black men have been accepted as *men* only since the Civil Rights Movement of the 1960s. Yet according to Michelle Wallace (1979), it is black *women* who, in a manner of speaking,

---

Box 5.4: Five black masculinities

The Conformist
The most common response to the above dilemma is to take up the challenge of trying to prove his masculinity through the pursuit of success (as defined by white, middle-class society). The Conformist either remains unaware of or ignores the knowledge that his chances of failure are high.

The Ritualist
Ostensibly the Ritualist behaves in the same way as the Conformist, except that he does so with little or no expectation of success. Unlike the above, he recognizes the hollowness of the 'American Dream', and yet, possibly for the lack of an obvious alternative, still abides by the rules of the game with neither purpose nor commitment.

The Innovator
Black males of this variety find ways of 'beating' a discriminatory system and achieving some level of success. Sometimes this is managed through quite harmless means (Franklin gives the example of the rap artists '2 Live Crew'). However, all too often the struggle for money and power is fought for through very dangerous and anti-social forms of activity such as drug dealing, murder and robbery.

The Retreatist
Like the Ritualists, these men are fully aware of the futility of their situation. However, rather than playing the game Retreatists withdraw from society, falling into long-term unemployment, homelessness and dependency on either drugs, alcohol or welfare payments.

The Rebel
This is the least common solution to the problem in which black men reject, rather than attempt to somehow resolve, the double bind. This central contradiction within American society (and to a lesser extent Britain also) would have to be laid open, and its twin assumptions questioned. As a result, such Rebels might be able to develop new understandings about the meaning of masculinity which sit more in line with their own interests.

(Franklin, 1993)

have had to pay their admission fee. As she points out, if being a man meant being head of the household (i.e. the sole protector and provider for the family) then this meant challenging the independence of black womenfolk. It became felt that in the past black women had been too dominant, too strong. They were seen as the cause of black men's problems, in preventing them from being able to fulfil the masculine role.

Just as the meaning of masculinity emerges out of a contrast between 'man' and 'child', so it is also defined in opposition to the concept of femininity. Being a man, in other words, is quite literally being *not* like a woman. Moreover, just as with the man/child distinction, masculinity represents the higher status term of the pair (i.e. masculinity is valued above femininity). There are numerous examples of this value asymmetry from cultures all around the world (*see* Gilmore, 1990). Time and again, the male who fails to live up to his culture's masculine ideal is likened to a woman. This is no less true, of course, in our own culture where a comment made to a sportsman such as, 'You played like a woman', is readily understood as an insult.

There are many parallels between the de-meaning of black men and that of women. The equation with children, for one thing, is common to both. For example, when the proverbial ship is sinking, it is the women and children who together climb aboard the first life-boats. The different (i.e. higher) status of the men is signalled by the fact that they must wait until all the others are safe. Even in the more 'politically correct' 1990s, this same symbolic ordering is evident in things like news reports of terrorist attacks, where the numbers of women and children killed or injured is offered as a separate statistic from those of men. Another similarity is that women, like black men, have been almost universally perceived as somehow closer to nature – as opposed to culture or civilisation (Ortner, 1974). Both have tended to be seen more in terms of their bodies rather than their minds: both, it was often felt, were born to obey rather than command.

For the last 300 years, the symbolic equation of women with nature and men with culture has had a tremendous impact in terms of the structure of power relations between the sexes. To a large extent this has been founded upon two basic assumptions: first, that reason or rationality is the only legitimate method of gaining knowledge about the world (Seidler, 1989) and second, that women have nothing like the same potential for rational and abstract thought compared with men (a theme which is very much still part of today's common sense – *see* Box 5.5). Enlightenment philosophers such as Emmanuel Kant and Francis Bacon argued that intuition and feelings were not to be trusted. They saw emotions and desires as clouding or obstructing the pursuit of knowledge. Indeed Bacon, considered by many to be the father of modern science, saw the aim of science as the conquering or domination of nature, both within and without (Hoch, 1979).

Women, in a sense, became identified as the enemy. They were seen as ruled over by dark and dangerous forces; motivated by primitive instincts (cf. Freud's assessment of femininity in Chapter 2). To some, they appeared to threaten, not only the pursuit of knowledge, but civilised society itself: women needed to be controlled. At its most violent, this control took the form of witch hunts. During the seventeenth century countless European and American women were tried and then burnt at the stake. The domination of women also occurred more subtly, with men forcing them into silence on account of their own (i.e. men's) supposedly privileged access to the Truth (Seidler, 1989).

A challenge to these notions of masculinity and femininity emerged in 1792 with the publication of Mary Wollstoncraft's book *Vindication of the Right of Women*. Inspired by the French Revolution, Wollstonecraft argued for equal rights to be extended to middle-class women. According to Catherine Hall (1992), she also criticised the idea of femininity. 'She saw women's inferior status as resulting from their environment – not from a lack of natural abilities. She argued for better education for women, to equip them for the world' (Hall, 1992, p.82).

However, the French Revolution had also jolted the ruling classes who, fearing a similar uprising by the English working classes, moved swiftly to impose a new moral order; one which saw women firmly located in the domestic sphere (Hall, 1992). Once again the church played an important ideological role in lending legitimacy to this new vision of society. Hall notes how Evangelical leaders, such as William Wilberforce and Hannah More, preached that there was no natural equality between the sexes. They spoke of women's natural 'delicacy, fragility and moral weakness'; qualities which made them better suited to life at home, away from the hostilities of the public sphere. The inequality of the sexes was also signified by the fact that men and women were made to sit in different sections of some Evangelical churches (Hall, 1992).

Hall insists that the development of the middle class between 1780 and 1850 must be thought of as 'gendered'.

> [T]he ideals of masculinity and femininity are important to the middle class sense of self and the ideology of separate spheres played a crucial part in the construction of a specifically middle class culture – separating them off from both the aristocracy and gentry above them and the working class below them. (p.95)

For the middle classes living during the early part of the nineteenth century, she explains, masculinity meant *having* dependents; conversely, the meaning of femininity was *being* dependent. By 1850 these values were clearly reflected in British law: a woman had become little more than her husband's possession; everything she owned passed over to him; she could only do business through him; her children and even her body were defined as his (Walby, 1990).

At the same time there was a shift in attitudes concerning the boundaries between men's and women's work. Middle-class women became steadily concentrated into certain trades such as dressmaking, school teaching and the retail industry. Similarly, in working-class society, concern over the employment of women in various 'unsuitable' industries, such as coal mining, led to their gradual exclusion from these areas of work (Hall, 1992). Pleck and Pleck (1980) paint a similar picture of late nineteenth-century America, where a growing emphasis upon the notion of sex differences in physical strength worked to exclude women from competing for certain kinds of manual jobs. Eventually, with the emergence of the concept of the 'family wage' (first in Britain and later in America), manliness became increasingly bound up with the idea of being able to support a wife and family, without her working at all.

In the same way that feminists have drawn attention to the power relations underlying dominant or 'hegemonic' constructions of masculinity, so have writers from the gay movement. Authors such as Gregory Lehne (1976) and Gary Kinsman (1987) have stressed that the dominant form of masculinity is substantially shaped and maintained by homophobia (Thompson, 1987).

> The limits of 'acceptable' masculinity are in part defined by comments like 'What are you, a fag?' As boys and men we have heard such expressions and the words 'queer', 'faggot', and 'sissy' all our lives. Those words encourage certain types of male behaviour and serve to define, regulate, and limit our lives, whether we consider ourselves straight or gay. (Kinsman, 1987)

The fear of being perceived as homosexual drives men, they argue, to engage in destructively competitive relationships. It also discourages them from participating fully in close, loving relations both with other adult men and even their own sons. 'Any kind of powerlessness or refusal to compete among men', write Carrigan *et al.* (1987), 'readily becomes involved with the imagery of homosexuality.' As a consequence, heterosexual men are constantly faced with the problem of proving that they are not gay (Lehne, 1976).

Jeffrey Weeks (1977; 1985) and Michel Foucault (1981) have both written about the social construction of homosexuality. According to their historical analyses, homosexuality emerged as a significant cultural concept only towards the end of the nineteenth century.

> That period witnessed the advent of new medical categorizations, homosexuality being defined as a pathology by the German psychiatrist Westphal in 1870. There were also new legal proscriptions. All male homosexual behaviour was subject to legal sanctions in Britain by the end of the century. (Connell, 1987)

This is not to suggest, of course, that prior to 1870 there was no such thing as homosexual behaviour. Indeed, it seems likely that homosexual acts of some kind have been a feature of virtually every culture throughout history. What Weeks and Foucault are highlighting is the fact that before 1870 homosexual acts were not seen as indicative of a specific type of personality. Instead they were perceived as the result of a lustful nature common to all men (Carrigan *et al.*, 1987).

Needless to say, the concept of the homosexual did not emerge in isolation. Rather, it was accompanied by its mirror or counter-concept: the heterosexual. As the terms suggest, both types of personality are defined by the objects of sexual desire, however, only one of these identities was treated as properly masculine. Heterosexuality became incorporated into the definition of the 'real' man, while homosexuality became seen as antithetical to the masculine ideal. Indeed, the idea of a 'homosexual man' became seen as a contradiction in terms (Carrigan *et al.*, 1987). Instead, the homosexual male became understood as an 'invert' (cf. Terman and Miles, 1936 – reviewed in Chapter 3); as a woman's soul trapped in a man's body.

During the 1970s and 1980s some sections of the gay movement strove to contest this equation of homosexuality with femininity. They reacted against the traditional view of gays as being, in some way, failed men. One way in which they attempted to resist this interpretation was to move from 'effeminate' or 'camp' modes of expression towards what Martin Humphries calls 'gay machismo' (Humphries, 1985). Gay machismo is the borrowing and exaggeration of traditional forms of (straight) male identity. A typical example is the 'clone' – check shirt, faded blue jeans, bovver boots, short hair and moustache; others include the all-leather and the all-denim man. In a very real sense these are *political* costumes, for at the same time as seeking to confirm gay men's masculinity, they also work to subvert the very codes themselves by disrupting the simple binary relationships between macho and heterosexual, camp and homosexual.

Carrigan *et al.* (1987) argue that the history of homosexuality represents 'the most valuable starting point' for those wishing to unravel the meaning of masculinity.

> [For it] obliges us to think of masculinity not as a single object with its own history but as being constantly constructed within the history of an evolving social structure, a structure of sexual power relations. It obliges us to see this construction as a social struggle going on in a complex ideological and political field in which there is a continuing process of mobilization, marginalization, contestation, resistance, and subordination. (p. 89)

In this section we have seen how the ability to define the meaning of masculinity has been an important element in the power relationships between many different groups in society. The history of the concept of masculinity stands as a testimony to these different battles, with each twist and transformation in its definition representing another chapter in the story. However, it is now time to consider the materialisation of this complex history. In other words, let us end this chapter by examining the way in which these cultural representations become part of individual men's subjective experience.

The cultural construction of the masculine subject

Masculine identities are lived out in the flesh but fashioned in the imagination. (Dawson, 1991)

In this section our aim is to look at how some of the themes evident in the different histories outlined above have been taken up or internalised by individual men living in contemporary Western societies. We begin by looking at the ways in which the equation of masculinity and rationality find reflection in the everyday lives of ordinary men like Carl and Jim (*see* Box 5.5 below).

It would be surprising if there were many male readers who would not at least recognise, if not directly identify, with the sentiments expressed by Carl and Jim. Men, it seems, are forever attempting to present themselves as the 'rock' in a crisis; calm and clear-thinking among the supposedly wild-running emotions of women. Jim's father probably tried to be a rock, and as likely his father before him. Indeed, so familiar is this pattern that it takes on the appearance of something natural, something built into men. However, as Seidler (1989) points out, what this pattern really represents is the successful internalisation by men of one established aspect of the masculine ideal.

> We have learnt to pride ourselves in our struggles against our own desires and natures, to be able to identify our sense of self with our reason. If successful, this denial can mean that we no longer have a sense of self which exists separately from our sense of male identity. We are so anxious as boys to prove that we are *not* girls – that is, that we are not emotional, not weak and not governed by our feelings – that we come to identify our sense of self directly with our sense of male identity. (p. 18 – emphasis in original)

As we have already seen, men's power, for some while now, has been bound up with their supposed immunity from emotions. To a great extent it is what signifies their difference from and superiority over women. However, according to Seidler, most men are painfully aware of the gap or mis-match between the way they *really* are and the way society expects them to be. 'Being a man' for these people is very much a case of shameful self-discipline; of squashing and denying the emotions which, had they been real men, they would not be feeling in the first place. For a minority, the identification with the masculine ideal is a much more complete process. With men such as these, there are no guilty secrets and efforts to conceal, as the ideal and their sense of self have become one and the same thing (*see* Box 5.6).

Box 5.5: Men and reason

JIM: If someone's trying to get at you and you cry, you let them know they've got at you. I mean that's ... I mean if you have an argument ...

CARL: It's a sign of weakness.

JIM: ... with a woman and she always ends up crying, I mean, you know you've got at her. And I think if you ... it *is* a sign of weakness, yeah if someone's just smashed into the back of your car and you get really annoyed about it, you're not gonna start crying about it ... I mean if a bloke starts crying about it, you've lost your insurance claim! (*Laughs*) That's the difference.

CARL: You've lost your initiative as well haven't you?

JIM: You *have* lost the initiative, you can't ... you've gotta say 'Well you hit the back of my car'. I mean, I know Jane, if she had somebody hit the back of the car, she gets out and cries. 'Ohhh what am I gonna say when I get home? Ohhhh!' Just cries, you know ... where, you say 'Oh right, it's your fault, name and number?'

JIM: You know, it would be much better if women didn't cry over stupid things, you know, dropping something or breaking something or denting the car or ...

NIGEL: Hmm.

JIM: I mean, that's like *stupid*, it's you know ...?

CARL: It's just an emotional release though, isn't it?

JIM: Yeah, it is, yeah, but it's a dented car. If your kid's just been run over, yeah, I can see you getting very upset about it. But a dented car, you know ... is it worth crying?

NIGEL: Hmm.

JIM: You know, especially when it's covered by insurance ...

NIGEL: Hmm.

JIM: It's not ...

CARL: Well is it the same sort of emotional release as a man will swear about it?

JIM: Yeah you go 'Shit!' (*Laughs*) You get a bit annoyed but you don't er ... you just get on with the situation, get the car off the road and deal with the situation. You know, the first thing you do is get the car off the road, nobody's hurt, get the insurance details and it's done.

(Wetherell and Edley, 1993)

Box 5.6: Men and emotions – two different accounts

NIGEL: Okay, do you ever see films for instance which upset you, sad movies? And have you ever experienced trying to sort of tough yourself out of feeling like crying?

KEITH: Yeah.

NEIL: I mean it's not so much as you think oh it's sissy to do this, it's sort of *pull yourself together* it's only a bloody film!

MARK: Another comment my wife would make is 'Why aren't you loving?' 'Why don't you cry?' 'Why don't you do that?' and to be honest, if you say 'Oh, your dad tells you not to cry', I couldn't cry if I *tried*. I never have. I've *never ever ever* felt the need to cry.

NIGEL: Hmm.

CHARLIE: You never cried as a kid?

MARK: No, not as far as I know. Well, everybody cried as a kid. I've had a good whacking. Pain brings tears to your eyes but in an emotional sense, no. When anyone's died or that, I've had *no* feelings to cry at all.
                                         (Wetherell and Edley, 1993)

Of all the current literature on men and masculinity Seidler's work provides some of the best illustrations of how various cults of masculinity have come to structure the ordinary, everyday lives of Western men. The way men behave in bed, in the office, on the tennis court, even their preferred choice of television programmes can all be linked up, Seidler argues, with the philosophical pronouncements of Descartes, Kant, Locke and Luther. Men might well fashion their own identities, but as Seidler clearly demonstrates, they invariably do so using the established or historically given set of raw materials traced in previous sections. They are what the Italian political theorist, Antonio Gramsci, called 'precis of the past' (Gramsci, 1971).

Seidler traces the roots of modern masculinity back to the time of Martin Luther and the Reformation (sixteenth century). From there, he argues, we inherit an idea of human nature as basically rotten. Luther believed that society, if left to its own devices, would disintegrate into chaos as people followed their own selfish inclinations (this idea also appeared in the writings of the seventeenth-century philosopher Thomas Hobbes). Civilisation, therefore, depends upon the ability of people to ignore their basic emotions and desires and to concentrate instead upon the dictates of reason. Indeed, without this discipline society could not hope to progress (progress being the central theme of the Enlightenment period). By portraying themselves as the much more rational gender, men managed to establish themselves as the guarantors of civilised society. At the same time, of course, their power as men became firmly bound up with their, at least apparent, lack of feeling. Seidler argues that one of the most profound consequences of this way of thinking is that men became alienated from their own body, and from their own sexuality.

> We inherit a Protestant tradition which has seen sex as basically evil. Like our other natural inclinations, it is seen as inevitably threatening to any kind of moral or civilised behaviour. There is a close identification of the sexual with the bestial, so that giving in to our sexual feelings is compromising our sense of ourselves as rational and 'civilised' men. (Seidler, 1989, p.58 – *see also* Box 5.7).

As a result of these cultural notions, Seidler argues, many men have an uncomfortable relationship with their own sexuality. The feeling of being

---

Box 5.7: Men, sexuality and the church

Hoch (1979) notes how the influence of Christian doctrine on attitudes towards sexuality can be traced back even further, to the time of the Middle Ages. He writes: 'The church had carefully curtailed the number of days on which intercourse might be performed, the allowable hours of the day, and even body positions (only the male superior – or missionary – position might avoid damnation). Later the *chemise cagoule* – a nightshirt with a suitably placed hole – was introduced so that husband and wife could avoid all bodily contact. Although all sex – marital or not – was officially regarded as sin, "fornication" (sex outside marriage) was held in some penitentials to be a sin worse than murder.' (p. 129)

Men, sexuality and the loss of control

DAN: Er, the thing about falling in love, I've never worried about the control of that because I've fell in and out of love so easily er, in and out during my life, you know. But as for when it comes down to control with sex, that's a difficult subject because er ... I was once asked by a woman or told by a woman to let go, because I wouldn't let go, you know, I wouldn't er, enjoy myself while I was having sex. It wasn't my wife, it was another woman ...

NIGEL: Hmm.

DAN: ... and she says 'You're not enjoying yourself, why don't you just let yourself go?' and I couldn't fi ... I couldn't ... I wasn't able to let go.
                                                         (Wetherell and Edley, 1993)

'turned on' can often be experienced as a weakness; as giving in to temptation. The sexual act itself can leave a man with a confusing sense of disgust, for at some deep level it reminds him of 'the beast from within'. The male orgasm is for many, a profoundly ambivalent event, comprising a mixture of intense physical pleasure and anxiety over the temporary loss of control. Feeling out of control, for whatever reason, terrifies men as it erodes their very sense of self and threatens to undermine the basis of their power (*see* references to the work of Stephen Frosh (1993) and Jessica Benjamin (1988) in Chapter 2). Consequently, Seidler claims, men have tried to shore up their gender identities by transforming their sex lives into a set of achievements. Boys 'see how far they can get' with girls. Adolescent males compare 'scores' of sexual 'conquests', and even within more mature, settled heterosexual relationships, the sexual act, as far as many men are concerned, is a matter of grimly hanging on until he gives the woman an orgasm.

Another way in which a man could regain some level of control over his body was by making it work hard. For example, Hoch (1979) notes how the fathers of the Calvinist churches preached that through constant, disciplined toil a man could prove his worthiness to God.

'The standing pool is prone to putrefaction' writes Richard Steele (1684), 'and it were better to beat down the body and keep it in subjection by a laborious calling, than through luxury to become a castaway.' (p. 134)

Seidler also notes how the internalisation of the Protestant (or Puritan) work ethic (which equates a person's value with their productivity) makes many men uneasy about relaxing. Men can feel agitated, even guilty if they are not working (*see* Box 5.8). Even their leisure hours have to be productive. They must either be watching the match or playing themselves, off down the pub or under the car: every second of every day, if possible, should be put to good use. Male friendships are typically based around activities; they *do* things together whereas women tend more just to *be* with one another (Sherrod, 1987). Men treat their bodies like machines, often driving them to the point of exhaustion and beyond (*see* David Jackson's account of his workaholicism in Box 4.3 of Chapter 4). As a result, men suffer a number of stress-related illnesses including insomnia, heart problems and stomach ulcers. Yet in an ironic and masochistic kind of way, these aches and pains are themselves the source of pleasure or satisfaction for many men, for they signify the victory of mind over body, spirit over flesh.

Sport, of course, offers men the same gratifications. Irrespective of whether it is on the football field, tennis court or in own's back yard, males of all ages derive an enormous amount of satisfaction from the precise execution of complex skills and movements. As boys they spend an inordinate amount of time honing these techniques; catching and throwing, running and dodging, day after day for years on end (*see* Box 5.9), and with each well-timed tackle and sweetly struck volley they gain in return a deeply reassuring sense of self-control. Putting one's body through a tough and demanding training

Box 5.8: Men and work

NICK: I was not technically unemployed last year, well I was but then I chose to do a part-time job. Erm, but I wasn't earning the money later on so my wife luckily has a job as a clerical assistant/secretary if you like at a local school, and she tends to be bringing a little bit more home, moneywise, than me. I mean I'm not earning very good money at all at the moment, doing this ... if ever you want to earn peanuts work for an agency. And, alright I've been out to work today and I'm out tomorrow and Friday hopefully but at the end of the week I don't feel as if I've provided for my family. And I felt *lousy* while I was only earning £30, £40 a week as a driving instructor. And it's alright there ... luckily she's understanding, we've been married 18 years and she keeps saying 'You can't help it, you're doing what you can, the right job will come along' after earning what ... without throwing money about when I was an Engineer, that was an 11 grand a year job and doing part-time driving instruction was probably another 4 or 5 for a couple of years before I did do it full-time ... you know, £100 a week on top of that. To suddenly have nothing and er, you're expected to accept it. Well I can't accept it.

DAVE: Can't you accept the ...

NICK: I can't ...

DAVE: ... the role that you could well be the ... ?

NICK: I can't accept role reversal really.

DAVE: No.

NICK: Even if my wife suddenly got a job tomorrow on £500 a week, I would still feel lousy. Which is pretty psychologically, isn't it, you know? I mean if the money's coming in, it doesn't really matter who earns it these days but I was brought up ... and my mum *had* to work part-time but the *main* job was dad's. This is the difference, now the main job at the *moment* is my wife's and I can't er ... it sort of ... well probably it's our age, I don't know. Probably the younger people don't give a damn who earns the money but erm, I do *personally*. There may be somebody else my age who's got different views but I can't really accept that this is normal to do as I'm doing at the moment. I don't feel as if I'm providing enough...

NIGEL: Hmm.

NICK: ... through no fault of my own, you know?

                                                    (Wetherell and Edley, 1993)

session offers a similar cocktail of pain and pleasure. The muscular, V-shaped build of the athlete is, therefore, a sign of male power and sexual difference (Hargreaves, 1986). It represents, not just physical strength (as an aspect of the masculine ideal), but also, quite literally, the embodiment of mind over matter.

Box 5.9: Men and sport

'All through my childhood I hardened my body through everyday sporting practice. Sometimes, while my sisters were doing the washing up, shopping, cleaning, I was developing my footballing skills and my throwing arm ... Occasionally I used to dribble a balding tennis ball along the pavement all the one and a half miles to school, learning to play wall-passes, selling dummies to lamp-posts, or sending the ball round one way and going the other way with my body. Then at primary school and later at grammar school I used to join in the rushing melee of playing football in boys-only yards, rarely connecting with the ball but hacking, lunging and swiping at it as it whizzed past. In the evenings I used to spend solitary hours kicking a ball against a garage door and learning to trap the rebound, bring the ball down under control and send it back against the door or a neighbouring brick wall.

'Thrusting for goal over the years has shaped my body in a particular way. It has taught me to impose my will on my body and other people, rather than listening to it and learning to acknowledge its needs. I have a tendency to treat my body as an external machine that carries out my clenched determination to achieve through work and, particularly, intellectual work. In this way, one specific version of masculinity – dominant heterosexuality – has become nat- uralised in my bodily relations. The clenched legacies of my past determination to win or achieve or score are there in the rigid way I tense and hold my body.'

(David Jackson, 1990)

There can be little doubt, therefore, that men's lives and experiences are influenced to a large degree by the cultural environment in which they are situated. The ways in which men perceive the world (including themselves), their behaviour, even to some extent their physical bodies can be seen as resulting from specific cultural notions and practices: as cultures change or evolve, so do the men who inhabit them.

Yet such a view implies that men are the victims of historical circum- stance, for it suggests that men get provided with their masculine identities in a way similar to a new recruit picking up his uniform; it all depends upon the style at the time. The problem with this view, however, is that it sits un- comfortably with some of the evidence from both this chapter and Chapter 4. For example, we have heard on numerous occasions how various groups of men have managed to advance their own interests through the successful manipulation of the meaning(s) of masculinity. 'Real' men are religious, 'real' men are good at sport, 'real' men dress up in fancy clothes and wear make-up and so on. From this perspective, the relationship between cults of masculinity and the men themselves appears quite different. Indeed, far from appearing to be the slaves of culture, they seem like its masters. However, the problem with this viewpoint is that it seems to deny the very possibility of cultural domination. Surely no-one would allow him or herself to be oppressed by a particular version of the world, if its legitimacy could be overturned so easily?

Structure or agency?

In trying to come to terms with this contradiction, we might usefully turn to the development of cultural studies itself. As Stuart Hall (1981) argues, the entire discipline can be seen to have emerged out of the tension between these same two opposing perspectives or paradigms. On one side stood the 'structuralist' theorists, such as Louis Althusser, who argued that people were very much the prisoners of culture (or ideology). According to them, people can never have a neutral or un-mediated perspective upon their social environment, rather they must always experience the world in terms of a cultural framework or set of meanings. On the opposing side stood the 'culturalists', such as Williams, Thompson and Hoggart. Complaining that the structuralists' view of culture was far too deterministic, they argued that people actively create culture in response to their social experience (Turner, 1992). In terms of the literature reviewed above, they might point to the cultural creativity of black men (or gay men) who respond to their powerlessness by finding new, if sometimes dangerous, ways of being 'manly'.

The work on masculinity, which can be seen as most clearly situated within the culturalist perspective, comes from Victor Seidler (Seidler, 1989, 1991a). Outspoken in his criticism of the structuralist tradition, Seidler thoroughly rejects the assumption that all experiences are culturally mediated, and invokes instead the idea of an extra-cultural space in which a person can experience the world in a kind of raw, unprocessed manner (like the stuff psychoanalysts see as the target of their enterprise – *see* Chapter 2).

> Language does not constitute individuality in the way structuralism has assumed ... Too often history is reduced to a theoretical construction with little sense of experience or reality existing beyond, or independent of, our theoretical constructions ... Oppressed people are constantly trying to make language their own, as they attempt to discover and redefine their experience. (1989, pp. xii and 134)

As far as Seidler is concerned, cultural change is impossible without such a space, insofar as it is invariably prompted by some sense of the inadequacy of existing cultural concepts. In other words, it is only the discrepancy between theory and experience which drives people towards trying to forge more 'accurate' or 'realistic' representations of the real. However, there are at least two problems with this argument. First, while one can easily make a conceptual distinction between accurate and inaccurate representations, in practice trying to categorise experiences into those which are culturally constituted and those which are not becomes virtually impossible. Indeed, as we have noted above, trying to present a particular version of the world as real, is precisely the name of the ideological game. Second, as Antonio Gramsci demonstrated, the possibility of cultural change can be explained without needing to invoke the existence of an extra-cultural domain of real and authentic experiences (Gramsci, 1971). The cultural environment in which people live is not coherent and integrated, as some theorists have assumed, but embodies a whole range of differences and contradictions. According to Gramsci, society's common sense represents one source of potentially subversive meanings. Being a fragmented body of ideas and practices, littered with the 'sediments' or 'deposits' of age-old ideas and theories, this established stock of taken-for-granted understandings can always provide the raw materials for the construction of markedly different world views.

We have seen, for example, how the exploitation of black men and women has been historically 'justified' through a chain of symbolic associations which links black people with nature, and then nature with brutishness and sexual depravity. This left the black population with two different strategies for action. First, they could contest the idea of their being closer to nature compared with whites or, second, they could aim to disrupt nature's negative associations (in practice they have almost certainly explored both strategies). The point is that the cultural resources necessary to pursue the second strategy were already available in the form of Darwin's theory of 'natural selection', and the related nineteenth-century American ideal of the Masculine Primitive (see earlier references to the work of Rotundo, 1987). By drawing upon these themes, the natural instincts of the black male became interpretable as a source of virtue rather than shame. As a result, Wallace (1979) argues, black men have come to see their bodies and their sexuality as something to be celebrated and emphasised rather than denied.

Gramsci insists that the rule or hegemony of the dominant culture is never absolute (as Althusser implied). It never fully achieves the position of being the only available way of making sense of an event or situation. Rather, the dominant culture continually has to defend its position as the most widely adopted frame of reference against the challenges from other, subordinate cultures. For example, while Chapman and Rutherford's (1988) 'Retributive Man' used to be the dominant cult of masculinity, over the last few decades it has been engaged in a struggle for supremacy with the 'New Man' alternative.

This implies, of course, that men of today are presented with the opportunity of inhabiting at least two different subject positions or identities. Consider, for instance, the conversation in Box 5.10.

There seems little doubt that we have here positive evidence of two, quite different ideals of masculinity engaged in a process of struggle. Clearly Harry is cast as the Retributive Man, trying to assert a Puritan ideal against the more liberal New Man version played by his son. Both men can be seen simply as the products of their different generations; dominated, as it were, by the leading definitions of their day. For Harry, brought up in the 1930s and 1940s, smelling sweetly and being a real man do not go together. Yet for his son, a child of the more 'permissive' 1960s and 1970s, the wearing of perfumed goods in no way threatens his masculine identity. Each might be invested in his own ideal, feeling strongly about the correctness of his own argument. Little do they realise that an almost identical scene was played out more than 300 years earlier, when fathers discovered their sons, fresh from the court of Louis XIV at Versailles, practising the 'French wallow' with their powdered peri-wigs.

Box 5.10: A clash of ideals

HARRY: When I was a young man if you used scented soap you were very, very funny! (*Laughs*) Do you know what I mean?

NIGEL: Right, yeah.

HARRY: It always used to be Fairy, you know Fairy Snow, you know, that doesn't smell but you know, if you had brilliantine on, you know the sweet smelling brilliantine or scented soap ...

NIGEL: Hmm.

HARRY: ... you was, you know, you were going that way to, you know, femininity. (*Laughs*).

NIGEL: So there was no such thing as, well men didn't use erm under-arm deodorant?

HARRY: No, no *never*!

NIGEL: What about aftershave, did they use that?

HARRY: No, I never, not even to this day!

NIGEL: You don't?

HARRY: No!

NIGEL: There's so many adverts trying to flog this stuff ...

HARRY: Hmm.

NIGEL: ... especially around Christmas, erm why not, why don't you give in to that? (*Laughing*).

HARRY: My son uses it and I keep saying 'You smell like a ponce!' (*Laughter*) You know what I mean?

NIGEL: Hmm.

HARRY: And I've never, as I say I've been brought up, you know, not to be, you know, one of the big muscle men sort of thing.

NIGEL: Right.

HARRY: You don't, you know, smell like that sort of thing.

NIGEL: Do you think, I mean, do you think it would, make you seriously uncomfortable if you did smell perfumy?

HARRY: It would. I've erm, well my sister-in-law, they bought me Grecian 3000 and Old Spice aftershave and I always throw it away. I never use it. I say 'Thank you, that's just what I wanted' but it's never, it never gets used, talcum powder ...

NIGEL: Right, O.K. So, you know, we talked about, I dunno, 20 minutes ago about erm learning some lessons about what it means to be masculine, yeah? Well it seems as though you've unsuccessfully tried to teach your son one, right? (*Laughing*) Which is that you should avoid perfume. I mean my *dad* doesn't wear those things.

HARRY: I don't, I don't tell him, you know, he should avoid it, I'm saying, he is a person on his own now. He's 23, he pleases himself what he does. But I'm always, when he goes out I say 'Phew! No more of that son, you smell like a ponce.'

(Wetherell and Edley, 1993)

Nevertheless, it is still a mistake to see Harry and his son as doing nothing more than playing out a preordained scene. To begin with, the struggle for hegemony between competing cults of masculinity is not restricted to a battle between different types of men. The same tensions and contradictions can also be observed at the level of the individual as he represents himself, either for others in the context of social interaction or, alternatively, for himself in the form of private voices or patterns of subjectivity (such as when he asks himself 'What kind of man am I?' or 'What kind of man should I be?'). While it might be the case that the framing of their dialogue is to some extent pre-structured, its outcome most certainly is not. Whether the struggle sees the New or the Retributive Man emerge triumphant is, actually, up to them: as such they are history makers.

In this chapter we have seen masculinities described as a collection of 'theories' which are handed down from one generation to the next. Men, it is argued, come to imagine themselves through these different discourses; in a sense, they are 'told' by them. Yet, at the same time men are also the authors of these narratives. It is they who decide what the meaning of masculinity shall be. The history of the concept of masculinity stands as a record of these 'decisions', representing hundreds of years of argument and negotiation between different groups in society, with each struggling to advance its own particular version of the concept. Therefore, one of the most important questions that we can ask in studying cults of masculinity is: who stands to benefit from a particular formulation? Who does it privilege and who (else) does it serve to marginalise or degrade? As we have shown, the victims of these battles to define manhood have included working-class men, black men, gay men, but most of all, perhaps, women. In Chapter 6, we turn to look at what feminism and feminist theorists have had to say about this process.

Chapter 6

Feminism and the politics of masculinity

> . . . in this century, it is feminism which represents *the* major change in social thinking and politics because only feminism radically questions our understanding of 'men' and 'women' and the social structures which maintain the differences.
>
> (Humm, 1992, p. xi)

The previous chapters in this book have covered a wide range of perspectives on men and masculinity from biology to sociology. These discussions have contained more than occasional echoes of feminism and the feminist critique of masculinity. Indeed, all the perspectives reviewed can be seen as developing a dialogue or debate with feminist theory in some way or other. Feminist influences were most explicit in Chapter 4 which introduced the concept of patriarchy, and in Chapter 5 which looked at how masculinity has been defined against femininity. In other chapters, too, the impact of feminism upon areas as diverse as psychoanalysis, role theory and genetic research has been clear.

In this final chapter we wish to bring the feminist presence to the fore – emphasising and re-emphasising the various ways in which feminism has made men and masculinity visible. We will be looking at men and masculinity from an explicitly political standpoint, from the viewpoint of women, and those oppressed by conventional forms of masculinity. What do men look like from this 'under-side'? What new interpretations and phenomena appear? We will look, too, at men's responses to feminism and at the kind of politics which have emerged from various men's movements.

Above all, feminism is a social movement for women. Its main topic and focus are the subordination of women. However, as the facts of this subordination and the extent of women's cultural and economic disadvantage became clear, it also became apparent that feminism concerns men too. From a feminist perspective, what defines men is their power in relation to women. Masculinity may have something to do with men's relationships with their mother in early childhood, it may have something to do with hormones, genes and physiology, but, above all, it must be enormously influenced by men's social advantages and privileges. Feminists argue that it is impossible to understand men and masculinity without taking stock of that social fact. The possession of power cannot help but have crucial consequences for those who possess it. Inevitably men's characters and psychologies will be structured and shaped through this relation with women.

Like all political movements, feminism takes a self-conscious moral and ethical line. It asks us to evaluate men and masculinity. Is it right that men are privileged? Should men behave in these ways? Which, if any, of the cults of masculinity discussed in Chapter 5 should be preferred to others? Feminists argue that, for social justice and in the interests of challenging inequalities, men must change. All feminists agree on this point, even if there is considerable disagreement about the kinds of politics which should flow from this recognition. Men have developed a variety of strategies in reply, ranging from the politics of anger and resistance to the politics of acceptance, support and self-criticism.

In trying to explain male domination, feminists have developed a number of different themes. It has become conventional to distinguish three traditions – liberal, socialist and radical varieties of feminism (cf. Jaggar, 1983). Liberal feminists have focused principally on the concept of rights, citizenship and equality, arguing that sexist attitudes and prejudice have resulted in a situation where women are under-represented in society. Socialist and radical feminists have argued that this emphasis on under-representation and bias in public life underestimates the systematic nature of women's oppression and the way it is organised through the very structures of society. These feminisms prefer the term patriarchy to sexism, indicating that the problem is not just one of reforming relatively ephemeral attitudes and prejudice, but an issue of how male rule has become entrenched. Socialist or Marxist feminists look to economic factors and the inter-twining of capitalism and gender divisions to explain male power, while radical feminists focus instead on sexuality and reproduction as the central axis of male control.

In the course of this chapter we will try to explicate these different threads within feminism which are mirrored, too, in debates among men concerning their sexual politics. We will begin by looking at the nature of male power, picking up two core themes in feminist research – the extent of male control of public life and men's objectification of women. This last theme will allow us to test the implications of that most characteristic feminist statement – the 'personal is political'. From there we will look in detail at feminist work on male sexuality, to indicate some of the cross-currents in feminist theorisations of masculinity, before considering the position of men in relation to feminist politics.

It is important to stress, first, that attention to feminist perspectives requires a considerable shift in everyday perceptions. Feminism launches a critique of ordinary life and the status quo, arguing that things are not as they seem. Feminism questions, for example, the differences between the sexes; it questions the legitimacy of men's and women's usual roles in society, and it also questions the ideas, beliefs and social practices which sustain normal patterns of motherhood, fatherhood, sexuality, consumerism, codes of appearance, militarism, and which underlie taken-for-granted rights, duties, and responsibilities.

The encounter with feminism can lead to a profound transformation in people's lives and perceptions. In Box 6.1, the Australian feminist Dale Spender describes her first meeting with feminist ideas through the work of Germaine Greer (1971). She notes that she felt like an anthropologist who finally understands the behaviours of a distant tribe, except that it was her own culture which was being illuminated.

Feminism also provokes great resistance, from both women and men.

Box 6.1: Encountering feminism

'At this point Germaine Greer entered my life. She gave me my mental health. Initally, reading *The Female Eunuch* was like reading a horror story: all those clues that I had ignored, all those awful connections I'd never dared make, all that evidence I had not been brave enough to examine; all put together, and pushed at me with great force. Some of it I wanted to deny, declare it exaggerated and yet I knew it was authentic. I have never forgotten my reaction to the chapter "Loathing and Disgust" which begins with the sentence "Women have very little idea how much men hate them". Recognition came with that line – but so too did some resistance.

'The easiest way to describe my response is to say that I started laughing. It was a mixed laugh – joy, relief, hysteria, satisfaction, suppressed anger, curiosity? I am sure that I was suddenly years younger. I know – from looking at photographs – my whole body posture changed. Without conscious effort I also became healthier, more active – and lost weight. I could say much about what I learned from Germaine Greer – about women being "oppressed" (I had never used that word before), about the extent to which we were confined, distorted, used, and abused. Women, I had been instructed directly and indirectly from the cradle, were passive; they wanted and needed to look up to men; they were only content when dominated and domesticated. And I had believed this, and had spent nearly thirty years trying to hide my deformity, to conceal my assertiveness, my lack of respect for most of the men I knew, to conceal my discontent with domination and domestication so that I would not be found out and branded a female failure. What Germaine Greer was asking me to see was that to be a true female in these terms was to be a *human* failure. The world turned on its head!'

(Spender, 1986, p. 214)

Many women, as Christine Griffin (1989) has pointed out, accept many feminist points, an awareness of unfairness, a sense that things are stacked against women, while at the same time expressing extreme reluctance about accepting the identity of 'feminist' ('I'm not a woman's libber, but ...). While many men report feeling both bemused and bruised by feminism. One of the reasons for men's bemusement may be that power and privilege are difficult to experience directly. When interviewed, many men say that they do not feel powerful or that they are not aware of being privileged (Griffin, 1991; Lips, 1981). What might be most salient to these men is their *lack* of power compared with other men (and some few women) who perhaps have more money, are higher up in status hierarchies, belong to more privileged social classes and races, or who are more physically forceful, aggressive or well-built, but, if power is not directly felt, if it is not absolute but only relative, does that mean it does not exist?

Men vary greatly in their participation in the subordination of women, but, from a feminist perspective, nearly all men can be seen to benefit directly or indirectly from a social system in which they are privileged *vis à vis* women.

A man may refuse to oppress the women he knows; they may share housework and childcare; he may reject every unsavoury element of machismo. Yet, if he makes more money than his female co-worker or is hired in preference to an equally qualified woman, or is promoted because he has a family to support, or qualifies for a job because of an irrelevant height requirement, or is listened to in a discussion because he is a man, or sees that men are featured in the mass media, or can pick up a textbook in his high school or college class and know that all human achievement is ascribed to him, or can routinely walk past strangers without being whistled at or propositioned or fearing rape, or doesn't have to cope with the horrors of trying to stretch welfare payments so that he and his children can survive another day, or need never worry about the ill-effects of contraceptives to his body – he is still part of a privileged group. (Ehrlich, 1977, pp.144–5).

The extent and nature of male control

As Carol Ehrlich's statement suggests, male power and privilege may be direct or indirect, actively sought or unwelcome, obvious or subtle, but it is evident across a range of social phenomena. The extent of male control perhaps emerges most clearly when inequalities between women and men in the public sphere are documented. In Box 6.2 Susan Faludi summarises the recent evidence as a series of questions which dispute the claim that women's disadvantage in social and economic life is a thing of the past.

Box 6.2: Second class citizens

'If women are now so equal, why are they much more likely to be poor, especially in retirement? Why are over 6.5 million of the 10 million workers in the UK who earn below the Council of Europe's decency threshold women? Why does the average working woman, in both the UK and US, still earn only just over two-thirds what men do for the same work? Why in 1990 was the average hourly rate for a part-time worker – and in the UK 86 per cent of part-time workers are women – little more than half that of male full-time earnings?

'If women have "made it", then why are 80 per cent of all workers in catering, cleaning, hairdressing and other personal services still women, and 78 per cent of all workers in clerical jobs? Conversely, why are there only 19 female circuit-court judges out of 426, two female high court judges out of 83, and no female Law Lords? Why, of 1,200 surgeons in the UK, are there only ten women? Why for every woman given a public appointment by the government are there four men? Why, of the 48 per cent non-industrial civil servants who are women, have only 3 per cent reached the top two grades? Why are there still only 44 women Members of Parliament in the House of Commons, out of 650 MPs? Why in the US are there only three female state governors and two female senators, the same number as in the 1930s? Why in the UK are there only two female general secretaries out of a total of 71 affiliated unions in the TUC? And why in 1989 were only 11 per cent of British managers women?'

(Faludi, 1992, pp.5–6)

These statistics and similar surveys demonstrate the large disproportion of men to women in positions of power, influence and control. This is so, even in those areas where women predominate such as health and welfare and in trade unions representing women workers. The standard pattern is for men to take up the majority of positions in bureaucratic, professional and managerial elites, while women staff the service industries on the ground. Some women, of course, do exert considerable power – women such as Margaret Thatcher in the UK and Hillary Rodham Clinton in the USA – but, as Faludi's summary suggests, these women are exceptions. Many have argued, perhaps less frequently now, that the spread and scope of male influence in politics, government, business, universities and the arts merely reflect men's greater ability, drive and genius. In response, feminists have argued that the cry, 'go on, show me a great woman artist', rests on the false premise of equal starting points and equal opportunities. This point was strongly taken up by early feminists such as Virginia Woolf and Simone de Beauvoir.

Woolf (1929) asked people to consider, as a hypothetical example, the case of Shakespeare's sister – 'Judith Shakespeare'. If Shakespeare had such a sister, equally talented and creative, what would have been her fate? Woolf argues that it is impossible to imagine Shakespeare's artistic productivity without his advantages of education, freedom of movement, independence from child-rearing and domestic duties, and without the support he received at every level. De Beauvoir summarises Woolf's point as follows:

> The first thing necessary in order to be able to write is to have a room of your own, a place to which you can retreat for a few hours; a place where without risk of interruption, you can think, write, re-read what you have written; criticise what you have done, be left to yourself. In other words, the room is at one and the same time a reality and a symbol. In order to be able to write, in order to be able to achieve anything at all, you must first of all belong to nobody but yourself. Now, traditionally, women are not independent, but rather the property of their husbands and their children. At any moment, their husbands or their children can come and demand explanations, support or assistance, and women are obliged to comply. Women belong to the family or the group; and not to themselves. And in such conditions, writing becomes, if not an impossibility, then at least a very difficult task indeed. (Simone de Beauvoir, reprinted in Kourany, Sterba and Tong, 1992)

Studies of those women who do become prominent in public life confirm that this picture applies, not just to artistic achievement or just to past times. Research on women politicians in the UK (cf. Currell, 1974; Kirkpatrick, 1974, described in Walby, 1990), notes that those women who succeeded in politics are a group with specific characteristics. Women MPs are typically older than their male colleagues, for instance, having entered parliament after child-rearing, or are privileged in terms of access to childcare. They often come from 'political families' and thus are already linked into the appropriate networks. Another common route is to enter parliament as a replacement for a close male relative MP who has died. These women succeed because they escape some of the usual material and ideological constraints women face, but their situation also reveals some of the 'extra' requirements it takes to become a successful woman, as opposed to a successful man.

From a liberal feminist perspective, such inequality would disappear if traditional prejudices against women could be removed. Liberal feminists have campaigned to increase the representation of women in parliament and for the introduction of equal pay legislation. This politics has worked through democratic avenues to reform the state, drawing upon discourses of equal rights and fairness to establish feminist arguments. Although some gains have been made, many of these campaigns seem, with hindsight, to have had mixed effects – the representation of women in high places, and in politics, has not increased substantially, for example. It is certainly true that more women are working than in the 1960s but, as Chapter 4 documented, women workers have been segregated into low pay areas of the economy and into part-time work. For this reason, because of occupational segregation, along with the way different kinds of work have been defined, it has been difficult for the legal concept of 'equal pay for equal work' to get a purchase on differentials in women's and men's pay and make much of a difference (Walby, 1990).

In trying to explain male dominance, radical and socialist feminists have argued that the problem is not simply one of removing the barriers created by prejudice. Rather, it reflects the organisation of society at all levels in favour of men. It is no coincidence or accident that women are under-represented, indeed this is only to be expected in societies organised around men's interests. Radical and socialist feminists are thus more pessimistic about reform. Although the concept of equality is an important one, these feminists doubt that acceptance of women's rights is sufficient if the underlying structures of society are not transformed.

As we saw in Chapter 4, feminists of these persuasions look to the way domestic and private life, paid and unpaid work, have been organised, and the role this plays in sustaining male power. Radical and socialist feminists have also drawn attention to the part played by the State and Government in consolidating men's interests and privileges (e.g. Connell, 1990; MacKinnon, 1982; 1983; 1987; Walby, 1990).

It is often assumed that the role of the State or Government in countries such as the UK and the USA is to act as a neutral ringmaster, co-ordinating the different interests of social groups, according to the wishes of the electorate that governments represent. The State distributes resources, makes laws, administers services, and uses force to keep order both internally and in relations with other states. The legal system, as Catharine MacKinnon (1983, p. 642) points out, can be seen from this point of view as the 'mind of society'. The law should incarnate 'disembodied reason' and apply it impartially. Liberal feminism, in seeking to reform the State, has often worked with this view – looking to the law and the principles it establishes for redress of inequality.

Marxist theorists, however, have long argued that such a liberal view of government overlooks the systematic way the State works through the legal system and the distribution of resources to advantage the middle and governing classes at the expense of the working class. Feminists have inquired whether the State may not operate similarly in favour of men.

> We need to know. What, in gender terms, are the state's norms of account-ability, sources of power, real constituency? Is the state to some degree auto-nomous of the interests of men or an integral expression of them? Does the state embody and serve male interests in its form, dynamics, relation to society, and specific policies? Is the state constructed upon the subordination of women? If so, how does male power become state power? Can such a state be made to serve the interests of those upon whom its power is erected? (MacKinnon, 1983, pp. 643–4)

Sylvia Walby (1990), while not addressing all of these questions, argues that there is strong evidence that the State has been interested on the behalf of men. Historical examples include the active blocking of women's demand for the vote, the maintenance of barriers to women's entry into higher education, the professions, and other forms of work. Through laws on divorce, children and inheritance, the State has acted to institutionalise men's rights within marriage. Walby (1986) argues that even legislation supposedly designed to protect women and children, through restricting the working day, acted in men's interests. These laws prevented women from continuing to work in the best jobs they had formerly held, while having little effect on conditions in the worst jobs held by women.

More contemporary examples include the recent priorities of government in the UK in relation to childcare and the provision of nurseries, community care policies in relation to the elderly, the legislation of discriminatory forms of income support, and the notion that married women's unemployment is in a different category from male unemployment. For black women, of course, these gendered features of State action are intertwined with the way the UK State and Governments in the USA have typically embodied the interests of white citizens over black citizens.

To some extent these ways in which State and Government have supported men's interests and the subordination of women are quite visible. Feminist scholars have argued, however, that these interests can work, in a more subtle fashion, through absences (the kinds of legislation and administrative actions which are missing) and through the very wording, constitution and assumptions of the law. It is in the areas of sexuality and violence in particular that these patterns have been traced.

One key absence concerns State intervention in domestic violence. A number of feminists researchers have noted how liberal democracies put up with a level of violence from men directed towards women, which in other contexts would certainly be described as terrorism, and would excite public outrage (cf. Hamner and Maynard, 1987; Kelly, 1988; Stanko, 1985). The fact that this violence is not understood in this fashion indicates how government procedures have been organised from a male perspective and with a male vision.

> Women who are beaten by their husbands or the men they live with are given very little assistance either by the criminal justice system or the welfare wing of the state. Police are slow to intervene to protect the women and very reluctant to prosecute the man for his criminal assault. Even enforcement of injunctions can be difficult. Welfare officials are often unhelpful in providing alternative accommodation or necessary payments. (Walby, 1990, p. 153)

Elizabeth Stanko (1985) has argued, on the basis of her research on the judicial systems in the UK and USA, that despite a strong belief in the importance of protecting women as members of the 'weaker sex', women, in actuality, are badly protected by the law. This failure is indicated by the difficulty of pressing charges for sexual assault, as well as by the inadequate response of the police and courts to male domestic violence in the home. Protectiveness is a rhetoric, Stanko concludes, rather than a reality. Women who press charges against men often feel that they have to endure a second process of assault by the courts. While women who lead 'unorthodox lives', and who do not appear to obey codes of 'suitable behavior', are sometimes seen as deserving a violent response from their male 'protectors'.

In a complex analysis Catharine MacKinnon (1983) takes apart the assumptions within laws on rape and argues that the very way the law is framed, its very mode of perception, similarly assumes male definitions and interests. The phallocentric construction of the law was most evident in the ruling that rape was not possible in marriage, and in the legal assumption that a husband owned his wife's sexuality and was thus entitled to unrestricted access. However, it is evident also, MacKinnon argues, in the way rape has been defined in terms of vaginal penetration.

Rape is defined, not in terms of *women's* experience of violation and invasion, which may or may not be associated with penetration, but from the moment when the act in question becomes such that *men* can recognise it as a sexual act. Rape is said to occur when the woman can be most obviously said to have been taken by another man. The framing of the law is based on the definition of sex as something which men normally do *to* women. It is thus instructive to speculate about what a sexual assault law written on the basis of woman's experience might look like, and the alternative criteria which might be proposed.

After extensive research on sexual assault, often feminist-inspired, it is now clear that most rapes are committed by men known to the women, rather than by anonymous strangers. Yet studies of the operation of the courts and judicial process indicate that rape prosecutions are easiest to obtain when women are assaulted by an unknown stranger (Stanko, 1985). MacKinnon asks if this reflects a male and legal confusion about consent and familiarity, harking back to the notion that husbands have rights of access to wives. To what extent do men assume that knowing a woman is equivalent to sexual consent? Adjudication on rape frequently seems to hang on the question of which man owns a woman's sexuality, and what is an unacceptable level of force in pursing sexual access to that woman.

MacKinnon concludes that from a woman's point of view, rape is not prohibited; it is merely regulated by the State (1983, p. 651). The law thus represents not the mind of all society, the voice of disembodied reason, but quite literally embodies the minds of men, and their reasoning.

The patterns documented here suggest that although governments have been elected by both men and women since the early twentieth century, and should, in theory, represent them equally, the State has in fact operated as a patriarchy. It has set up and defended an 'aristocracy of sex' and has thus been based on a gender hierarchy (Connell, 1990). Connell argues that this gendered organisation of State action should not be seen as a chance imperfection due to outmoded traditions. Rather, it indicates that men have a continuing collective interest which the State maintains.

Although it is convenient to refer to the State as a thing or as an actor and agent, as we have done through this discussion, we must be clear, as Connell points out, that we are dealing with a set of continually changing processes of regulation, along with established but continually changing institutions such as the courts, the tax offices, welfare agencies, police, government bureaucracies which make regulation possible.

It is also doubtful that men's collective interests and their disproportionate power and influence are maintained through active and self-conscious male conspiracies. Connell wonders if we should embark on a search for 'Patriarch Headquarters' to try to find the co-ordinating centre from which State and governmental processes are directed. He concludes that, although there may be many localised 'patriarch headquarters', or groups of men using their power to protect their gendered interests, the general process of regulation which supports male power is likely to be much more complex, indirect and subtle.

Connell, as we noted in Chapter 4, prefers the view that social processes and structures are more haphazard and uneven, the outcome of historical compromises and current struggles on a number of levels between conflicting interest groups. This process happens to benefit men because of their greater dominance throughout society, sometimes male interests may be overtly and deliberately promoted and co-ordinated by government agencies, but the process can also be unself-conscious – simply a matter of what seems reasonable and obvious to those in power, including those few women in power. We will return to this debate about how male power works later in the chapter, in relation to arguments over the nature of male sexuality.

Sylvia Walby (1990) also prefers a view of the State as the outcome of multiple processes and multiple struggles. She is concerned to stress that women have not been passive victims here. Every legislative change has been fought for and women, despite limited resources and access, have consistently tried to intervene. Walby also stresses the extent to which patriarchy is open to change – mutating as we move through history. Walby argues that we have moved, for example, from a situation of 'private patriarchy' where women were directly controlled by their husbands and fathers within the family to a new modernised form of 'public patriarchy'.

As an example of 'private patriarchy', Walby asks us to consider the position of women in the mid-ninteenth century in relation to the legal procedures of the State.

> Before 1857 divorce was impossible (except by an Act of Parliament). At this time a woman had no legal rights as an independent person when married, since the law conceptualised the married couple as one, and that one was represented by the husband. The husband's rights over his wife were extensive. He had the right to insist that she lived with him; runaway wives could be returned by force

and legally held in the husband's house against their will. He had the right to beat her. He legally owned all her goods, for instance, any wages she earned or property she inherited. He had the right to care and custody of the children and to determine their education. He had the right of sexual access to his wife's body. A wife could not engage in any financial or legal transaction except as the agent of her husband. (1990, p. 163)

Patriarchal control, in other words, at this period, was direct and personal, mediated through family relationships. The main patriarchal strategy here was the exclusion of women from public life along with tight control on female sexuality. This form, as Walby notes, was most prevalent among the middle class, the ways in which working-class women and women in other cultural and ethnic groups in different countries experienced patriarchy had some features in common, but also their own specificities. Women, of course, developed their own strategies for accommodating and resisting this kind of patriarchy.

Women, now, are free to divorce, they can obtain custody of their children, and they are freer to enter a range of sexual relationships, with 'serial monogamy' becoming a new norm. Women are now no longer actively excluded by law from public life. So does this mean that society is no longer patriarchal, and there has been substantial progress for women? Walby argues that there have certainly been changes, many of which women have campaigned for, and which in some areas have lessened oppressive practices. She also argues, however, that the main changes have been in the *mode* of patriarchy rather than in its existence.

Modern patriarchy is much less personal in the sense that it is not so commonly experienced as administered by one man (husband or father) who is the direct beneficiary. This new public form of patriarchy, Walby argues, works not by the exclusion of women from public life, but by the segregation of women within public life. Women are allowed to enter paid work and public life, but on a basis where women's jobs carry least pay and power. Within the family, women are free to divorce, but they are still largely responsible for domestic labour and child-rearing, and are expected to service the men with whom they have relationships.

Some women are better off, but it is debatable whether the majority can be described as beneficiaries. Women's new freedom, for instance, has been accompanied by a massive 'feminisation of poverty' as women lose the kinds of financial security private patriarchy offered, and as men increasingly flee from the financial and other responsibilities of fatherhood. Furthermore, while it may be much easier now for women to enter into the public sphere, there still appears to be relatively little chance of them rising up through the ranks to positions of authority and influence (Walby, 1990).

There are many consequences for women from these historical changes in forms of patriarchy, and, crucially, changes, too, in expressions of masculinity and in men's lives. New cults of masculinity emerge as forms of patriarchy change, with shifting expectations about how 'real men' should behave. In Chapter 5, for instance, we saw some of these changes as the 'private patriarchy' of the Victorian middle classes emerged from earlier forms of social relations and, more recently, as 'public patriarchy' has begun to predominate with its modernisation of masculinity.

As feminist research into the nature and extent of male power has developed, what has become clearer is women's alienation from public life and from centres of power, influence and control. Women are not only under-represented in positions of authority, placed in domestic situations which curtail their opportunities to compete for these positions, but they are also alienated by the very procedures of the State. As radical feminists have pointed out, national public culture has to be seen as male culture (cf. Jaggar, 1983, ch. 9). Public government is substantially men's government, while the economy, including patterns of both paid and unpaid work, is largely male-run, reflecting men's material interests. To the extent there is a woman's culture, it has to exist on the margins, in the interstices, and around the edges of male-controlled public life: invalidated, disempowered and under-resourced. The meaning of the phrase, 'it's a man's world', has become more apparent, and with it some of the implications for understanding men and masculinity.

The personal and the political

The distinction between public life and private life is a useful one for sociologists, economists, and political scientists, as it describes the different kinds of activities which occur inside and outside the home. Feminist scholars, too, have found this terminology useful, but they also want to challenge many of the conventional assumptions which go along with this distinction. Feminist theorists argue that the existence of private and public spheres, linked to paid and unpaid forms of work, is not natural or inevitable; it is a social construction. Indeed, one of the main ways women have been subordinated is through the organisation of society around a private world of domestic work (the province of women), and a public world seen as the province of men.

Feminists, particularly radical feminists, also want to challenge the assumption that real politics happens only in the public sphere – that politics occurs only in the world of public meetings, committees, through diplomatic, governmental and inter-governmental negotiations, in places where men wear suits and report back on television. This is the meaning of the feminist claim that the personal is also political. By this statement, feminists wish to draw attention to the fact that when women and men meet in the bedroom, over the breakfast table, when they play with their children, social and political business is also occurring – political business on which the edifice of public politics depends. From a feminist point of view, therefore, politics has strongly psychological, inter-personal and cultural dimensions.

This is an important point for studies of men and masculinity. It suggests that the kinds of patterns and inequalities in power found in public life will percolate through the rest of life. The characters of men in the smallest details will be formed by the economic and material advantages the majority of men experience, whether working-class or middle-class, in relation to comparable groups of women. If, as Carrigan *et al.* suggest, 'masculinity is constructed in a very complex and tense process of negotiation mostly with women [stretching] right through adult life' (1985, p. 563), then the social position of women will have profound consequences for the outcome of the negotiation.

As many feminists have noted, everyday interactions and negotiations between men and women take place in a context where masculinity is defined as normal and usùal, and where femininity is defined as otherness – the devalued contrast. 'To be human is to be male and to be male is in a sense to be all right' (Lynne Segal, cited in Wetherell and Griffin, 1991, p. 385). Masculinity becomes defined as the norm to which women should aspire, while femininity becomes treated as a falling short of the standards set by men. This cultural law – which Dale Spender (1980) describes as the 'plus male, minus female phenomenon' – can be detected, for instance, in the diverse evaluations of the 'tomboy' and the 'sissy', in the standard practice of using 'he' and 'man' to stand linguistically for humans in general, as well as in the different reactions to instances of 'cross dressing' (i.e. comedy ensues when men dress up in women's clothes, but not when the reverse situation occurs).

Simone de Beauvoir argued in her classic work of the 1940s, *The Second Sex*, that in philosophy, the arts, and in all major cultural pursuits men tend to become defined as 'the Subject', while women are persistently understood as the alterity, 'the Other'. Men, de Beauvoir pointed out, define their masculinity in opposition to, or in terms of their distance from, what is seen as a base femininity. Masculinity becomes identified with transcendence, with culture, and the development of civilisation, while women become identified with nature and with the forces which hold back the transcendent spirit (cf. also Mary Ellman, 1979). Some of the psychological effects of this cultural arrangement were discussed in Chapter 2 in relation to psychoanalytic assessments of men's flight from femininity, and in the later sections of Chapter 5.

What these lines of argument point to is a process of objectification of women along with the denigration and cultural contempt of femininity which come to structure women and men's psychologies. Misogyny can be subtle, as part of a generalised framework of taken-for-granted assumptions, or it may be entirely explicit as in the extracts in Box 6.3. The objectification and devaluation of women are evident, not just in the content of what men say but evident, too, in gaze, and what Rosalind Coward calls 'the look' described in Box 6.4.

Box 6.3: 'Groping towards sexism'

These extracts from adolescent boys come from a fascinating study conducted by Julian Wood in a London school. Wood (1984) argues that material like this demonstrates the category system that the boys he studied adopted to describe women ('dogs', 'horny birds' and 'right whores'), their tendency to assess women by their bodies and 'component parts', and their sometimes precarious assumption that 'we are the gender superior enough to judge women' (p. 61). Wood cites the extracts below as part of a conversation between some of the boys about which girls they 'fancied'. He comments also that this conversation occurred at a time when the boys were trying, in the most heavy-handed fashion, to obtain sexual contact with the girls.

JAKE: I reckon Helen's got a nice face, she's good looking but her body, man! If she was slim... like her sister... she used to be really ugly didn't she, really fat? But now she's really slim, 'aint half nice now, she's got a nice body now... Lorraine though, she's big. She ain't got a nice personality, too much mouth. She thinks she can rule everybody just because she is big.

The conversation passes on to assessing the younger sister of one of the girls in the centre. Jake urges Don to consider fancying her:

DON: What's the sister like?

JAKE: Lovely! Ginger hair, ginger minge. ["minge" = pubic hair]
Don demurs, indicating he is not attracted.

JAKE: Oh my good God! Don't worry, you don't fuck the face! She's got a nice body.

(Wood, 1984, pp.59–60)

As feminist work in this area has advanced, the consequences for women of being objectified in this way in terms of self-presentation and self-esteem have become clear, along with the difficulty of using appearance to make statements (cf. Chapkis, 1986). Less has been said about the consequences for men of this organisation of the visual environment, although, as we will shortly discuss, the consequences for male sexuality have been explored in some detail. This work has led, too, to sophisticated analyses of movies and television and the process of spectating through the camera (Mulvey, 1975).

The film camera also normally looks from a male position, from the implied viewpoint of a male watcher. Films are often structured on the premise of identification with the active male hero. We look at objects and other people, therefore, with his gaze. Richard Dyer (1993) argues that frequently gaze in film is also structured around the rapist-watching-in-the-shadows position. Many films, for example, particularly in thriller or horror genres, depend for their excitement on a heroine in jeopardy. She might be pictured, for instance, going through a daily routine which slowly goes wrong

---

Box 6.4: The male gaze

'The preoccupation with visual images strikes at women in a very particular way. For looking is not a neutral activity. Human beings don't all look at things in the same way, innocently as it were. In this culture, the look is largely controlled by men. Privileged in general in this society, men also control the visual media. The film and television industries are dominated by men, as is the advertising industry. The photographic profession is no less a bastion of the values of male professionalism. While I don't want to suggest there's an intrinsically male way of making images, there can be little doubt that entertainment as we know it is crucially predicated on a masculine investigation of women, and a circulation of women's images for men.

'The camera in contemporary media has been put to use as an extension of the male gaze at women on the streets. Here, men can and do stare at women; men assess, judge and make advances on the basis of these visual impressions. The ability to scrutinize is premised on power. Indeed the look confers power; women's inability to return such a critical and aggressive look is a sign of subordination of being the recipients of another's assessment. Women in the flesh often feel embarrassed, irritated or downright angered by men's persistent gaze. But not wanting to risk male attention turning to male aggression, women avert their eyes and hurry on their way. Those women on the billboards, though; they look back. The fantasy women stare off the walls with a look of urgent availability.'

(Coward, 1984, pp.75–6)

---

and turns to terror, or pictured, as Dyer notes, walking down a corridor at night having heard a noise, or, perhaps, running away, tripping and falling while the monster comes ever closer. In these cases the camera becomes the pursuer, the psychopathic rapist about to strike, and we see the woman from his view. We are usually not encouraged to identify with the 'rapist-in-the-shadows' but, crucially, women are represented in a way which continues a process of objectification and disempowerment.

Many studies have demonstrated how gender further organises everyday life in the form of conversational patterns and non-verbal behaviour. Men tend to monopolise and dominate conversational space as well as other forms of personal space. Typically, men talk for longer than women, interrupt women to a much greater extent than women interrupt men, use less positive reinforcement, self-disclose less, and are less supportive of the conversational topics women initiate (cf. Jacklin, 1992; Spender, 1980; Tannen, 1991; 1993; Thorne, Kramarae and Henley, 1983, for reviews of this work.) On the basis of her research into conversational strategies of heterosexual couples, Pamela Fishman (1978) argues in an evocative phrase, that women are typically left with the 'shit work of conversation'. Just as women conduct most of the housework, preparing spaces for domestic events, they are left,

Figure 6.1 Space and place: gendered postures.

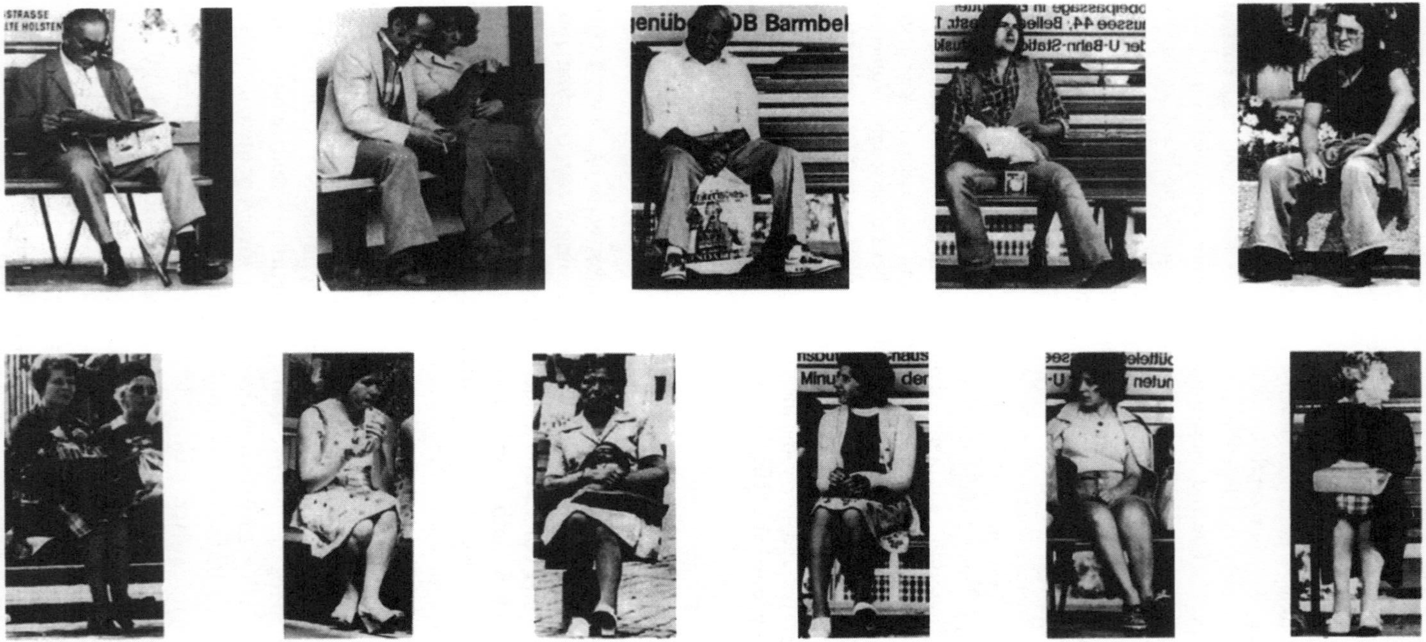

too, to set up conversations, to support and service their conversational partners through shows of interest, enthusiasm and agreement while frequently not receiving these conversational services in return.

Other research has demonstrated how men dominate non-verbal space as well as the geography of public spaces. Men, for example, touch women more than women touch men, some of this touching can be interpreted as sexual in nature, but much of it seems to be line with the general finding that high-status people initiate touch and similar 'invasions' of others' body space more than subordinates. Men similarly dominate public space through posture, as Marianne Wex's (1979) photographs from the 1970s demonstrates (*see* Figure 6.1). Men adopt more open and sprawling postures while women can be seen curling themselves into more confined and tighter spaces. Research on children confirms this pattern, with the boys monopolising common playground space, pushing girls and their games to the peripheries (Thorne, 1993).

Feminist researcher, Nancy Henley (1973) has suggested that it is possible through this work to identify a kind of 'micro-politics' of gender encounters. She and other feminist researchers have argued persuasively that these kinds of interactional patterns reflect status, and thus power differences, between women and men, rather than any inherent sex differences. Most researchers expect, for example, that if power relations in society between women and men were reversed overnight, differences in non-verbal behaviour and conversational strategies would change rapidly in line with new status patterns.

The important aspect of this work is the demonstration of how power relations come to discipline the body, the smallest movement, and the most mundane practices of social life. Patriarchy has a strongly material dimension, but it also has a phenomenology (Bartky, 1990). In other words, it organises people's consciousness, their daily experience, and their sense of normal life. In the next section, we want to look in more detail at one aspect of this phenomenology – sexuality – continuing to explore the ways in which men's dominance and women's subordination set the context in which men's characters are formed. Sexuality has also been a crucial area of debate for feminists, and thus begins to highlight some of the diverse political strategies that feminists advocate.

Sexuality and male violence

One of the most significant achievements of feminism has been to draw attention to the strong and uncomfortable links between male sexuality and male violence. As Deborah Cameron and Elizabeth Fraser point out in their study, *The Lust to Kill*, the conjuncture of desire, sexual climax and murder, to take just one example, is almost entirely a male preserve.

> There has never been a female Peter Sutcliffe (the Yorkshire Ripper). Women have committed very brutal murders; they have killed repeatedly; they have killed at random. But in all the annals of recorded crime, no woman has done what Peter Sutcliffe did (or Jack the Ripper, or Christie, or the Boston Strangler). (1987, p. 1)

This discrepancy is striking, but what is also striking is the sheer prevalence of less extreme and more mundane forms of sexual violence against women. Feminist-inspired research since the early 1970s has convincingly demonstrated the relative 'normality' of rape and other forms of sexual assault (Kelly, 1988; Russell, 1975; Stanko, 1985). As noted earlier, it has become clear, for example, that most rapes and forms of sexual abuse are committed by people known to the woman or child, rather than by the archetypal 'mad stranger' or 'sex maniac'. It has also become evident that while there are differences between men who rape and those who do not, the two groups are not nearly as distinct as once was thought. It is no longer suggested, for example, that rapists can be unequivocally distinguished from other men by their psycho-pathology (by their deviant personalities). Rather, researchers point instead to a culture of rape and to the social situation as a more important predictor.

As Liz Kelly (1988) notes, studies of random samples of women (mostly conducted in the USA) find that anywhere from 5 per cent to 40 per cent of women questioned report incidents of rape. The figures vary depending on the method of questioning, the wording of questions, and whether attempted rape is also included. Studies which ask women about their experiences of sexual harassment in general find even higher patterns of incidence. Studies of men similarly discover a high prevalence of reported sexual aggression, although, perhaps not surprisingly, men's admissions tend to be significantly less than women's reports.

Typical research by Mary Koss, for instance, described by Kelly (1988), investigated 1846 male students and found that 22.4 per cent admitted using verbal coercion to obtain sex, 4.9 per cent admitted sexual abuse (using physical force to attempt to obtain sex), while 4.3 per cent admitted actual sexual assault. Kelly also notes the American research finding that less than 15 per cent of recorded rapes reach trial, and argues that since estimates of the incidence of unreported rapes vary from 4 to 40 per cent, it seems likely that only one rapist in 250 or one rapist in 2500, depending on which estimates are used, ends up being convicted.

One way feminist researchers have understood these patterns is to see sexual assault and associated beliefs and myths as symptomatic of a much more generalised male sexual culture, commensurate with the forms of male power described in this chapter. Liz Kelly (1988), for example, building on a long tradition of feminist theorising (cf. Brownmiller, 1976; Dworkin, 1981; MacKinnon, 1982; Millett, 1972) argues for a 'continuum of sexual violence'. This continuum ranges from the most extreme serial sexual murders to misogynistic pornography, pin-ups, wolf whistling and men's routine sexual surveillance and harassment of women in the street and workplace. What connects these events, Kelly argues, is an underlying contempt for women and a series of shared assumptions about male sexual rights.

This type of argument has been associated mainly with radical feminist traditions of thought and aspects of these claims have been strongly disputed by feminists working within other traditions (e.g. Segal, 1990, Segal and McIntosh, 1992; Wilson, 1992). The alternative view will be discussed shortly, but first we wish to develop further the theory of masculinity, power and sexual expression beginning to emerge here.

The radical feminist analysis suggests that men, consciously and unconsciously, use their sexuality in the service of their general social interests. Male sexuality is seen as one further, and sometimes, the main weapon by which men attempt to control women and maintain male domination (MacKinnon, 1982). Coveney et al. (1984) point out that any ruling group will adopt a range of strategies to protect its position, such as the use of force (often as the last resort), the control of ideology so that the ruling group's interests are presented as natural and universal, joint action to protect important sites, and the alienation and disparagement of alternative points of view. They note that not all members of a dominant group need demonstrate all these behaviours. It is sufficient that many men demonstrate some of them. This way, all men, irrespective of their particular behaviour patterns, stand to gain from the power of their gender as a whole.

Seen in this light what becomes evident is the way in which women are routinely 'policed' by men (Radford, 1987). Women's actions, resistance and autonomous organisation are circumscribed by the threat or reality of male sexual violence (see Box 6.5). Rape and murder simply represent the most extreme example of this policing. As Susan Brownmiller maintains in her classic statement of the 1970s – 'From prehistoric times to the present ... rape has played a critical function. It is nothing more or less than a conscious process of intimidation by which *all men* keep *all women* in a state of fear' (1976, p. 15).

Brownmiller argues that rape is an example of force used by a dominant group as the last resort. It is not necessary that every man rapes: rapists are simply an 'advance guard' doing the 'dirty work' from which all men benefit indirectly, whether they approve of these tactics or otherwise. Crucially, this analysis suggests that rape is only partly about sexual satisfaction, and studies of the accounts of rapists have confirmed that sexual desire becomes fused in the act of rape, with desires to control and punish women (Scully, 1990).

Box 6.5: The policing of women

'The concept of sexual terrorism captured my attention in an "ordinary" event. One afternoon I collected my laundry and went to a nearby laundromat. The place is located in a small shopping center on a very busy highway. After I had loaded and started the machines, I became acutely aware of my environment. It was just after 6:00 p.m. and dark; the other stores were closed; the laundromat was brightly lit; and my car was the only one in the lot. Anyone passing by could readily see that I was alone and isolated. Knowing that rape is a crime of opportunity, I became terrified. I wanted to leave and find a laudromat that was busier, but my clothes were well into the wash cycle, and, besides, I felt I was being "silly", "paranoid". The feeling of terror persisted, so I sat in my car, windows up, doors locked. When the wash was completed, I dashed in, threw the clothes into the drier, and ran back to my car. When the clothes were dry, I tossed them recklessly into the basket and hurriedly drove away to fold them in the security of my own home.'

(Carole Sheffield in Kourany, Sterba, and Tong, 1992, p. 61)

A more routine policing of women and girls is evident in sexual harassment in the workplace (*see also* Box 4.4 in Chapter 4, and Boxes 6.3 and 6.4 in this chapter). As Sue Wise and Liz Stanley (1987) argue, women on the street, girls in schools, and women at work are subjected to a relatively relentless and varying barrage of sexual comment, all of which seems mostly concerned to establish women's place and men's power in relation to women (*see also* MacKinnon, 1979; Hearn and Parkin, 1987; Pringle, 1989). Women are sexualised in these encounters in a way men rarely are. Men typically regard themselves as the rightful 'connoisseurs' of a sexual spectacle, where the woman is the object and the man the legitimate viewer. It is much less usual for men's own sexuality and appearance to become objectified as a spectacle in return, which women could reasonably comment upon and evaluate.

As Sylvia Walby (1990) notes, these feminist analyses of male sexuality in terms of power relations could be combined with either a biological or a social constructionist explanation of sexual behaviour, and indeed also meshed with either a psychoanalytic account of sexual socialisation (*see* Chapter 2) or a role theory explanation (*see* Chapter 3). The biological and more conservative point of view was reviewed in Chapter 1. If sexual violence is seen as biologically determined, as an intrinsic and unavoidable part of masculinity, then debate within feminism begins to turn around the containment of masculinity, and the channelling of male sexuality in directions which are less harmful to women. It makes sense, too, for feminists to take a separatist line in relation to men.

Most radical feminists, however, as Walby points out, argue strongly for a social constructionist rather than a biological approach. It is suggested that there is no necessary or natural form to male or female sexuality. Rather, sexual expression always takes place in a cultural and historical context, strongly influenced by available social scripts. Male sexuality does not have to take violent forms, and the fact it often does reveals something about our particular social organisation around gender divisions. Some consequences of this social context for cultural scripts can be seen in Box 6.6. The ways in which male genitalia have been symbolised are revealing about the social construction of male preoccupations. The penis is often represented as a club or dangerous instrument, yet these are social representations not natural associations. Here gay men have perhaps done most to question and undermine these patterns of symbolisation.

The emphasis on the construction of symbols and scripts stresses that

---

Box 6.6: Symbolising the penis

'One of the striking characteristics about penis symbols is the discrepancy between the symbols and what penises are actually like. Male genitals are fragile, squashy, delicate things; even when erect, the penis is spongy, seldom straight, and rounded at the tip, while the testicles are imperfect spheres, always vulnerable, never still. There are very exceptional cases where something of the exquisiteness and softness of the male genitals is symbolized. Constance Beeson in her film of male gay love, uses the imagery of the flower's stamen . . . to evoke the male genitals. Jean Genet . . . also uses flowers to symbolize the penis and writes of an erection being like a flower unfolding . . . Yet such examples are marginal. Far more commonly the soft, vulnerable charm of male genitals is rendered as hard, tough and dangerous. It is not flowers that most commonly symbolise male genitals but swords, knives, fists, guns. One of the steamiest images of male sexual arousal in the cinema occurs near the beginning of the classic Japanese film *Rashomon*. The warrior, played by Toshiro Mifune, lies half-naked and unshaven under a tree. A beautiful woman passes by escorted by her husband. Mifune does not move, but his eyes stare at her off-screen, and gradually the sword that is dangling over his knee rises up at an angle to his body. A hard, gleaming weapon is at once understood to be like a penis; impossible to imagine flower imagery being used as a prelude to this tale of rape and seduction. (. . .)

'Visual symbolism not only reduces male sexuality to the penis, cutting us off from other erotic pleasures, and placing on the penis a burden of being driving, tough, aggressive, it also tends to separate men from their sexuality. The penis is seen to have a life of its own, leading the man on almost despite himself. At best the man is seen as the possessor or owner of this object, but it is an object over which he does not have full control. It is the beast below.'

(Richard Dyer, 1993, pp. 112–13)

male sexuality is no less socially controlled or moulded than female sexuality. In that sense, men could be said to be equally victims of a social process or equally alienated as the range of possible modes of sexual expression become narrowed to a few conventional and acceptable forms. Of course, from a feminist perspective it is very clear that this social organisation and regulation of sexual expression work most obviously to the disadvantage of women.

Exploring the social constructionist argument further, feminists began to question some of the masculine heterosexual scripts found in many bedrooms (Feminist Review Collective, 1987). Why, for example, is heterosexual sex so narrowly focused on the male penetration of the woman? Why are other forms of sexual contact, which women might find more pleasurable, so often defined as not 'proper' sex? The extent of female sexual dissatisfaction became evident with the publication, among other things, of the Hite Report, and feminists argued that even the most mundane heterosexual encounters have been largely organised around themes in male sexual culture, and around usual forms of male pleasure (cf. Kitzinger, Wilkinson and Perkins, 1992). As Diane Richardson (1993) points out, the challenge of AIDS has lent force to this discussion as women and men have begun to re-conceptualise what counts as erotic activity, in the light of the imperative for safe sex.

What has also become apparent from a feminist social constructionist perspective, is the role the 'eroticisation of domination' has come to play in our culture in the development of the male sexual psyche (MacKinnon, 1987). Again, this eroticisation can be found in the most extreme forms in the accounts of rapists and sex murderers and in the symbolisation of the phallus, but similar themes extend in more muted forms throughout many masculine cultures. Diana Scully's investigations of the stories of convicted rapists include the following common accounts of this pleasure through mastery.

> Rape gave me the power to do what I wanted to do without feeling I had to please a partner or respond to a partner. I felt in control, dominant. Rape was the ability to have sex without caring about the woman's response. I was totally dominant.

> Seeing them laying there helpless gave me the confidence that I could do it . . . With rape I felt totally in charge. I'm bashful, timid. When a woman wanted to give in normal sex, I was intimidated. In the rapes I was totally in command, she totally submissive.

> (Scully, 1990, pp.149–50)

In trying to explain the actions of the Yorkshire Ripper and other serial sex murderers, Cameron and Fraser (1987) take up Andrea Dworkin's (1981) recognition of the strong cultural association between masculinity and tran-scendence. Men, Cameron and Fraser argue, have become used to seeing themselves as the prime subjects and agents. Indeed, as we noted, the human subject and male subject are often treated as interchangeable; to be a human agent is to be male, to be female is a falling from this norm. Such subjectivity is defined in the West through mastery, through the transcending of material constraints.

> 'Man' has been seen as a subject engaged in a struggle to master and subdue his object, nature, to know and act upon it (upon *her*, of course, in traditional parlance). This view is reflected in many ancient myths: the story of Prometheus who stole fire from the gods, of Faust and Satan, the overreachers, of quest narratives like the romance of the Holy Grail . . .
>
> Since sexuality does not stand apart from the rest of culture, these themes have been echoed in erotic practice and in the definition of masculine sexuality. The motifs of that sexuality are *performance, penetration, conquest.*
>
> (Cameron and Fraser, 1987, pp.168–9)

This analysis can, of course, be linked with the psychoanalytic approaches to masculinity considered in Chapter 2. As the characteristics of the Yorkshire Ripper suggest, and the words from the rapists interviewed by Diana Scully, it is perhaps those men most in doubt of their capacity to transcend and dominate in other areas who turn to violent methods of asserting control over women, and to child abuse (Frosh, 1993).

The eroticisation of domination is equally evident, Andrea Dworkin (1981) argues, in pornography, both soft-core and hard-core. This characteristic of pornography has lead some radical feminists into alliances with other anti-pornography groups to campaign for greater censorship and control of sexual imagery (cf. Itzin, 1992; MacKinnon, 1987). It has led, too, to a re-evaluation of the sexual liberation and permissiveness of the 1960s. Was this in fact a sexual liberation or just the emergence of another twist in men's control of women? John Stoltenberg, speaking from a radical feminist platform, puts this argument eloquently.

> Let's say you understand people should be free to be sexual and that one way to guarantee that freedom is to make sure people are not punished for the individuality of their sexuality. And then you find a magazine showing page after page of bodies with their genitals garrotted in baling wire and leather thongs, with their genitals tied up and tortured, with heavy weights suspended from rings that pierce their genitals, and the surrounding text makes it clear that this mutilation and punishment are experienced as sex acts. And you might wonder in your mind . . . where's the sexual freedom?
>
> If you look at the books and magazines and movies that have been produced in the USA in the name of sexual freedom over the past two decades, you have to wonder: *Why has sexual freedom come to look so much like sexual repression? Why has sexual freedom come to look so much like unfreedom?* (1992, pp.146–7)

One man's freedom, in other words, is frequently woman's oppression and men, in freeing themselves for sexual licence, have in many cases freed themselves also from domestic commitment. In commenting on this debate, Sylvia Walby (1990) argues that while radical feminists rightly question the advantages of sexual permissiveness for women, it is important to recognise the double-edged nature of changes in sexual mores since Victorian times. In Walby's view, there have been some important benefits for women from the development of more reliable birth control, freedom to divorce and greater acceptance of female sexual activity.

What has changed, in Walby's view, is the strategy of male sexual control. Formerly, women were tightly controlled by their dependence on one man, by the enormous emphasis placed on sexual purity, and stringent safeguards against infidelity. The consequence, Walby notes, was often to reduce women's interest in sexual activity, even within marriage. Women are now encouraged freely to participate in sexual activity, yet this sexual revolution has not resulted in much change in the long-term balance of power between women and men. Women now simply service men within the patriarchal institution of heterosexuality in different ways.

One important focus for Walby is the varying ways in which women's resistance to patriarchal pressures has changed over time. Her stress, as we noted earlier, is on the continuing struggle between men and women as opposed to an image of domination as straightforward, in the face of women's supposed passivity and men's overwhelming power. From a somewhat different frame of reference, Naomi Wolf (1993) has also recently argued against what she calls 'victim feminism', or the tendency to underestimate women's strengths by dwelling on the details of their subjugation.

These themes would strike a chord with other feminists who have wished to moderate or challenge aspects of radical feminist analyses of male sexuality, despite their many points of agreement with this tradition. Here we will focus on some of the arguments developed by the British-based feminist Lynne Segal (1990), as her comments particularly highlight the implications of these debates for analyses of masculinity (*see also* Vance, 1989).

Segal's main request is for a more complex analysis of male sexuality. She argues that radical feminists such as Andrea Dworkin and Catharine MacKinnon are in danger of ignoring key differences *between* men, and important shifts over time, when they seek to find in male sexuality 'one transhistorical basis for male domination' (1990, p. 207). Segal argues that there is no *one* male sexuality, but multiple male sexualities, just as there are multiple types of masculinity. Male sexuality is not *the* sole cause of the subordination and policing of women, but one arena among many through which patriachal social relations are expressed. Sexuality is currently very important and salient in maintaining gender divisions, but we should not conclude from this that it has always been the main route to the assertion of patriarchy.

In Segal's view, understanding the differences between men who rape, for example, and men who do not should be a vital part of feminist campaigns for social change. Overall, Segal favours a less pessimistic analysis of gender relations. If men are seen as all the same, and if the history of relations between women and men is seen as invariant – structured around an intrinsically controlling male sexuality – then it is difficult to see how change might take place. Segal concludes that there are some men feminists need to work with, and many more men feminists need to work against, but these differences are blurred when men are assumed to have a common dominating sexuality.

In this respect her approach resembles Connell's (1987) arguments reviewed in Chapter 4 (cf. also Carrigan, Connell and Lee, 1985). Connell and his colleagues similarly oppose views of women and men as two homogeneous groups or 'gender classes' standing one against the other. Both Connell and Segal wish to investigate the ways in which certain groups of men manage to control the concept of masculinity, and the meaning of male sexuality. They wish to study how this 'hegemonic masculinity' is then used to subordinate or repress both women and other groups of men.

It is worth considering Segal's specific points concerning sexuality in more detail. She accuses many radical feminists of confusing cultural fantasies (such as those evident in Box 6.6) with actual lived realities and in this way possibly strengthening, rather than undermining, male sexual illusions. The cultural fantasy in the case of male sexuality is what Segal describes as 'the power of the phallus', meaning the representation of men as driven by all-consuming sexual needs – as striving to conquer, overpower, penetrate, and pursue the passive woman. This image of male sexuality is highly pervasive and very powerful, Segal notes, but there is no perfect match here with men's actual sexual behaviour and the reality of their sexual experiences. Instead, many men aspire to this impossible dream of power, while their actual sexual lives are structured by the gap between the fantasy and reality.

> Heterosexual performance may be viewed as the mainstay of masculine identity, but its enactment does not in itself give men power over women. (Even in violent situations, it is the use of muscular force or weapons which give men power to sexually abuse other men, women, or children.) Most of the men who can talk honestly about their heterosexual experiences, admit to considerable confusion, often feeling it is the woman who has all the power . . . Whatever the meanings attached to 'the act' of sexual intercourse, for many men it confirms a sense of ineptness and failure: the failure to satisfy women . . . Unsurprisingly then, for many men it is precisely through sex that they experience their greatest uncertainties, dependence and deference in relation to women – in stark contrast, quite often, with their experience of authority and independence in the public world. (Segal, 1990, pp. 211–12)

Some men do manage to act out the cultural fantasy of the power of the phallus, and their violent or harassing behaviour presents real problems for women and for those men who may also become their victims. Segal is suggesting, however, that male sexuality is not naturally, inevitably or essentially organised around domination and control. The problem is the way in which male sexual expression (which could go in many different directions) is currently bound up and preoccupied with one particular cultural construction.

Segal is thus reinforcing the social constructionist view of sexuality which is also found in radical feminism. She combines this view, too, with some feminist psychoanalytic speculations on the roots of these cultural fantasies of domination and subordination in early childhood such as Wendy Hollway's (1989) studies of men's sexual anxieties discussed in Chapter 2 (cf. Cowie, 1992).

This view draws attention to some of the costs for men of contemporary cultural constructions of male sexuality as well as the major ways this form of sexuality disadvantages women. Men are in some senses to be pitied as they struggle to match the impossible standards of 'the power of the phallus'. As others have noted (*see* Chapter 2) much male sexual dysfunction is concerned with impotence and failures of performance; problems which are precisely tuned to worries about the expectation that men control, act out, and take charge. Male writers on men, such as Victor Seidler (1989; 1991a), have also developed this theme of the disadvantages for men of current formulations of masculinity (*see* Chapter 5).

Developing her analysis further, Segal notes that studies of male sexual fantasies often reveal a preponderance of masochistic rather than sadistic themes. One strongly expressed male desire is for passivity and subordination in the sexual act; a fact which is hard to reconcile with the assumption that male sexuality is uniformly oriented towards power over women (although it does also seem to be the case that sadism is a more common feature of male sexuality than female sexuality – *see* Kappeler, 1992).

Similarly, Segal argues that while the pornography industry expresses strong contempt for women and objectifies them, men, too, are being controlled and exploited by its 'eroticisation of domination'. She quotes Deidre English and Henry Schipper's point that pornography shops and similar venues hardly present celebrations of powerful male sexuality. Rather, these writers claim, the sense of sexual failure and joylessness is palpable in such places. The pornography industry actively builds on and exploits men's anxieties about their sexual performance to sell its products. Schipper comments, 'As they open the door [of the adult 'entertainments' centre] [men's] faces twist into expressions at once helpless and bitter' (cited in Segal, 1990, p. 220).

Segal, too, wishes to qualify the feminist assumption of a 'continuum of sexual violence'. She argues that while this notion has been very useful in understanding sexual violence from a woman's point of view, and the kinds of fears expressed in Box 6.5, for instance, it has not been helpful in understanding men's involvement in such violence. From a woman's perspective, it is the case that sexual violence is unpredictable; there is no method for telling in advance in daily encounters which men are most dangerous, and thus all men, known and unknown, have to be treated with care. The fears which keep women off the streets at night result from the experience of a continuous pattern of intimidation.

However, to understand how rape can be combatted, it is important to examine the historical and anthropological evidence, which suggests that the incidence of rape varies across societies and across historical periods in our own society. Typically the incidence seems highest, Segal argues, when there is a generally high level of violence, and where male sexuality is defined as active – as a form of conquest – while female sexuality is defined as passive – a matter of enticement and coy resistance. Not all men, therefore, should be treated as potential rapists and placed on a continuum. The choice for rape and other forms of abuse as sexual solutions depends on the immediate cultural and social environment. This environment also includes the local community of the men involved in terms of class, race, and region. More specific analyses of sexual violence are thus required, which look at variation as well as continuity.

Overall, then, feminist analyses of male sexuality give us an insight into the links between the generalised forms of male power, exemplified in men's control of public life, and male behaviour in one core area of private life. The principal tension in feminist accounts of this link, as we have seen, concerns reconciling universality (the things men have in common) with men's diversity. As Segal (1990) ruefully comments, when feminists face the continuing practical problem men present to women, universality and the characteristics men share as a group are most salient. In the light of women's disadvantage, a focus on the differences between men can seem like letting men 'off the hook'. Yet the analysis of masculinity (and the political goals of feminism) may often best be served by acknowledging diversity among men, just as in recent years feminists have worked hard to recognise the diversity in women's experiences. This dilemma is one, of course, for which there is no magic wand or easy solution.

Some questions for men

Through exploring these different themes in feminist scholarship, some of the contrasts in feminist politics in relation to men have also become apparent. Some feminists have worked closely with men as equal allies. If the problem is seen to lie in conventional sex-roles, gender stereotypes and socialisation, then this is an entirely reasonable response. Liberal feminists of the 1970s such as Gloria Steinem and Betty Friedan in the USA argued that both women *and* men are oppressed and damaged by sexism and thus reform is in the interest of both groups (a view echoed by many 'men's liberationists' – *see* Chapter 3). To become fully rounded human beings, both men and women must change. Men need to learn from women, while women need to become more like men.

From radical and socialist points of view, this argument ignores the power relation which exists between men and women and the extent to which men benefit from women's subordination. It is naïve, these critics suggest, to expect a powerful and privileged group to give up their advantages without a struggle. Radical and socialist feminists expect considerable resistance from men. Resistance comes about not just because men, like many women, are blinkered by gender ideologies, but because, in some sense, men's real interests are challenged by feminism (cf. Goode, 1982).

If men are seen as a coherent 'gender class', with similar vested interests in patriarchy and in controlling women's sexuality, then the political prognosis is pessimistic. If men *per se* are the enemy, then it is difficult to imagine a feminist politics which might work closely with men. Radical feminists, in particular, have emphasised the importance of building women's cultures and spaces just for women, and these women-only events, campaigns, and movements have been very important to the general development of feminism. Socialist feminists, as Lynne Segal's arguments concerning male sexuality suggest, have been more optimistic about the process of building alliances across gender divides. To the extent that men are seen as internally divided by race, sexuality and class, there is scope for coalitions between men and feminists on particular issues.

This debate, however, is by and large contained among the political left, and, running alongside the politics of feminism is a strong right-wing backlash. Conservative politics, as Bea Campbell (1987) notes, has traditionally been a politics of the feminine rather than feminism. Right wing-women have stressed the value of traditional family life, what they see as the power of women within the domestic sphere, and women's economic and psychological interests in maintaining the traditional relationship between the sexes.

There are some important choices here for women in building individual responses to changing social circumstances and also a collective politics, but there are some real challenges here, too, for men. Can a man be feminist? How should men respond to feminism and the social changes in women's position since the 1960s? This is a social movement which is not going to go away. It has developed a powerful critique of some forms of masculinity and men's actions. It is also linked to quite profound shifts in social organisation such as employment patterns. The question for men is how to be a man in this new context, let alone a 'real man'. Some men have been more perturbed by these issues than others, but since men and women exist only in relation to one another, changes in the position of one group cannot help but cause ripples in the lives of the other (Segal, 1990).

In this section we want to describe some of the responses of men to these dilemmas, focusing mostly on men active in the various men's movements of recent years. A tremendous amount has been written by men about their position (cf. Clatterbaugh, 1990, for an excellent summary) and this review is intended to be symptomatic rather than exhaustive. The main trends we pick out should not be seen as mutually exclusive strategies. As Jeff Hearn (1993) notes, men move between various and sometimes contradictory responses and the politics of any particular men's group can be equally wide-ranging.

One obvious response for men is anti-feminism. The attack on feminism can be more or less virulent. Some male writers (e.g. Farrell, 1994; Lyndon, 1992) argue that men, not women, are the real victims of the 'sex war'. Men within the 'men's rights' movement have suggested that it is men's position, rather than women's, which is under threat and needs to be protected. The main focus of this movement both in the UK and USA has been on divorce and child custody legislation, along with opposition to the criminalisation of rape within marriage. These men claim that feminism has undermined the rights of fathers and the position of men in the family. They see themselves as a victimised and disadvantaged social group, and argue that the political establishment is now entirely under the thumb of the feminist lobby (Baker, 1994). Feminists, of course, would be only too delighted if this was the case, but can see little evidence for the power attributed to them by this strand of male politics (cf. Chesler, 1991).

Warren Farrell (1994) suggests, along similar lines, that male power is a myth rather than a reality. Men, in his view, are enslaved by current work practices and the responsibilites of being the breadwinner. They are also brutalised by self-destructive macho cults, especially young black and working-class men. The consequence, Farrell argues, is that men die younger, commit suicide more frequently than women, are forced to go to war, learn to hate themselves, and find that there is no space in which their disturbances can be acknowledged.

This work claims that feminism is misleading about the relationship and balance of power between the sexes. Anti-feminist writers suggest either that patriarchy is imaginary, a feminist fantasy, or, alternatively, that it is a highly desirable form of social organisation which is in such a fragile and parlous state that it requires rescue. As Kenneth Clatterbaugh (1990) notes, other conservatives, from a more academic perspective, have argued a third and more self-confident position, based on biological theories. These authors propose that patriarchy and women's subordination are inevitable because of the biological make-up of women and men (e.g. Goldberg, 1973 – *see* Chapter 1).

The so-called men's 'mytho-poetic movement' can be viewed as a somewhat different line of conservative argument. This movement, which is more predominant in the USA than the UK, also sees masculinity as under threat and wants to restore lost male glories. However, its focus is therapeutic and spiritual, concentrating on the lives of individual men and their psychological development. Some of the anxieties expressed by this movement are evident in Box 6.7 as Robert Bly, author of *Iron John*, bewails the fate of the 'soft men' of modern times (*see also* Kean, 1992).

Box 6.7: Soft men and nice boys

'[T]he feminist movement encouraged men to actually look at women, forcing them to become conscious of concerns and sufferings that the Fifties male laboured to avoid. As men began to examine women's history and women's sensibility, some men began to notice what was called their *feminine* side and pay attention to it. This process continues to this day, and I would say that most contemporary men are involved in some way.

'There's something wonderful about this development – I mean the practice of men welcoming their own "feminine" consciousness and nurturing it – this is important – and yet I have a sense that there is something wrong. The male in the past twenty years has become more thoughtful, more gentle. But by this process he has not become more free. He's a nice boy who pleases not only his mother but also the young woman he is living with.

'In the seventies I began to see all over the country a phenomenon that we might call "the soft male". Sometimes even today when I look out at an audience, perhaps half the young males are what I'd call soft. They're lovely, valuable people – I like them – they're not interested in harming the earth or starting wars. There's a gentle attitude toward life in their whole being and style of living.

'But many of these men are not happy. You quickly notice the lack of energy in them. They are life-preserving but not exactly life-giving. Ironically, you often see these men with strong women who positively radiate energy.

'Here we have a finely tuned young man, ecologically superior to his father, sympathetic to the whole harmony of the universe, yet he himself has little vitality to offer.'

(Bly, 1990, pp. 2–3)

The argument (cf. Clatterbaugh, 1990; Fee, 1992) seems to be that feminism, although good for women, has been damaging for men. This damage is compounded by modern work patterns and the absence of fathers as active presences in the lives of young boys. Bly argues that the cure for the 'anguish' of the soft male is to discover through myths, story-telling, 'wild-man' workshops and a type of Jungian therapy, a more vigorous and authentic masculinity. Other writers in similar 'spiritual' traditions have taken a more pro-feminist line. The British writer John Rowan (1987), for example, argues that men have indeed been deeply wounded by feminism, but this wound is necessary and highly positive. He advocates that men should get in touch with a female goddess tradition as a source of strength.

The mytho-poetic movement with its strongly nostalgic and conservative, yet 'New Age', feel has proved enormously attractive to many men in the

USA. It combines a response to feminism and a pro-masculine stance, together with contemporary enthusiasm for individual therapy and 'work on the self'. Dwight Fee (1992), commenting on the movement, notes that this has become a very appealing identity politics for privileged white hetero-sexual men. Power relations are obscured in a rhetoric of individual loss and self-development which need not ruffle or question male privilege.

Men, however, have also responded in much more positive ways to feminism, and the remainder of this chapter will touch on these responses. The 1960s and 1970s were periods of intense activity for women, paralleling earlier waves of feminism such as the suffragette campaigns at the beginning of the twentieth century. Men, especially those already involved in left-wing politics, inevitably also became caught up by and interested in these develop-ments. In much smaller numbers, men similarly became involved in con-sciousness-raising groups, in developing critiques of gender stereotypes, in theorising gender inequality, in campaigns for equal pay, abortion rights, for childcare, and became active within trade unions.

Some of the flavour of this activity has been captured in various antho-logies of men's writings of the period, such as Jon Snodgrass's (1977) *For Men Against Sexism*, Pleck and Sawyer's (1974) collection *Men and Mascu-linity*, and Victor Seidler's (1991b) recent selection of men's writings, pub-lished in the British men's magazine *Achilles Heel* (from 1978 to 1984). These articles contain a fair amount of self-exploration, as men speculate on their life histories and choices. There is also considerable self-criticism as men began to re-evaluate their sexual histories, their avoidance of domestic work, complicity with pornography and other practices demeaning to women. Some moments of political strategy-making can also be seen in these collec-tions, as men discuss the development of manifestos (such as 'The effeminist manifesto', Dansky, Knoebel and Pitchford, 1977) or the advantages and limits of men's consciousness-raising groups.

This political activity was paralleled by an extensive academic reconcep-tualisation of men and masculinity, as well as a new wave of research on men which has continued into the 1990s. Much of this work has been reviewed already in this book (*see also* particularly collections by Brod, 1987; Hearn and Morgan, 1990; Kaufmann, 1987; Kimmel, 1987; 1989; Metcalf and Humpheries, 1985). Kenneth Clatterbaugh (1990) argues that although there are strong continuities in this men's politics of recent times, one important division occurs between the 'men's liberationists' who have taken a more liberal feminist stance and 'men against sexism' who, like radical and socialist feminists, have tried to focus on patriarchy and male power.

Men's liberationists are those who have taken to heart the message that men have much to gain from women's liberation, since men are also seen as restricted and confined by conventional sex-roles. Male socialisation and gender ideologies are thought to produce an incomplete and inadequate human being, stifled by social expectations of masculinity. Men are chained, too, by current social practices. They are unable to nurture and care for others for fear of being seen as unmanly. They are trapped within competitive relationships with other men, and always fearful of never being masculine enough. In the UK, the writer Victor Seidler (1989; 1991a) has done much to develop this analysis, although he also writes as a socialist (*see* Chapter 5).

Unlike the more conservative approach of the mytho-poetic movement, male liberationists are not encouraging men to recapture some lost male essence. Instead, they are urged to take the movement towards androgyny further, by questioning all aspects of masculine cults. Furthermore, unlike the men's rights movement, male liberationists see feminism, not as a threat, but as a welcome release for men. Male liberationists argue that men are, indeed, victims of masculinity, but they explore, too, how this conventional masculinity leads men to victimise others.

Thus Miller (1974), in a good example of this analysis, describes in an article entitled 'The making of a confused middle-aged husband' how his early egalitarian perspective translated into a conventional marriage. He candidly describes his own failings and the difficulty of giving up his privileges, despite the fact he could see the injustice from his wife's point of view. Much of this 'male liberationist' work draws upon role theory and the assumption, discussed in Chapter 3, of a split between social roles and a 'real' authentic underlying self. The assumption is that if men could work through their social conditioning to liberate their real feelings, emotions and reactions, then, by learning to act in line with different values, the lives of both men and women would be improved.

Men who prefer a more radical politics of gender have been critical of this tendency within men's movements on several counts. First, as radical and socialist feminists noted about liberal feminism, this approach underestimates the social structural basis of male power. Gender inequality is not a matter of individual wishes and choices, but organised through social institutions and social practices at all levels. Work on the self, although vital, is secondary to organising for social change. Men involved in 'men against sexism' groups have criticised men's consciousness-raising groups, in particular, for eschewing difficult political tasks in favour of the more interesting and absorbing tasks of self-exploration.

This tendency within men's movements is cruelly parodied in Box 6.8 by Mick Cooper, a member of the editorial collective of *Achilles Heel*, the British men's anti-sexist magazine. Cooper's point is that without a clear and constant focus on male power, men's groups are in danger of backsliding and developing an incoherent politics. At the same time, however, Cooper's critique also seems to buy into and reproduce popular stereotypes of pro-feminist men as wishy-washy and ineffectual. How much of this in the popular media, if not in Cooper's case, is part of the backlash against feminism; a way of undermining the activities of pro-feminist men? The most persistent charge against men who explore feminist ideas is that they are

Box 6.8: Liberating men

'The clearest conclusion that came out of my history of the men's movement (Cooper, 1990) was that for men, *talking about men is a lot more rewarding than talking about women.* Even when men get together to explicitly challenge sexism, what seems to happen in men-only groups is that they slowly veer towards forgetting about sexism and ending up talking about men ... I was at a conference once discussing "The Way Forward for Men" and I think what happened is fairly common for what happens at a lot of these events. Someone stands up and says, "we need to challenge sexism!", and everyone nods their heads furtively and mutters into their woolly beards and then the room goes quiet. And then someone else says that we need to run more creches and people begin to look around a bit nervously because they've got crochet evening on Wednesday night and the anti-sexist rugby group on Fridays and every other Tuesday Pat comes around for a drink and the idea of wiping a few smelly behinds isn't very appealing. So everyone nods nervously and hopes the idea will go away. Which it does. And then someone says that men are always *doing* things and that the idea of *doing* creches and *doing* political work is just so *typically male* and everyone breathes a sigh of relief because now they don't have to ask Phil and Bill whether it's all right to bring a couple of toddlers along to the Sunday quiz night. And then to put the icing on the cake, someone says that doing creches is just a product of male guilt and that if men *really* want to challenge sexism what they need to do is to sort themselves out and learn to live with and feel OK with other men. So someone suggests a game of sardines as an all-out attack on patriarchy and there's some debate over this because Derek has sprained his ankle in the session on men's ballet and it's decided that it would be oppressive to him if everyone else played sardines so the group decide that they'll play "everyone sitting on everyone else's lap in a circle" at the end of the session and get back to debating fighting sexism. Now the guy who first denounced creches chirps up that maybe what men need is a better communication network of anti-sexist men's groups so that they can co-ordinate their activities more effectively. And someone suggests how about a travelling library so that everyone can share the same books. What about a national men's centre, a TV programme on men, how about a men's publishing co-op, men's studies on the national curriculum, what we need is more men in child-rearing, more men in teaching, more men in parliament. And then someone hits upon it. The little shifty guy at the back who nobody wanted to be a partner with in the trust games because no one trusted him slowly rises to his feet, "why don't we have", he says in his meekest, most anti-sexist voice, *'a men's political party'.* The room screams with delight. The "touchy-feely" men touchy-feely each other, the intellects stroke their beards and wonder why they weren't the ones who came up with such a novel idea, and the session finishes with an exhilarating game of "sitting in a circle on each other's laps" which collapses into a beaming heap on the floor. Patriarchy is quaking at the knees.'

(Cooper cited in Griffin and Wetherell, 1992, pp.143–4)

insufficiently 'masculine'. They are seen as too liberal, indecisive and effeminate.

From another angle, Connell (1983) and Segal (1990) have asked what evidence there might be for the claim that men are damaged by patriarchy and conventional sex-roles. Is it the case, Connell asks, that masculinity is an impoverished character structure? Do men need liberating for the sake of their own mental health? Segal argues that although psychological research suggests there are some distinctive masculine fears and anxieties, there are no signs, in terms of measures of self-confidence and self-esteem, of men's greater psychological disadvantage compared with women.

> When we know that from schooldays onwards boys collectively succeed in getting more attention, talking more, demanding more, showing off, occupying public spaces in more relaxed and confident ways than women, it seems hard to sustain the notion of 'masculinity' as inherently oppressive to men. (Segal, 1990, p. 289)

Men, Segal and Connell argue, are indeed the 'favoured sex'. The problem is that this favouring, or this privileged position, rests on the domination of women. If we take this message on board, it suggests that for most men, particularly heterosexual men, there may be little intrinsic reason for change, except the claims of social justice.

As Cooper notes, it is very difficult for men to come to terms with their participation in patriarchy. Many men report that one of the main challenges in working out a perspective on feminism is coming to terms with the fact that *you* are the object of the critique. Much men's politics, therefore, is uneasy and fraught. 'Feminism makes things unsafe for men, unsettles assumed positions, undoes given identities' (Stephen Heath, 1987, p. 6). Heath argues that men's relationship with feminism is an impossible one. Men cannot *be* feminists since feminism is a social movement for women. For a man to argue that he is a feminist is to risk being seen as appropriating the movement (cf. Canaan and Griffin, 1990). What is open to men then, Heath argues, is to try to learn from feminism and to avoid being anti-feminist in any way. Men have to acknowledge their own complicity with forms of masculinity which disadvantage women. There is thus no easy 'holier than thou' or 'politically correct' position here. The consequence can be political paralysis as people dwell too long on the difficulties rather than the possibilities for action. Once again, Segal proves incisive on this point.

> I don't really think it is so hard at all to see what men should do and one reason why men can think that is if they see change simply in terms of personal change, but my whole point is that change in gender relations certainly isn't going to be just a question of personal change, it's going to be creating the possibilities for greater choice in women's lives particularly for women when they have dependent children, when they're carers. It's going to be changes in social policy which enable far greater choice in women's lives as well as men's lives, like more

flexible working conditions and shorter working hours. It's not hard for men to know, say if they're in trade unions – which they should be if they're concerned at all about other people. Then there are certain policies they should be pursuing, and to say, 'Well I don't know what women really want'. I think it's not really so tricky at that level to see what women really want. When you come back precisely to the bedroom or the kitchen – I think in the kitchen it's not necessarily so hard to see what women want either, while maybe in the bedroom it can get trickier, and although again I suppose I shouldn't over-simplify things. I suspect it's disingenuous when men say it's not so clear and we should tell them what to do ... I am quite happy to tell them what to do, I would very much like men to be tackling issues of other men's violence ... I think it's very crucial to have men there at the cutting edge of where some of the issues around men's abuse of power are. (Interview with Lynne Segal in Griffin and Wetherell, 1992, p. 153)

Segal's view is that men should stop agonising and get on with negotiating with the women and men with whom they live and work, acting in both the public and private spheres to make women's lives better. Although there might not be much to be gained here in terms of 'psychological liberation', Segal suggests some clear incentives in terms of material changes for men (such as more flexible working patterns) as well as better relationships with women.

The radical pro-feminist John Stoltenberg (1990) gives three reasons why men should become committed to feminism. First, he notes that for many men, feminist convictions develop from loyalty to particular women (friends, sisters, mothers, partners). He states that once a man has experienced male supremacy from the inside through the experiences of women, there is a strong incentive to be her ally and stand by her. Second, Stoltenberg argues, men might come to feminism through their own experience of abuse (physical and/or sexual) or because their own sexuality is not, in Stoltenberg's words, 'standard issue'. Third, men may come to feminism because of their broader political principles, for if they are engaged in other struggles for human rights, the refusal to acknowledge the rights of women seems both inconsistent and intellectually dishonest.

Stoltenberg's own position is summed up in the title of his book *Refusing to be a Man*. What does this mean – how is it possible for a man to *refuse* to be so constituted? Stoltenberg argues (*see* Box 6.9) that masculine identity is not a natural state but an idea, a set of choices which men have to work at adopting. Since masculinity within patriarchal societies is premised on male supremacy, based on sexual injustice, then to choose to adopt this identity and to work hard at being masculine is also to choose an ethics of domination. In a subtle analysis, Stoltenberg focuses on rape and sexual violence, arguing that rapist ethics are maintained through men's everyday choices for certain kinds of sexuality and patterns of sexual objectification of women. It is precisely the ways in which men have to struggle to be men that result in rape and sexual violence, since the mind set of 'the man' involves, by definition, the attempt to control and dominate others, no matter how difficult and intimidating this might be in practice.

Box 6.9: Refusing to be a man

'Sexual identity is a political idea. Its force derives entirely from the human effort required to sustain it, and it requires the lifelong, nearly full-time exertion of everybody for its maintenance and verification. Though everyone, to some extent, plays their part in keeping the idea of sexual identity real, some people, it should be noted, work at this project with more fervor than do others.'

(Stoltenberg, 1990, p. 10)

'To act convincingly a male sexual identity requires:

an unfailing belief in one's own goodness and the moral rightness of one's purposes, regardless of how others may value what one does;

a rigorous adherence to the set of behaviors, characteristics and idiosyncrasies that are appropriately male (and therefore inappropriate for a female);

an unquestioning belief in one's own consistency, notwithstanding any evidence to the contrary – a consistency rooted, for all practical purposes, in the relentlessness of one's will and in the fact that, being superior by social definition, one can want whatever one wants and one can expect to get it.'

(Stoltenberg, 1990, p. 17)

'[T]here is enormous promise in perceiving gender as an ethically constructed phenomenon – a belief we create by how we decide to act, not something that we automatically "are" on account of how we were born.'

(Stoltenberg, 1990, p. 24)

Heterosexual men can learn a great deal here from gay men and gay male cultures (Carrigan, Connell and Lee, 1985; Dollimore, 1991; Harrison, 1985; Kinsman, 1987), since, on a daily basis, it is gay men who have had the most experience of choosing to behave differently (Kleinberg, 1987). To be gay is to be already in confrontation with male sexual identity. Despite a sometimes fraught relationship with feminism (cf. Stanley, 1982), many gay men have been in the vanguard of attempts to forge new identities in response to the categories constructed for them by political and medical establishments, such as 'the deviant', 'the pervert', 'the sick', 'the unhealthy'. These identities have at times been powerfully anti-sexist and anti-masculinist.

Stoltenberg's politics is in no sense defeatist. He sees men as complicit with patriarchy, but with the freedom to choose differently. Although this strong action-orientation would be applauded by socialist feminists, women and men in this tradition might also question Stoltenberg's voluntarism. Is it just a matter of individual choice? What else might be involved? To what extent can individual men overcome their socialisation? Is male sexual identity just an idea, a social construction? Or are there sets of social and economic practices which make masculinity a material force? What is the relationship between ideas and social forces? Is there just one masculine identity or many masculinities?

We have now come full circle to the questions which sustain the perspectives and debates considered in this book. Politics and academic research are intertwined in the study of gender. In this chapter we have raised questions for men but, as we have tried to demonstrate, these are more than questions; they are also choices which summarise ways of living. The task for all men is to negotiate these decisions both individually and collectively across the personal and the political.

Conclusion

Summaries and key debates

It is worth repeating the point that, in viewing men from a number of different theoretical perspectives, we are trying to emphasise that there is no single, correct theory of masculinity. Perspectives cannot be labelled right and wrong. As one walks around a sculpture or any other three-dimensional object, the views one obtains are all, in some sense, equally valid. However, this in no way implies that they are always equally useful or insightful. Looking at the back of a television set, for example, is much less stimulating than directly facing the screen. Indeed, unless one is in the process of trying to repair the set, such a view is completely irrelevant to the very point of television.

In order to assist in making judgements about the relative adequacy of the various perspectives on men and masculinity, each chapter sought to address the same basic set of questions. These were, we might recall, first, what is the *substance* of masculinity? What is it that binds men together as a distinctive group? Second, why does masculinity takes the particular shape (or shapes) that it does? Why, in other words, do men behave in certain ways rather than others? Third, what are the mechanisms by which males become masculine? How does masculinity 'get into' men? Fourth, how can we account for the fact that, while men may form a distinctive social group, there are always those who deviate from these patterns of commonality? In the first section of this conclusion we will work our way through the six perspectives systematically, again beginning with the biological position, in each case providing summary answers to the above.

For those working from within the biological perspective, the substance of masculinity is chromosomal, hormonal and possibly even determined at the level of the single gene. Men are defined by their possession of a Y chromosome. Masculinity, they argue, follows as a consequence of this organic structure, particularly through the stimulation of the production of male sex hormones (androgens) which act directly upon the body's vital organs – especially the brain. Masculinity does not so much 'get into' men as 'emerge out' of them. It flourishes like an oak tree from the acorn of the Y chromosome. Differences between men are only to be expected from a biological perspective. Indeed, not only does every species contain variations in physical and behavioural characteristics across its membership, but they also rely upon these differences for their continued ecological 'fitness'.

Psychoanalytical theorists argue that masculinity is a specific organisation of psychical structures within the mind of the individual male. It consists of a multi-layered and contradictory collection of desires, fantasies and emotions. On the question of why masculinity takes the particular shape that it does, different branches of psychoanalysis offer different kinds of explanations. However, all see the relationships which the boy enters into (typically) with his parents as being central. For example, those belonging to the object relations school of thought see masculinity as a product of the boy's initial identification with the mother, and subsequent re-identification with his father. Masculinity gets into the boy via a range of psychological processes, including identification, introjection and repression. It is a development – driven either by the boy's fear of castration or by the socialising practices of the mother – again depending which version of the theory one takes. Variations between men are accounted for either in terms of some malfunction in the socialisation process (e.g. the boy 'fails' to switch identification from mother to father), or else as a by-product of differences in the basic organisation of the family unit (depending upon whether the boy is primarily looked after by his mother, father or both taking equal shares).

Role theorists see the substance of masculinity as a set of social scripts; a collection of 'stage directions' telling men how to act like men. Generally speaking, role theorists have not concerned themselves with the question of why these scripts take the form that they do. Where the issue has been addressed, theorists have suggested that the constitution of the male sex-role is determined by the needs of society. If, in other words, a society requires people to defend against aggressors, look after dependents and generate wealth, it must tailor people's behaviour to suit. Sex-roles reflect the specific division of labour between men and women in meeting these needs. The male individual learns to be manly. He has it drummed into him. The existence of differences between men is a thorny problem for many sex-role theorists. However, just as with psychoanalytical theory, one way of accounting for such variations is to argue that sometimes the process goes wrong. The boy, for some reason, fails to learn his lessons. The only alternative explanation is that there is not just one, but several different male sex-roles available at any given time.

The social relations perspective on men sees masculinity as a set of distinctive practices which emerge from men's positioning within a variety of social structures (such as work and the family). As such, masculinity takes its shape from the institutions in which men are embedded. Being much more of a social than a psychological theory, it remains agnostic as regards the processes by which masculinity gets into men (although it would imply that men are not born with masculinity). The social relations perspective is relatively 'strong' on explaining differences between men, for insofar as society is seen as divided into different social groups (e.g. race and class) the masculinities which emerge from these conditions are unlikely to be the same.

The cultural perspective on men sees the substance of masculinity in terms of theory or ideology. Masculinity is a concept which gets transmitted from one generation to the next through talk and texts. Different cultural theorists disagree about the forces which underpin the construction of masculinities. Some suggest, once again, that masculinities simply evolve to meet the general needs of society. Others insist that while masculinities might be functionally oriented, they invariably serve the interests, not of the whole of society, but of particular sub-groups. They point to the ways in which the ability to control the meaning of masculinity has played an important part in the securing of social, political and economic power by certain sections of society. Like the previous perspective, the cultural viewpoint does not specify a particular model of the male subject. As such, it does not compete with the psychoanalytical and role perspectives in explaining how boys become men. However, it does imply that the meaning(s) of masculinity have to be learned or somehow internalised, for they come to structure the very ways in which men perceive both themselves and their social environments. The cultural perspective is also well capable of accounting for differences between men, since it posits the simultaneous existence of multiple and even contradictory cults of masculinity, some of which might be more dominant than others.

Finally, the feminist perspective on men sees the substance of masculinity as a set of power relations. The primary factor determining the shape of masculinity is politics. Men, that is, adopt those forms of activity and identity which bring them the maximum rewards, both materially and in terms of self-esteem. Once again the feminist viewpoint has no implicit theory of the male subject. As we have seen, feminists have often drawn upon the ideas of psychoanalysis, role theory and even biology to explain how males become constituted as men. The issue of differences between men is a live one for many feminists. Some argue that such differences are superficial; all men, they claim, benefit from the subordination of women, irrespective of whether they themselves are actively involved. Others maintain that it is too simple to think of men as a unitary gender class. Instead, they suggest, we should see men as divided into various sub-groupings, some of whom wield a great deal of power and others who are relatively powerless.

So what are we to make of this mixed bag of different perspectives? Can we fit them all together to produce a total picture of men and masculinity? Surely the spatial metaphor of perspectives implies that we could (given views from 'all sides'). Unfortunately things are not so straightforward. The main problem is that different perspectives often lay claim to explaining the same phenomena. In other words, they stand as competing explanations. For example, in Chapter 1, we described the struggle between different social scientists to have masculinity seen as a consequence of natural or social forces (i.e. the 'nature-nurture debate'). Role theorists and psychoanalysts offer competing versions of male socialisation which are similarly difficult to reconcile. There are also tensions between social and cultural theorists over the issue of whether the essence of masculinity is material or ideal, and whether the economic organisation of society is more important than the cultural. While, in feminism, there are debates between radical and socialist feminists about the relative importance of capitalism versus patriarchy as the key social structure organising gender relations.

Clearly, there is no way in which these different perspectives can be simply tacked on to one another, although this is no way means, of course, that they are all mutually exclusive. Indeed, we have already seen how theorists such as Talcott Parsons have brought together or synthesised different kinds of theory into a single account. It might be worthwhile, therefore, spending some time looking at a few of the key issues which need to be addressed by anyone seeking to develop a broader theoretical understanding of men and masculinity. It is to this task that the remainder of this brief conclusion is dedicated.

The first issue that we would like to raise concerns the origins of masculinity. Where does it actually come from? Most of our six perspectives see masculinity as having its origins in society. That is, they see masculinity, not as growing out of men, but as descending onto them from above. The obvious exception to this rule comes from the adherents of a strongly biological approach. As we have already mentioned, this perspective sees masculinity written into the very cells of a man's body. All his potentials are already 'in there', just waiting to be realised. However, it is also the case that certain strands of psychoanalytic writing similarly rely upon essentialist notions of sex (i.e. that the sexes are different in essence). Hudson and Jacot (1991), for instance, argue for the existence of a biological foundation which is then subsequently reinforced by child-rearing. The issue of the origins of masculinity has been, and remains, tremendously important politically, for as we pointed out in Chapter 1, the belief that masculinity represents a genuinely natural state of being frequently serves to help justify the continuation of societies in which men enjoy a disproportionate level of power and privilege.

If we accept, for the moment, that masculinity (the traits and characteristics of men as opposed to their distinctive organs) has its main origins in society, we are still faced with a closely related question about the (eventual) *location* of masculinity. Upon this key issue there is also something of a division or split between our main theoretical approaches. Psychoanalysts, for example, see masculinity as 'inscribed' into the young boy's psyche. He may not come into the world masculine, but during his first few years, they argue, the characteristics of the male mind continue to develop until, around the age of six, they set like a blancmange. A similar notion appears in the work of cognitive developmentalists who see masculinity in terms of specific mental structures located within the brains of individual males. In both cases, therefore, masculinity seems to exists as some kind of entity which almost could be extracted surgically and held aloft.

On the other hand, there are theorists who see masculinity, not as a thing, but as an on-going process or system of relations located in history. For example, social learning theorists might claim that masculinity is little more than a predictable response to stable schedules of reinforcement. The moment displays of masculine behaviour fail to elicit rewards is, they insist, the moment when men will begin to change their ways. Masculinity, there-fore, is not so much something that someone *is*, as something that someone *does*. A similar conclusion is drawn by those who portray masculinity as a collection of situated performances in relation to the social institutions in which men are inserted. In both cases, masculinity is every bit as much a product of the contexts in which men act as it is a possession of the indi-viduals themselves (assuming that it is possible even to separate the two things meaningfully).

While many readers would probably be quite happy to accept the idea that masculinity is a social construction (i.e. men are not born with their masculinity already *in situ*), it is much less likely that they would feel so comfortable with the assumption that there is no such thing as a continuous masculine personality. To many it might seem obvious that there has to be some substance to a person's identity, otherwise it would be impossible to recognise them (or even oneself) as a distinctive human being. In response to this argument, a number of different theorists (including Bob Connell) have suggested that personalities represent, not descriptions of something inherent within the person, but accounts of life histories; that is, stories told either to oneself or to others which make historical sense of a person's social relationships.

> Life histories are ... artifacts of writing; they are the upsurge of the narrative imagination ... We too, *as selves*, are artifacts of the narrative imagination. *We*, literally, would not exist, save as bodies, without imagining who and what we have been and are: kill the imagination and you kill the self. (Freeman, 1993, p. 223 – emphasis in original)

These stories often remain the same, thereby affording the impression of a coherent biography. However, as these writers insist, it is always possible to construct new stories which make a completely different sense of a person's life history.

The idea that masculine identities are 'fashioned in the imagination' (Dawson, 1991) leads us neatly into another key debate around the issue of human agency, for it would seem to imply that men can construct themselves as they like. This assumption is, of course, challenged by most of our theoretical perspectives. Psychoanalysts see men as determined by their in-fantile experiences, role theorists see them as moulded and manipulated into 'sex-appropriate' kinds of displays, while sociologists of gender see men as the products of various institutional structures. Similarly, cultural theorists argue that men are constrained by the range of different theories of mascu-linity made available by a culture. They may be able to pick and choose to some extent, but only within the confines of the 'menu'. What is more, the individual man might have further constraints placed upon him by the fact of his physical shape and occupational status. For example (and here we begin to get an idea of how different theoretical approaches might be combined), it may be much more difficult for a fat boy to represent himself in terms of an Arnold Schwarzenegger-style macho masculinity compared to some of his slimmer friends. Similarly, an unemployed man has nothing like the same access to a masculine identity, built around the demonstration of power and wealth (e.g. dressing in designer clothes and driving a Ferrari). Indeed, the only way in which these identifications can be carried off successfully is in fantasy.

> Representations furnish a repertoire of cultural forms that can be drawn upon in the imagining of lived identities. These may be aspired to, rather than actually ever being achieved, or achievable. And into this gap flows the element of desire. The forms furnished by representations often figure ideal and desirable mascu-linities, which men strive after in their efforts to make themselves into the man they want to be. Imagined identities are shot through with wish fulfilling fantasies. (Dawson, 1991, pp.188–9)

Here we see something of how the cultural and psychoanalytic perspectives might intersect, for while cultural theorists might be able to specify the different representations of masculinity made available by a particular cul-ture, they are not so adept at explaining the emotional investments which men make in such images. As a consequence, we need an approach such as psychoanalysis to help us theorise the complex structuring of the male mind, and to understand the processes by which cultural voices become appropri-ated in the fashioning of individual selves (*see* Easthope, 1990, for another example of how these two theoretical perspectives can be combined).

In general terms, the relationship between ideology and practice (or broader still, between culture and society) is a central issue for any thorough-going analysis of men and masculinity. On the one hand, there are those who would want to argue that masculinities are, first and foremost, ideological constructs. They might claim, for example, that the equation of manliness with physical strength and endurance has helped bring into being a whole range of different working and leisure-related practices, in which men are expected to participate. Conversely, others would want to uphold the pri-macy of practice over ideology. For them, ideologies operate in the service of practices, by producing accounts or justifications for why certain kinds of work, play and so on, are appropriate activities for men to perform. A third group of theorists (of which we are a part) would want to challenge the theoretical separation of ideology and practice by pointing to the ways in which accounts and justifications can have quite significant practical effects.

A final, paradoxical issue (given that it comes at the very end of a book on men and masculinity) concerns the question of whether there really is something which social scientists can call 'men'. In other words, is there something ultimately which binds this group of people together and sets them apart from another collectivity called 'women'? Once again we are back to the issue of the *substance* of masculinity. As far as the biologist is concerned, man is a category grounded in the reality of the physical body. However, as far as the other perspectives are concerned, the assumption of a universal basis to masculinity is a lot less obvious. Indeed, as we have seen, advocates of all of the alternative perspectives (from psychoanalysis to feminist theory) admit at least the potential for a range of different masculinities. Yet this implies that whatever men are like, they can only ever be some kind of 'variation on a theme', whether that theme is defined by personality, power, social practices or social scripts. It begs the question: is there an underlying coherence? Does masculinity reduce to biology after all? Is the most basic theme around which men vary the possession of a Y chromosome or penis? If this is the case, then it suggests that the concept of masculinity is of severely limited use to most social scientists, for, as we have tried to show, it would fail to capture so much of what is most interesting about the lives of men.

References

Adorno, T. W., E. Frenkel-Brunswik, D. J. Levinson and R. N. Sanford (1950), *The Authoritarian Personality*, New York: Harper and Row.

Allen, E. *et al.* (1977), 'Sociobiology: a new biological determinism', in Sociobiology Study Group of Boston (eds), *Biology as a Social Weapon*, Minneapolis: Burgess.

Althusser, L. (1969), *For Marx*, Harmondsworth: Penguin.

Althusser, L. (1971), *Lenin and Philosophy and Other Essays*, London: New Left Books.

Archer, J. (1976), 'Biological explanations of psychological sex differences' in B. B. Lloyd and J. Archer (eds), *Exploring Sex Differences*, New York: Academic Press.

Archer, J. and B. B. Lloyd (1985), *Sex and Gender*, Cambridge: Cambridge University Press.

Ardrey, R. (1966), *The Territorial Imperative*, New York: Atheneum.

Backett, K. (1987), 'The negotiation of fatherhood', in C. Lewis and M. O'Brien (eds), *Reassessing Fatherhood*, London: Sage.

Baker, P. (1994), 'Who's afraid of the big bad women?', the *Guardian*, 24 January, 12–13.

Bandura, A. (1977), *Social Learning Theory*, Englewood Cliffs, N.J: Prentice Hall.

Bandura, A., D. Ross and S. A. Ross (1961), 'Transmission of aggression through imitation of aggressive models', in *Journal of Abnormal and Social Psychology*, 63, 575–82.

Bandura, A., D. Ross and S. A. Ross (1963), 'A comparative test of the status envy, social power, and secondary reinforcement theories of identification learning', in *Journal of Abnormal and Social Psychology*, 67, 527–34.

Bandura, A. and R. H. Walters (1963), *Social Learning and Personality Development*, New York: Holt, Rinehart and Winston.

Bardwick, J. (1971), *The Psychology of Women: A study of bio-cultural conflicts*, New York: Harper and Row.

Barnes, H. (1974), *Sartre*, London: Quartet Books.

Bartky, S. (1990), *Femininity and Domination: Studies in the phenomenology of oppression*, New York: Routledge.

Baudrillard, J. (1992), 'The vanishing point of communication', paper presented to the Department of Social Sciences, Loughborough University, England.

Bem, S. L. (1974), 'The measurement of psychological androgyny', in *Journal of Consulting and Clinical Psychology*, 42, 155–62.

Bem, S. L. (1981), 'Gender schema theory: a cognitive account of sex-typing', in *Psychological Review*, 88, 354–64.

Bem, S. L. (1985), 'Androgyny and gender schema theory: a conceptual and empirical integration', in T.B. Sonderegger (ed.), *Nebraska Symposium on Motivation 1984: Psychology and Gender*, Lincoln, Nebraska: University of Nebraska Press.

Bem, S. L. (1987), 'Gender schema theory and the Romantic Tradition', in P. Shaver and C. Hendrick (eds), *Sex and Gender*, Newbury Park: Sage.

Benjamin, J. (1988), *The Bonds of Love: Psychoanalysis, feminism and the problem of domination*, New York: Pantheon.

Benjamin, J. and A. Rabinbach (1989) 'Foreword', in K. Theweleit, *Male Fantasies. Volume Two: Male Bodies: Psychoanalyzing the white terror*, Cambridge: Polity.

Bennett, T. (1981), *Popular Culture: Themes and issues*, Milton Keynes: Open University Press.

Bhachu, P. (1988), 'Apni Marzi Kardhi: Home and Work: Sikh women in Britain', in S. Westwood and P. Bhachu (eds), *Enterprising Women: Ethnicity, economy, and gender relations*, London: Routledge.

Biddle, B. J. and E. J. Thomas (eds) (1966), *Role Theory: Concepts and research*, New York: Wiley.

Blizard, D. A. (1983), 'Sex differences in running-wheel behaviour in the rat: the inductive and activational effects of gonadal hormones', in *Animal Behaviour*, 31, 378–84.

Block, J. H. (1978), 'Another look at sex differentiation in the socialisation behaviours of mothers and daughters', in J. Sherman and F. Denmark (eds), *Psychology of Women: Future directions of research*, New York: Psychological Dimensions.

Bloor, D. (1976), *Knowledge and Social Imagery*, London: Routledge.

Bly, R. (1990), *Iron John*, New York: Addison-Wesley.

Boulton, M. G. (1983), *On Being a Mother*, London: Tavistock.

Braham, P., A. Rattansi and R. Skellington (1992), *Racism and Anti-Racism: Inequalities, opportunities and policies*, London: Sage.

Brannen, J. and J. Collard (1982), *Marriages in Trouble*, London: Tavistock.

Brannen, J. and P. Moss (1987), 'Fathers in dual-earner households – through mothers' eyes', in C. Lewis and M. O'Brien (eds), *Reassessing Fatherhood*, London: Sage.

Brannon, R. (1976), 'The male sex role: our culture's blueprint of manhood, and what it's done for us lately', in D. David and R. Brannon (eds), *The Forty-Nine Percent Majority: The male sex role*, Reading, MA: Addison-Wesley.

Brimer, M. A. (1969), 'Sex differences in listening comprehension', in *Journal of Research and Development in Education*, 3, 72–9.

Brittan, A. (1989), *Masculinity and Power*, New York: Blackwell.

Brod, H. (ed) (1987), *The Making of Masculinities*, Boston, MA: Allen and Unwin.

Brod, H. (1987), 'The case for men's studies', in H. Brod (ed.), *The Making of Masculinities*, Boston, MA: Allen and Unwin.

Brown, R. (1986), *Social Psychology: The second edition*, New York: The Free Press.

Brownmiller, S. (1976), *Against Our Will: Men, women and rape*, Harmondsworth: Penguin.

Bruegel, I. (1989), 'Sex and race in the labour market', in *Feminist Review*, 32, 49–68.

Bunker-Rohrbaugh, J. (1981), *Women: Psychology's puzzle*, London: Abacus.

Burian, R. M. (1977), 'A methodological critique of sociobiology', in A. L. Caplan (ed.), *The Sociobiology Debate: Readings on the ethical and scientific issues concerning sociobiology*, New York: Harper and Row.

Cameron, D. and E. Fraser (1987), *The Lust to Kill*, Cambridge: Polity.

Campbell, A. (1984), *The Girls in the Gang*, Oxford: Blackwell.

Campbell, B. (1987), *The Iron Ladies: Why do women vote Tory?*, London: Virago.

Canaan, J. and C. Griffin (1990), 'The new men's studies: part of the problem or part of the solution?', in J. Hearn and D. Morgan (eds), *Men, Masculinities and Social Theory*, London: Unwin Hyman.

Caplan, A. L. (ed.) (1978), *The Sociobiology Debate: Readings on the ethical and scientific issues concerning sociobiology*, New York: Harper and Row.

Carby, H. (1982), 'White woman listen! Black feminism and the boundaries of sisterhood', in Centre for Contemporary Cultural Studies, *Empire Strikes Back*, London: Hutchinson.

Carrigan, T., R. W. Connell and J. Lee (1985), 'Towards a new sociology of masculinity', in *Theory and Society*, 14, 551–604.

Carrigan, T., R. W. Connell and J. Lee (1987), 'Hard and heavy: toward a new sociology of masculinity', in M. Kaufman (ed.), *Beyond Patriarchy: Essays by men on pleasure, power and change*, New York: Oxford University Press.

Chapkis, W. (1986), *Beauty Secrets*, London: Women's Press.

Chapman, R. and J. Rutherford (eds) (1988), *Male Order: Unwrapping masculinity*, London: Lawrence and Wishart.

Chesler, P. (1991), 'Mothers on trial: the custodial vulnerability of women', in *Feminism and Psychology*, 1, 409–27.

Chodorow, N. (1978), *The Reproduction of Mothering: Psychoanalysis and the sociology of gender*, Berkeley, Calif.: University of California Press.

Chodorow, N. (1989), *Feminism and Psychoanalytic Theory*, New Haven: Yale University Press.

Cicone, M. V. and D. N. Ruble (1978), 'Beliefs about males', in *Journal of Social Issues*, 34 (1), 5–16.

Clarke, J., S. Hall, T. Jefferson and B. Roberts (1981), 'Sub-cultures, cultures and class', in T. Bennett, G. Martin, C. Mercer and J. Woollacott (eds), *Culture, Ideology and Social Process*, Milton Keynes: Open University Press.

Clatterbaugh, K. (1990), *Contemporary Perspectives on Masculinity*, Oxford: Westview Press.

Cockburn, C. (1981), 'The material of male power', in *Feminist Review*, 9, 41–57.

Cockburn, C. (1983), *Brothers: Male dominance and technological change*, London: Pluto.

Cohen, B. (1988), *Caring for children: Services and policies for childcare and equal opportunities in the United Kingdom*, London: Family Policy Studies Centre.

Cohen, D. (1990), *Being a Man*, London: Routledge.

Collinson, D. L. and M. Collinson (1989), 'Sexuality in the work-place: the domination of men's sexuality', in J. Hearn, D. Sheppard, P. Tancred-Sheriff and G. Burrell (eds), *The Sexuality of Organisation*, London: Sage.

Connell, R. W. (1979), 'The concept of the "role" and what to do with it', in *Australian and New Zealand Journal of Sociology*, 15, 7–17.

Connell, R. W. (1983), *Which Way is Up? Essays on Class, Sex and Culture*, Sydney: Allen and Unwin.

Connell, R. W. (1987), *Gender and Power*, Cambridge: Polity Press.

Connell, R. W. (1990), 'The state, gender, and sexual politics', in *Theory and Society*, 19, 507–44.

Cooper, A. (1986), 'What men fear: the facade of castration anxiety', in G. Fogel, F. Lane and R. S. Liebert (eds), *The Psychology of Men: New psychoanalytic perspectives*, New York: Basic Books.

Cooper, H. M. (1979), 'Statistically combining independent studies: a meta-analysis of sex differences in conformity research', in *Journal of Personality and Social Psychology*, 37, 131–46.

Cooper, M. (1990), *Searching for the Anti-Sexist Man: A study of the British men's movement*, Sheffield: Achilles Heel.

Coveney, L., M. Jackson, S. Jeffreys, L. Kay and P. Mahoney (1984), *The Sexuality Papers: Male sexuality and the social control of women*, London: Hutchinson.

Coward, R. (1983), *Patriarchal Precedents: Sexuality and social relations*, London: Routledge and Kegan Paul.

Coward, R. (1984), *Female Desire*, London: Paladin.

Cowie, E. (1992), 'Pornography and fantasy: psychoanalytic perspectives', in L. Segal and M. McIntosh (eds), *Sex Exposed: Sexuality and the pornography debate*, London: Virago.

Croghan, R. (1991), 'First-time mothers' accounts of inequality in the division of labour', in *Feminist Psychology*, 1, 221–47.

Culp, R. E., A. S. Crook and P. C. Housley (1983), 'A comparison of observed and reported adult-infant interactions: effects of perceived sex', in *Sex Roles*, 9, 475–9.

Currell, M. (1974), *Political Woman*, London: Croom Helm.

Dahrendorf, R. (1973), *Homo Sociologicus*, London: Routledge and Kegan Paul.

Dansky, S., J. Knoebel and K. Pitchford (1977), 'The effeminist manifesto', in J. Snodgrass (ed.), *A Book of Readings for Men Against Sexism*, New York: Times Change Press.

David, D. and R. Brannon (eds) (1976), *The Forty-Nine Percent Majority: The male sex role*, Reading, MA: Addison-Wesley.

Davis, A. (1982), *Women, Race and Class*, London: The Women's Press.

Dawson, G. (1991), 'The Blond Bedouin: Lawrence of Arabia, imperial adventure and the imagining of English-British masculinity', in M. Roper and J. Tosh (eds), *Manful Assertions: Masculinities in Britain since 1800*, London: Routledge.

De Beauvoir, S. (1953), *The Second Sex*, London: Cape.

Delphy, C. (1984), *Close to Home: A materialist analysis of woman's oppression*, London: Hutchinson.

Demos, J. (1975), 'The American family in past time', in *American Scholar*, 43, 422–46.

Devaney, K. (1991), 'Mining: a world apart', in V. Seidler (ed.), *The Achilles Heel Reader: Men, sexual politics and socialism*, London: Routledge.

De Vries, G. J. et al. (eds) (1984), *Sex Differences in the Brain: The relation between structure and function*, Progress in Brain Research, vol. 61, New York: Elsevier.

Doering, C. H., H. K. H. Brodie, H. Kraemer, H. Becker and D. A. Hamburg (1974), 'Plasma testosterone levels and psychologic measures in men over a 2 month period', in R. C. Friedman, R. M. Richart and R. L. Vande Wiele (eds), *Sex Differences in Behaviour*, New York: Wiley.

Dollimore, J. (1991), *Sexual Dissidence*, Oxford: Clarendon Press.

Dover, K. J. (1978), *Greek Homosexuality*, Cambridge, MA: Harvard University Press.

Dunning, E. (1986), 'Sport as a male preserve', in *Theory, Culture and Society*, 3 (1).

Dworkin, A. (1981), *Pornography: Men possessing women*, London: The Women's Press.

Dyck, N. (1980), 'Booze, barrooms and scrapping: masculinity and violence in a western Canadian town', in *Canadian Journal of Anthropology*, 1, 191–8.

Dyer, R. (1993), *The Matter of Images: Essays on representations*, London: Routledge.

Eagly, A. H. (1983), 'Gender and social influence: a social psychological analysis', in *American Psychologist*, (September).

Eagly, A. H. (1994), 'On comparing women and men', in *Feminism and Psychology: An international journal*, 4 (4), 513–23.

Eagly, A. H. and L. L. Carli (1981), 'Sex of researchers and sex-typed communications as determinants of sex differences in influenceability: a meta-analysis of social influence studies', in *Psychological Bulletin*, 90, 1–20.

Easthope, A. (1990), *What a Man's Gotta Do: The masculine myth in popular culture* 2nd edn, Winchester, MA: Paladin.

Ehrlich, C. (1977), 'The reluctant patriarchs: a review of men and masculinity', in J. Snodgrass (ed.), *A Book of Readings for Men Against Sexism*, New York: Times Change Press.

Eichenbaum, L. and S. Orbach (1982), *Outside In and Inside Out: Women's psychology: A feminist psychoanalytic approach*, Harmondsworth: Penguin.

Eisenstein, Z. (1979), *Capitalist Patriarchy and the Case for Socialist Feminism*, New York: Monthly Review Press.

Ellis, A. (1945), 'The sexual psychology of human hermaphrodites', in *Psychosomatic Medicine*, 7, 108–25.

Ellman, M. (1979), *Thinking about Women*, London: Virago.

Eysenck, H. J. (1985), *Decline and Fall of the Freudian Empire*, Harmondsworth: Viking.

Fagot, B. I. (1974), 'Sex differences in toddlers' behaviour and parental reaction', in *Developmental Psychology*, 4, 554–8.

Fagot, B. I. (1977), 'Consequences of moderate cross-gender behaviour in pre-school children', in *Child Development*, 48, 902–7.

Fairweather, H. (1976), 'Sex differences in cognition', in *Cognition*, 4, 31–80.

Faludi, S. (1992), *Backlash: The undeclared war against women*, London: Chatto and Windus.

Farrell, W. (1974), *The Liberated Man*, New York: Random House.

Farrell, W. (1994), *The Myth of Male Power*, New York: Fourth Estate.

Fasteau, M. F. (1974), *The Male Machine*, New York: McGraw-Hill.

Fee, D. (1992), 'Masculinities, identity and the politics of essentialism', in *Feminism and Psychology*, 2, 171–7.

Feminist Review Collective (1987), *Sexuality: A Reader*, London: Virago.

Filene, P. (1975), *Him/Her/Self: Sex Roles in Modern America*, New York: Harcourt Brace Jovanovich.

Firestone, S. (1971), *The Dialectic of Sex*, London: Paladin.

Fishman, P. (1978), 'Interaction: the work women do', in *Social Problems*, 25, 397–406.

Fiske, J. (1987), *Television Culture*, London: Methuen.

Fling, S. and M. Manosevitz (1972), 'Sex typing in nursery school children's play interests', in *Developmental Psychology*, 7, 146–52.

Fogel, G., F. Lane and R. S. Liebert (1986), *The Psychology of Men: New psychoanalytic perspectives*, New York: Basic Books.

Formaini, H. (1991), *Men: The darker continent*, London: Mandarin.

Foucault, M. (1981), *The History of Sexuality: An introduction*, Harmondsworth: Penguin.

Franklin, C. W. (1984), *The Changing Definition of Masculinity*, New York: Plenum.

Franklin, C. W., II (1988), *Men and Society*, Chicago: Nelson Hall.

Franklin, C. W. (1993), 'Ain't I a Man?: The Efficacy of Black Masculinities for the Men's Studies in the 1990s', in R. Major and J. V. Gordon (eds), *The American Black Male: His present status and his future*, Chicago, Il: Nelson Hall.

Freeman, M. (1993), *Rewriting the Self: History, memory, narrative*, London: Routledge.

Frosh, S. (1987), *The Politics of Psychoanalysis: An introduction to Freudian and post-Freudian theory*, London: Macmillan.

Frosh, S. (1993), 'The seeds of male sexuality', in J. Ussher and C. Baker (eds), *Psychological Perspectives on Sexual Problems*, London: Routledge.

Galton, F. (1962), *Hereditary Genius: An inquiry into its laws and consequences*, Cleveland: Meridian (Originally published 1896).

Garai, J. E. and A. Scheinfeld, (1968), 'Sex differences in mental and behavioural traits', in *Genetic Psychiatry Monographs*, 77, 169–299.

Garvey, C. (1977), *Play*, Cambridge, MA: Harvard University Press.

General Household Survey (1990), *Office of Population Censuses and Surveys, Preliminary Results for 1989*, London: HMSO.

Gilbert, A. T. (1807), 'Remonstrance', in L. Davidoff and C. Hall, *Family Fortunes: Men and Women of the English Middle Class, 1780–1850*, Hutchinson and Chicago University Press: London and Chicago, 1987.

Gilmore, D. (1990), *Manhood in the Making: Cultural concepts of masculinity*, New Haven, CT: Yale University Press.

Glass, G. V., B. McGraw and M. L. Smith (1981), *Meta-analysis in Social Research*, Beverley Hills, California: Sage.

Goffman, E. (1959), *The Presentation of Self in Everyday Life*, New York: Doubleday Anchor.

Goldberg, H. (1976), *The Hazards of Being Male*, New York: Nash.

Goldberg, S. (1973), *Inevitability of Patriarchy*, New York: William Morrow.

Goode, W. (1982), 'Why men resist', in B. Thorne and M. Yalom (eds), *Rethinking the Family: Some feminist questions*, New York: Longman.

Graham, H. (1987), 'Being poor: perceptions and coping strategies of lone mothers', in J. Brannen and G. Wilson (eds), *Give and Take in Families*, London: Allen and Unwin.

Gramsci, A. (1971), *Selections from the Prison Notebooks*, ed. and trans. by O. Hoare and G. Nowell-Smith, London: Lawrence and Wishart.

Gray, J. A. and R. F. Drewett (1977), 'The genetics and development of sex differences', in R. B. Cattell and R. M. Dreger (eds), *Handbook of Modern Personality Theory*, New York: Halsted Press.

Greenberg, J. R. and S. A. Mitchell (1983), *Object Relations in Psychoanalytic Theory*, Cambridge, MA: Harvard University Press.

Greenson, R. (1968), 'Dis-identifying from mother: its special importance for the boy', in *International Psychoanalytic Journal*, 49, 370–4.

Greer, G. (1971), *The Female Eunuch*, London: McGibbon and Kee.

Griffin, C. (1989), ' 'I'm not a women's libber but...': feminism, consciousness and identity', in S. Skevington and D. Baker (eds), *The Social Identity of Women*, London: Sage.

Griffin, C. (1991), 'Experiencing power: dimensions of gender, 'race' and class', in *British Psychological Society Psychology of Women Section Newsletter*, 8, 43–58.

Griffin, C. and M. Wetherell (1992), 'Feminist psychology and the study of men and masculinity Part Two: politics and practices', in *Feminist Psychology*, 2, 133–69.

Hall, C. (1992), *White, Male and Middle Class: Explorations in feminism and history*, Cambridge: Polity Press.

Hall, J. A. (1984), *Nonverbal sex differences: Communication accuracy and expressive style*, Baltimore, Virginia: John Hopkins University Press.

Hall, S. (1977), 'Culture, the media and the "Ideological Effect"', in J. Curren, M. Gurevitch and J. Woollacott (eds), *Mass Communications and Society*, London: Edward Arnold in association with the Open University.

Hall, S. (1981), 'Cultural studies: two paradigms', in T. Bennett, G. Martin, C. Mercer and J. Woollacott (eds) (1981), *Culture, Ideology and Social Process*, Milton Keynes: Open University Press.

Hall, S., D. Hobson, A. Lowe and P. Willis (eds) (1980), *Culture, Media, Language*, London: Hutchinson.

Hamner, J. and M. Maynard (1987), *Women, Violence and Social Control*, London: Macmillan.

Hampson, J. L. (1965), 'Determinants of psychosexual orientation', in F. A. Beach (ed.), *Sex and Behaviour*, New York: Wiley.

Hantover, J. P. (1978), 'The Boy Scouts and the validation of masculinity', in *Journal of Social Issues*, 34 (1), 184–95.

Haraway, D. (1990), 'A manifesto for cyborgs: science, technology, and socialist feminism in the 1980s', in L. Nicholson (ed.), *Feminism/Postmodernism*, New York: Routledge.

Hargreaves, D. J. (1986), 'Psychological theories of sex-role stereotyping', in D. J. Hargreaves and A. M. Colley (eds), *The Psychology of Sex Roles*, London: Harper and Row.

Hargreaves, D. J. and A. M. Colley (eds) (1986), *The Psychology of Sex Roles*, London: Harper and Row.

Hargreaves, J. A. (1986), 'Where's the virtue? Where's the grace? A discussion of the social production of gender relations in and through sport', in *Theory, Culture and Society*, 3 (1).

Harrison, B. (1985), 'Misogyny and homophobia: the unexplored connections', in C. Robb (ed.), *Making the Connections: Essays in feminist social ethics*, Boston, MA: Beacon.

Harrison, J. (1978), 'Warning: the male sex role may be dangerous to your health', in *Journal of Social Issues*, 34 (1), 65–86.

Hartley, D. (1981), 'Infant-school childrens' perception of the behaviour of same and opposite sex classmates', in *British Journal of Social Psychology*, 20, 141–3.

Hartmann, H. (1979), 'The unhappy marriage of marxism and feminism: towards a more progressive union', in *Capital and Class*, 8, 1–33.

Hearn, J. (1987), *The Gender of Oppression: Men, masculinity and the critique of Marxism*, Brighton: Harvester Wheatsheaf.

Hearn, J. (1993), 'The politics of essentialism and the analysis of the "men's movement(s)"', in *Feminism and Psychology*, 3, 405–10.

Hearn, J. and D. Morgan (eds) (1990), *Men, Masculinities and Social Theory*, London: Unwin Hyman.

Hearn, J. and W. Parkin (1987), *'"Sex" at "Work": The power and paradox of organisation sexuality*, Brighton: Harvester Wheatsheaf.

Heath, S. (1987), 'Male feminism', in A. Jardine and P. Smith (eds), *Men in Feminism*, New York: Methuen.

Henley, N. (1973), 'Status and sex: some touching observations', in *Bulletin of the Psychonomic Society*, 2, 91–3.

Henriques, J., W. Hollway, C. Urwin, C. Venn and V. Walkerdine (1984), *Changing the Subject: Psychology, social regulation and subjectivity*, London: Methuen.

Henwood, M. (1987), 'Family care', in M. Henwood, L. Rimmer and M. Wicks (eds), *Inside the Family: The changing roles of men and women*, London: Family Policy Studies.

Henwood, M., L. Rimmer and M. Wicks (eds) (1987), *Inside the Family: The changing roles of men and women*, London: Family Policy Studies.

Herbert, J. (1976), 'Hormonal basis of sex differences in rats, monkeys, and humans', in *New Scientist*, 70, 284–6.

Hirst, P. and P. Woolley (1982), *Social Relations and Human Attributes*, London: Tavistock.

Hite, S. (1981), *The Hite Report on Male Sexuality*, New York: Knopf.

Hoch, P. (1979), *White Hero, Black Beast: Racism, sexism and the mask of masculinity*, London: Pluto Press.

Hoggart, R. (1957), *The Uses of Literacy*, London: Chatto and Windus

Hollway, W. (1983), 'Heterosexual sex, power and desire for the other', in S. Cartledge and J. Ryan (eds), *Sex and Love: New thoughts on old contradictions*, London: Women's Press.

Hollway, W. (1984), 'Gender difference and the production of subjectivity', in J. Henriques *et al.* (eds), *Changing the Subject*, London: Methuen.

Hollway, W. (1989), *Subjectivity and Method in Psychology*, London: Sage.

Hooks, B. (1982), *Ain't I a Woman?*, London: Pluto.

Hudson, L. and B. Jacot (1991), *The Way Men Think*, New Haven, CT: Yale University Press.

Humm, M. (1992), *Feminisms: A reader*, Hemel Hempstead: Harvester Wheatsheaf.

Humphries, M. (1985), 'Gay machismo', in A. Metcalf and M. Humpheries (eds) (1985), *The Sexuality of Men*, London: Pluto.

Hunter, A. (1992), 'Same door, different closet', *Feminism and Psychology*, 2, 367–87.

Husband, C. (1982), *'Race' in Britain*, London: Hutchinson.

Hutt, C. (1972), *Males and Females*, Harmondsworth: Penguin.

Hutt, C. (1978), 'Sex-role differentiation in social development', in H. McGurk (ed.), *Issues in Childhood Social Development*, London: Methuen, 171–202.

Hyde, J. (1981), 'How large are cognitive gender differences? A meta-analysis using W_2 and D', in *American Psychologist*, 36, 892–901.

Hyde, J. (1990), 'Meta-analysis and the psychology of gender differences', in *Signs: Journal of women in culture and society*, 16, 55–73.

Imperato-McGinley, J., R. E. Peterson, T. Gautier and E. Sturla (1979), 'Androgens and the evolution of male-gender identity among male pseudohermaphrodites with 5-reductase deficiency', in *New England Journal of Medicine*, 300, 1233–7.

Itzin, C. (ed.) (1992), *Pornography: Women, violence and civil liberties*, Oxford: Oxford University Press.

Jacklin, C. N. (1992), *The Psychology of Gender,* (IV), Aldershot, Hants: Elgar Reference.

Jacklin, C. N., E. E. Maccoby and C. H. Doering (1983), 'Neonatal sex-steroid hormones and timidity in 6–18 month-old boys and girls', in *Developmental Psychobiology*, 16, 163–8.

Jacklin, C. N., E. E. Maccoby, C. H. Doering and D. King (1984), 'Neonatal sex-steroid hormones and muscular strength of boys and girls in the first three years', in *Developmental Psychobiology*, 17, 301–10.

Jacklin, C. N., K. T. Wilcox and E. E. Maccoby (1988), 'Neonatal sex-steroid hormones and cognitive abilities at six years', in C. N. Jacklin (ed.) (1992), *The Psychology of Gender*, (I), Aldershot: Edward Elgar.

Jackson, D. (1990), *Unmasking Masculinity: A critical autobiography*, London: Unwin Hyman.

Jaggar, A. (1983), *Feminist Politics and Human Nature*, Brighton: Harvester Press.

Janson-Smith, D. (1980), 'Sociobiology: so what?', in L. Birke, W. Faulkner, S. Best, D. Janson-Smith, K. Overfield (eds), *Alice Through the Microscope: The power of science over women's lives*, London: Virago

Jarman, D. (1992), *At Your Own Risk*, London: Hutchinson.

Jourard, S. (1971), *The Transparent Self*, New York: D. Van Nostrand.

Jourard, S. (1974), 'Some lethal aspects of the male role', in J. H. Pleck and J. Sawyer (eds), *Men and Masculinity*, Englewood Cliffs, N.J.: Prentice Hall.

Kappeler, S. (1992), 'Pornography: the representation of power', in C. Itzin (ed.), *Pornography: Women, violence and civil liberties*, Oxford: Oxford University Press.

Kaufmann, M. (ed.) (1987), *Beyond Patriarchy: Essays by men on pleasure, power and change*, Toronto: Oxford University Press.

Kean, S. (1992), *Fire in the Belly: On being a man*, London: Piatkus.

Kelly, L. (1988), *Surviving Sexual Violence*, Cambridge: Polity Press.

Kessler, S. and W. McKenna (1978), *Gender: An ethnomethodological approach*, New York: Wiley.

Kimmel, M. S. (1987a), 'The contemporary "crisis" of masculinity in historical perspective', in H. Brod (ed.), *The Making of Masculinities*, Boston, M: Allen Unwin.

Kimmel, M. S. (ed.), (1987b), *Changing Men: New directions in research on men and masculinity*, Newbury Park: Sage.

Kimmel, M.S. (ed.), (1989), *Men Confront Pornography*, New York: Crown Press.

Kinsman, G. (1987), 'Men loving men: the challenge of gay liberation', in M. Kaufmann (ed.), *Beyond Patriarchy: Essays by men on pleasure, power and change*, Toronto: Oxford University Press.

Kirkpatrick, J. (1974), *Political Woman*, New York: Basic Books.

Kitzinger, C., S. Wilkinson and R. Perkins (eds) (1992), *Special Issue on Heterosexuality: Feminism and psychology*, (2).

Kleinberg, S. (1987), 'The new masculinity of gay men, and beyond', in M. Kaufmann (ed.), *Beyond Patriarchy: Essays by men on pleasure, power and change*, Toronto: Oxford University Press.

Kline, P. (1981), *Fact and Fantasy in Freudian Theory* 2nd edn, London: Methuen.

Kohlberg, L. (1966), 'A cognitive developmental analysis of children's sex role concepts and attitudes', in E. E. Maccoby (ed.), *The Development of Sex Differences*, Stanford: Stanford University Press.

Komarovsky, M. (1976), *Dilemmas of Masculinity*, New York: W. W. Norton.

Kourany, J., J. Sterba and R. Tong (eds), (1992), *Feminist Philosophies*, Englewood Cliffs, N.J.: Prentice Hall.

Kreuz, L. E. and R. M. Rose (1972), 'Assessment of aggressive behaviour and plasma testosterone in a young criminal population', in *Psychosomatic Medicine*, 34, 321–32.

Kuhn, D., S. C. Nash and L. Brucken (1978), 'Sex role concepts of two and three year olds', in *Child Development*, 49, 445–51.

Land, H. (1983), 'Poverty and gender: the distribution of resources within the family', in M. Brown (ed.), *The Structure of Disadvantage*, London: Heinemann.

La Rossa, R. and M. La Rossa (1981), *Transition to Parenthood: How children change families*, Beverley Hills, California: Sage.

Latour, B. (1987), *Science in Action*, Milton Keynes: Open University Press.

Lee, D. and H. Newby (1984), *The Problem of Sociology: An introduction to the discipline*, London: Hutchinson.

Lehne, G. (1976), 'Homophobia among men', in D. David and R. Brannon (eds), *The Forty-Nine Percent Majority: The male sex role*, Reading, MA: Addison-Wesley.

Leonard, P. (1984), *Personality and Ideology*, London: Macmillan.

Levine, S. (1966) 'Sex differences in the brain', in *Scientific American*, 214, (April), 84–90.

Levitas, R. (ed.) (1986), *The Ideology of the New Right*, Cambridge: Polity Press.

Lev-Ran, A. (1974), 'Gender role differentiation in hermaphrodites', in *Archives of Sexual Behaviour*, 3, 391–424.

Lewis, C. (1986), *Becoming a Father*, Milton Keynes: Open University Press.

Lewis, C. and M. O'Brien (1987), 'Constraints on fathers: research, theory and clinical practice', in C. Lewis and M. O'Brien (eds), *Reassessing Fatherhood: New observations on fathers and the modern family*, London, Sage.

Lewis, M. (1975), 'Early sex differences in the human: studies of socio-emotional development', in *Archives of Sexual Behaviour*, 4: 329–35.

Linton, R. (1936), *The Study of Man*, New York: Appleton-Century.

Lips, H. (1981), *Women, Men and the Psychology of Power*, Englewood Cliffs, N.J.: Prentice Hall.

Lorber, J. and S. A. Farrell (eds) (1991), *The Social Construction of Gender*, London: Sage.

Lorenz, K. (1967), *On Aggression*, New York: Harcourt, Brace and World.

Lyndon, N. (1992), *No More Sex War: The failures of feminism*, London: Sinclair Stevenson.

Maccoby, E. and C. N. Jacklin (1974), *The Psychology of Sex Differences*, London: Oxford University Press.

MacKenzie, J. M. (1987), 'The imperial pioneer and hunter and the British masculine stereotype in late Victorian and Edwardian times', in J. A. Mangan and J. Walvin (eds), *Manliness and Morality: Middle class masculinity in Britain and America 1800–1940*, Manchester: Manchester University Press.

MacKinnon, C. (1979), *Sexual Harassment of Working Women*, New Haven, CT: Yale University Press.

MacKinnon, C. (1982), 'Feminism, marxism, method, and the state: an agenda for theory', in *Signs*, 7, 515–44.

MacKinnon, C. (1983), 'Feminism, marxism, method, and the state: toward feminist jurisprudence', in *Signs*, 8, 635–59.

MacKinnon, C. (1987), *Feminism Unmodified: Discourses on life and law*, Cambridge, MA: Harvard University Press.

Mangan, J. A. (1987), 'Social Darwinism and upper-class education in late Victorian and Edwardian England', in J. A. Mangan and J. Walvin (eds), *Manliness and Morality: Middle class masculinity in Britain and America 1800–1940*, Manchester: Manchester University Press.

Mangan, J. A. and J. Walvin (eds) (1987), *Manliness and Morality: Middle class masculinity in Britain and America 1800–1940*, Manchester: Manchester University Press.

Marable, M. (1983), *How Capitalism Underdeveloped Black America*, Boston, MA: South End.

Martin, J. and C. Roberts (1984), *Women and Employment: A life-time perspective*, London: HMSO.

Marx, K. and F. Engels (1989), *The German Ideology*, Student Edition, London: Lawrence and Wishart.

McGlone, J. (1980), 'Sex differences in human brain asymmetry: a critical survey', in *Behavioural and Brain Sciences*, 3, 215–27.

McGuiness, D. (1976), 'Sex differences in the organisation of perception and cognition', in B. B. Lloyd and J. Archer (eds), *Exploring Sex Differences*, New York: Academic Press.

McLellan, D. (1986), *Ideology*, Milton Keynes: Open University Press.

Mead, G. H. (1934), *Mind, Self and Society*, Chicago: University of Chicago Press.

Mead, M. (1935), *Sex and Temperament in Three Primitive Societies*, New York: William Morrow.

Mead, M. (1949), *Male and Female*, New York: William Morrow.

Metcalf, A. and M. Humpheries (eds) (1985), *The Sexuality of Men*, London: Pluto.

Miles, R. (1989), *Racism*, London: Routledge.

Miles, R. (1992), *The Rites of Man: Love, sex and death in the making of the male*, London: Paladin.

Miller, P. H. (1983), *Theories of Developmental Psychology*, San Francisco, California: W. H. Freeman.

Miller, S. M. (1974), 'The making of a confused middle-aged husband', in J. Pleck and J. Sawyer (eds), *Men and Masculinity*, Englewood Cliffs, N.J.: Prentice Hall.

Millett, K. (1972), *Sexual Politics*, London: Abacus.

Mischel, W. (1966), 'A social learning view of sex differences', in E. E. Maccoby (ed.), *The Development of Sex Differences*, Stanford, California: Stanford University Press.

Mischel, W. (1970), 'Sex-typing and socialisation', in P. H. Musson (ed.), *Carmichael's Manual of Child Psychology* 3rd edn, vol. 2, New York: Wiley.

Mitchell, J. (1971), *Woman's Estate*, Harmondsworth: Penguin.

Mitchell, J. (1975), *Psychoanalysis and Feminism*, Harmondsworth: Penguin.

Moir, A. and D. Jessell (1989), *Brainsex: The real difference between men and women*, London: Mandarin.

Money, J. and A. A. Ehrhardt (1972), *Man and Woman, Boy and Girl*, Baltimore: John Hopkins University Press.

Money, J., J. G. Hampson and J. L. Hampson (1955), 'An examination of some basic sexual concepts: the evidence of human hermaphroditism', in *Bulletin of John Hopkins Hospital*, 97, 301–19.

Montemayor, R. (1978), 'Men and their bodies: the relationship between body type and behaviour', in *Journal of Social Sciences*, 34 (1), 48–63.

Morawski, J. G. (1987), 'The troubled quest for masculinity, femininity and androgyny', in P. Shaver and C. Hendrick (eds), *Sex and Gender*, Newbury Park: Sage.

Morgan, D. (1992), *Discovering Men*, London: Routledge.

Morris, D. (1967), *The Naked Ape*, London: Jonathan Cape.

Morris, D. (1977), *Manwatching: A field guide to human behaviour*, London: Jonathan Cape.

Moss, P. (1980), 'Parents at work', in P. Moss and N. Fonda (eds), *Work and the Family*, London: Temple Smith.

Moye, A. (1985), 'Pornography', in A. Metcalf and M. Humpheries (eds), *The Sexuality of Men*, London: Pluto.

Mulkay, M. (1979), *Science and the Sociology of Knowledge*, London: Allen and Unwin.

Mulvey, L. (1975), 'Visual pleasure and narrative cinema', in *Screen*, 16, 6–19.

Myers, D. G. (1988), *Social Psychology* 2nd edn, New York: McGraw-Hill.

Naftolin, F. (ed.) (1981), 'The dimorphic brain', in *Science*, 211, 1263–324.

Nicholay, C. (1991), 'Computer games', in V. Seidler (ed.), *The Achilles Heel Reader: Men, sexual politics and socialism*, London: Routledge.

Nichols, J. (1975), *Men's Liberation*, New York: Penguin.

Nicholson, J. (1979), *A Question of Sex: The differences between men and women*, London: Collins.

Nicholson, L. (ed.) (1990), *Feminism/Postmodernism*, New York: Routledge.

Notes from the Collective (1991), 'The sexual politics of men's work', in V. Seidler (ed.), *The Achilles Heel Reader: Men, sexual politics and socialism*, London: Routledge.

Oakley, A. (1979), *Becoming a Mother*, Oxford: Martin Robertson.

O'Brien, M. (1981), *The Politics of Reproduction*, London: Routledge and Kegan Paul.

Ohno, S. (1979), *Major Sex-Determining Genes*, New York: Springer-Verlag.

O'Leary, V. E. and J. M. Donoghue (1978), 'Latitudes of masculinity: reactions to sex-role deviance in men', in *Journal of Social Issues*, 34 (1), 17–28.

Olivier, C. (1989), *Jocasta's Children: The imprint of the mother*, London: Routledge.

Olweus, D., A. Mattson, D. Schallin and H. Low (1980), 'Testosterone, aggression, physical and personality dimensions in normal adolescent males', in *Psychosomatic Medicine*, 42, 253–69.

Ortner, S. B. (1974), 'Is female to male as nature is to culture?', in M. Z. Rosaldo and L. Lamphere (eds), *Woman, Culture and Society*, Stanford, California: Stanford University Press.

Ortner, S. B. and H. Whitehead (1981), *Sexual Meanings: The cultural construction of gender and sexuality*, Cambridge: Cambridge University Press.

Pahl, J. (1980), 'Patterns of money management within marriage', in *Journal of Social Policy*, 9 (3), 313–35.

Park, R. J. (1987), 'Biological thought, athletics and the formation of a "man of character": 1830–1900', in J. A. Mangan and J. Walvin (eds), *Manliness and Morality: Middle class masculinity in Britain and America 1800–1940*, Manchester: Manchester University Press.

Parmar, P. (1982), 'Gender, race and class: Asian women in resistance', in Centre for Contemporary Cultural Studies, *Empire Strikes Back*, London: Hutchinson.

Parsons, T. (1942), 'Age and sex in the social structure of the United States', in *American Sociological Review*, 7, 604–16.

Parsons, T. and R. F. Bales (1953), *Family, Socialisation and the Interaction Process*, Glencoe, Ill: Free Press.

Patt, D. I. and G. R. Patt (1975), *An Introduction to Modern Genetics*, Addison-Wesley.

Persky, H., K. D. Smith and G. K. Basu (1971), 'Relation of psychologic measures of aggression and hostility to testosterone production in man', in *Psychosomatic Medicine*, 33, 265–77.

Piaget, J. (1928), *Judgement and Reasoning in the Child*, London: Routledge and Kegan Paul.

Piaget, J. (1955), *The Child's Construction of Reality*, London: Routledge and Kegan Paul.

Pleck, E. H. and J. H. Pleck (1980), *The American Man*, Englewood Cliffs, N.J.: Prentice Hall.

Pleck, J. H. (1981), *The Myth of Masculinity*, Cambridge, M: MIT Press.

Pleck, J. H. (1987a), 'The theory of male sex-role identity: its rise and fall, 1936 to the present', in H. Brod (ed.), *The Making of Masculinities: The new men's studies*, Boston, MA: Allen and Unwin.

Pleck, J. H. (1987b), 'American fathering in historical perspective', in M. S. Kimmel (ed.), *Changing Men: New directions in research on men and masculinity*, Newbury Park: Sage.

Pleck, J. H. and J. Sawyer (eds) (1974), *Men and Masculinity*, Englewood Cliffs, N.J.: Prentice Hall.

Pleck, J. H. and E. H. Thompson (1987), 'The structure of male norms', in M. S. Kimmel (ed.), *Changing Men: New directions in research on men and masculinity*, London: Sage.

Potter, J. and M. Wetherell (1987), *Discourse and Social Psychology: Beyond attitudes and behaviour*, London: Sage.

Pringle, R. (1989), 'Bureaucracy, rationality and sexuality: the case of secretaries', in J. Hearn, D. Sheppard, P. Tancred-Sherriff and G. Burrell (eds), *The Sexuality of Organisations*, London: Sage.

Radford, J. (1987), 'Policing male violence: policing women', in J. Hamner and M. Maynard (eds), *Women, Violence and Social Control*, London: Macmillan.

Remy, J. (1990), 'Patriarchy and fratriarchy as forms of androcracy', in J. Hearn and D. Morgan (eds), *Men, Masculinities and Social Theory*, London: Unwin Hyman.

Renzetti, C. and D. Curran (1992), 'Sex-role socialisation', in J. A. Kourany, J. P. Sterba and R. Tong (eds), *Feminist Philosophies*, Englewood Cliffs, N.J.: Prentice Hall.

Reynolds, V. (1976), *The Biology of Human Action*, Reading and San Francisco: Freeman.

Rheingold, H. and K. Cook (1975), 'The contents of boys' and girls' rooms as an index of parents' behaviour', in *Child Development*, 46, 459–63.

Richards, J. (1987), '"Passing the love of women": manly love and Victorian society', in J. A. Mangan and J. Walvin (eds), *Manliness and Morality: Middle class masculinity in Britain and America 1800–1940*, Manchester: Manchester University Press.

Richardson, D. (1993), 'The challenge of AIDS', in S. Jackson (ed.), *Women's Studies: A reader*, Hemel Hempstead: Harvester Wheatsheaf.

Rogers, B. (1988), *Men Only: An inquiry into men's organisations*, London: Pandora.

Rose, S., L. J. Kamin and R. C. Lewontin (1984), *Not In Our Genes: Biology, ideology and human nature*, Harmondsworth: Pelican Books.

Ross, J. Munder (1986), 'Beyond the phallic illusion: notes on man's heterosexuality' in G. Fogel, F. Lane and R. S. Liebert (eds), *The Psychology of Men: New psychoanalytic perspectives*, New York: Basic Books.

Rotundo, E. A. (1987), 'Learning about manhood: gender ideals and the middle-class family in nineteenth century America', in J. A. Mangan and J. Walvin (eds), *Manliness and Morality: Middle class masculinity in Britain and America 1800–1940*, Manchester: Manchester University Press.

Rowan, J. (1987), *The Horned God*, London: Routledge.

Rubin, G. (1975), 'The traffic in women: notes on the "political economy" of sex', in R. R. Reiter (ed.), *Toward an Anthropology of Women*, New York: Monthly Review Press.

Rubin, J. Z., F. J. Provenzano and Z. Luria (1974), 'The eye of the beholder: parents' views on the sex of new borns', in *American Journal of Orthopsychiatry*, 44, 521–19.

Ruse, M. (1979), *Sociobiology: Sense or nonsense?*, Dordrecht: D. Reidel.

Russell, D. (1975), *The Politics of Rape*, New York: Stein and Day.

Russell, G. (1983), *The Changing Role of Fathers*, Milton Keynes: Open University Press.

Rutherford, J. (1992) *Men's Silences: Predicaments in masculinity*, London: Routledge.

Ryan, T. (1985), 'The roots of masculinity', in A. Metcalf and M. Humpheries (eds), *The Sexuality of Men*, London: Pluto.

Santayana, G. (1922), *Soliloquies in England and Later Soliloquies*, London: Constable.

Sayers, J. (1992), *Mothering Psychoanalysis*, Harmondsworth: Penguin.

Scully, D. (1990), *Understanding Sexual Violence: A study of convicted rapists*, Boston, MA: Unwin Hyman.

Secrett, D. (1991), 'Homogenized', in V. Seidler (ed.), *The Achilles Heel Reader: Men, sexual politics and socialism*, London: Routledge.

Segal, L. (1987), *Is the Future Female?: Troubled thoughts on contemporary feminism*, London: Virago.

Segal, L. (1990), *Slow Motion: Changing men, changing masculinities*, London: Virago.

Segal, L. and M. McIntosh (eds) (1992), *Sex Exposed: Sexuality and the pornography debate*, London: Virago.

Seidler, V. J. (1989), *Rediscovering Masculinity: Reason, language and sexuality*, New York: Routledge.

Seidler, V. J. (1991a), *Recreating Sexual Politics: Men, feminism and politics*, London: Routledge

Seidler, V. J. (ed.), (1991b), *The Achilles Heel Reader: Men, sexual politics and socialism*, London: Routledge.

Serbin, L. A., K. D. O'Leary, R. N. Kent and I. J. Tonick (1973), 'A comparison of teacher response to the preacademic problems and problem behaviour of boys and girls', in *Child Development*, 44, 796–804.

Sheffield, C. (1992), 'Sexual terrorism', in J. Kourany, J. Sterba and R. Tong (eds), *Feminist Philosophies*, Englewood Cliffs, N.J.: Prentice Hall.

Sherrod, D. (1987), 'The bonds of men: problems and possibilities in close male relationships', in H. Brod (ed.), *The Making of Masculinities: The new men's studies*. Boston, MA: Allen and Unwin.

Singleton, C. H. (1986), 'Biological and social explanations of sex-role stereotyping', in D. J. Hargreaves and A. M. Colley (eds), *The Psychology of Sex Roles*, London: Harper and Row.

Smith, P. K. (1986), 'Exploration, play and social development in boys and girls', in D. J. Hargreaves and A. M. Colley (eds), *The Psychology of Sex Roles*, London: Harper and Row.

Snodgrass, J. (ed.) (1977), *A Book of Readings for Men Against Sexism*, New York: Times Change Press.

Snow, M. E., C. N. Jacklin, and E. E. Maccoby (1983), 'Sex-of-child differences in father-child interaction at one year of age', in *Child Development*, 54, 227–32.

Sommerville, J. (1989), 'The sexuality of men and the sociology of gender', in *Sociological Review*, 37, 277–308.

Spelman, E. V. (1988), *Inessential Woman: Problems of exclusion in feminist thought*, Boston, MA: Beacon Press.

Spence, J. T. and R. L. Helmreich (1978), *Masculinity and Femininity: Their psychological dimensions, correlates and antecedents*. Austin, TX: University of Texas Press.

Spender, D. (1980), *Man Made Language*, London: Routledge and Kegan Paul.

Spender, D. (1986), 'What is feminism? A personal answer', in J. Mitchell and A. Oakley (eds), *What is Feminism*. Oxford: Blackwell.

Springhall, J. (1987), 'Building character in the British boy: the attempt to extend Christian manliness to working class adolescents, 1880 to 1914', in J. A. Mangan and J. Walvin (eds), *Manliness and Morality: Middle class masculinity in Britain and America 1800–1940*, Manchester: Manchester University Press.

Stanko, E. (1985), *Intimate Intrusions: Women's experience of male violence*, London: Routledge.

Stanley, L. (1982), 'Male needs: the problems and problems of working with gay men', in S. Friedman and E. Sarah (eds), *On the Problem of Men*, London: Women's Press.

Staples, R. (1978), 'Masculinity and race: the dual dilemma of black men', in *Journal of Social Issues*, 34 (1) 169–83.

Staples, R. (1985), *Black Masculinity: The black male's role in american society*, London: Black Scholar Press.

Steele, R. (1684), *The Tradesman's Calling*, London.

Sternglanz, S. H. and L. A. Serbin (1974), 'Sex-role stereotyping in children's television programmes', in *Developmental Psychology*, 10, 710–15.

Stoller, R. J. (1974), 'Facts and fancies: an examination of Freud's concepts of bisexuality', in J. Strouse (ed.), *Women and Analysis: Dialogues on psychoanalytic views of femininity*, New York: Grossman.

Stoller, R. (1975), *Perversion*, New York: Pantheon.

Stoller, R. (1985), *Presentations of Gender*, New Haven, CT: Yale University Press.

Stoltenberg, J. (1990), *Refusing to be a Man*, New York: Meridan.

Stoltenberg, J. (1992), 'Pornography, homophobia and male supremacy', in C. Itzin (ed.), *Pornography: Women, violence and civil liberties*, Oxford: Oxford University Press.

Stone, K. (1983) 'Motherhood and waged work: West Indian, Asian, and white mothers compared', in A. Phizacklea (ed.), *One Way Ticket: Migration and female labour*, London: Routledge.

Tannen, D. (1991), *You Just Don't Understand: Women and men in conversation*, London: Virago.

Tannen, D. (1993), *Gender and Conversational Interaction*, New York: Oxford University Press.

Taylor, M. L. and J. A. Hall (1982), 'Psychological androgyny: a review and reformation of theories, methods and conclusions', in *Psychological Bulletin*, 92, 347–66.

Terman, L. and C. Miles (1936), *Sex and Personality*, New York: McGraw-Hill.

Theweleit, K. (1987), *Male Fantasies. Volume One: Women, floods, bodies and history*, Cambridge: Polity Press.

Theweleit, K. (1989), *Male Fantasies. Volume Two: Male Bodies: Psychoanalyzing the white terror*, Cambridge: Polity.

Thomas, G. and L. Zmroczek (1985), 'Household technology: 'the "liberation" of women from the home', in P. Close and R. Collins (eds), *Family and Economy in Modern Society*, London: Macmillan.

Thompson, E. P. (1968), *The Making of the English Working Class*, Harmondsworth: Penguin.

Thompson, M. (1987) (ed.), *Gay Spirit: Myth and meaning*, New York: St. Martin's.

Thompson Woolley, H. (1910), 'A review of the recent literature on the psychology of sex', in C. N. Jacklin (ed.), *The Psychology of Gender*, (I), Aldershot: Edward Elgar.

Thorne, B. (1993), *Gender Play: Girls and boys in school*, Buckingham: Open University Press.

Thorne, B., C. Kramarae and N. Henley (eds) (1983), *Language, Gender and Society*, Rowley, MA: Newbury House.

Thornhill, R. and N. Wilmsen Thornhill (1992), 'The evolutionary psychology of men's coercive sexuality', in *Behavioural and Brain Sciences*, 15 (2), 363–75.

Timpanaro, S. (1976), *The Freudian Slip*, London: New Left Books.

Tolson, A. (1977), *The Limits of Masculinity*, London: Tavistock.

Toran-Allerand, C. D. (1984), 'On the genesis of sexual differentiation of the central nervous system: morphogenetic consequences of steroidal exposure and possible role of alpha-feroprotein', in G. J. De Vries, *et al*. (eds), *Sex Differences in the Brain: The relation between structure and function*, Progress in Brain Research, vol. 61, New York: Elsevier.

Tortora, G. J. and N. P. Anagnostakos (1984), *Principles of Anatomy and Physiology* 4th edn, New York: Harper and Row.

Tosh, J. (1991), 'Domesticity and manliness in the Victorian middle-class', in M. Roper and J. Tosh (eds), *Manful Assertions: Masculinities in Britain since 1800*, London: Routledge.

Touhey, J. C. (1974a), 'Effects of additional men on prestige and desirability of occupations typically performed by women', in *Journal of Applied Social Psychology*, 4, 330–5.

Touhey, J. C. (1974b), 'Effects of additional women professionals on ratings of occupational prestige and desirability', in *Journal of Personality and Social Psychology*, 29, 86–9.

Treadwell, P. (1987), 'Biologic influences on masculinity', in H. Brod (ed.), *The Making of Masculinities: The new men's studies*, Boston, MA: Allen and Unwin.

Turner, G. (1992), *British Cultural Studies: An introduction*, London: Routledge.

Vance, C. (ed.) (1989), *Pleasure and Danger: Exploring female sexuality*, London: Pandora Press.

Veyne, P. (1985), 'Homosexuality in ancient Rome', in P. Aries and A. Bejin (eds), *Western Sexuality*, trans. A. Forster, Oxford: Blackwell.

Walby, S. (1986), *Patriarchy at Work*, Cambridge: Polity Press.

Walby, S. (1990), *Theorising Patriarchy*, Oxford: Blackwell.

Walkerdine, V. and H. Lucey (1989), *Democracy in the Kitchen*, London: Virago.

Wallace, M. (1979), *Black Macho and the Myth of the Superwoman*, New York: Dial Press.

Warrier, S. (1988), 'Marriage, maternity and female economic activity: Gujerati mothers in Britain', in S. Westwood and P. Bhachu (eds), *Enterprising Women: Ethnicity, economy, and gender relations*, London: Routledge.

Weeks, J. (1977), *Coming Out: Homosexual politics in Britain, from the nineteenth century to the present*, London: Quartet.

Weeks, J. (1985), *Sexuality and its Discontents*, London: Routledge and Kegan Paul.

Wesley, F. and C. Wesley (1977), *Sex-Role Psychology*, New York: Human Sciences Press.

Westwood, S. (1990), 'Racism, black masculinity and the politics of space', in J. Hearn and D. Morgan (eds), *Men, Masculinities and Social Theory*, London: Unwin Hyman.

Wetherell, M. and N. Edley (1993), 'Men and masculinity: a socio-psychological analysis of discourse and gender identity', ESRC grant No. R000233129.

Wetherell, M. and C. Griffin (1991), 'Feminist psychology and the study of men and masculinity: Part One: Assumptions and perspectives', in *Feminism and Psychology*, 1, 361–93.

Wetherell, M. and J. Potter (1992), *Mapping the Language of Racism: Discourse and the legitimation of exploitation*, Hemel Hempstead: Harvester Wheatsheaf.

Wex, M. (1979), *Let's Take Back Our Space*, Hamburg and Longmead, Dorset: Element Books.

White, D. and A. Wollett (1981), 'The family at birth', paper presented at British Psychological Society London Conference, December.

Williams, J. E. and S. M. Bennett (1975), 'The definition of sex stereotypes via the adjective check list', in *Sex Roles*, 1, 327–37.

Williams, R. (1963), *Culture and Society, 1780–1950*, Harmondsworth: Penguin.

Willis, P. (1977), *Learning to Labour*, Farnborough: Saxon House.

Wilson, E. (1977), *Women and the Welfare State*, London: Tavistock.

Wilson, E. (1992), 'Feminist fundamentalism: the shifting politics of sex and censorship', in L. Segal and M. McIntosh (eds), *Sex Exposed: Sexuality and the pornography debate*, London: Virago.

Wilson, E. O. (1975), *Sociobiology*, Cambridge, MA: Harvard University Press.

Wilson, G. (1987), *Money in the Family: Financial organisation and women's responsibility*, Aldershot: Avebury.

Wise, S. and L. Stanley (1987), *Georgie Porgie: Sexual harassment in everyday life*, London: Pandora Press.

Wood, J. (1984), 'Groping towards sexism: boys' sex talk', in A. McRobbie and M. Nava (eds), *Gender and Generation*, London: Macmillan.

Woolf, N. (1993), *Fire With Fire: The new female power and how it will change the 21st century*, London: Chatto and Windus.

Woolf, V. (1929), *A Room of One's Own*, London: Hogarth Press.

Woollett, A. and A. Phoenix (1991), 'Psychological views of mothering', in A. Woollett, A. Phoenix, and E. Lloyd (eds), *Motherhood: Meanings, practices and ideologies*, London: Sage.

Yalom, I. D., R. Green and N. Fiske (1973), 'Parental exposure to female hormones: effect on psychosexual development in boys', in *Archives of General Psychiatry*, 28, 554–61.

Zammuner, V. L. (1987), 'Children's sex-role stereotypes: a cross cultural analysis', in P. Shaver and C. Hendrick (eds), *Sex and Gender*, Newbury Park: Sage.

Zuger, B. (1970), 'Gender role determinism: a critical review of the evidence from hermaphroditism', in *Psychosomatic Medicine*, 32, 449–67.

Name index

Subject index

aggression, 9, 12, 21, 23, 24, 26, 29, 33, 35, 41, 43, 48, 49, 52, 56, 76, 85, 86, 88, 89, 99, 106, 141, 142, 143, 149, 151, 172, 183, 186, 189; the aggressive gene, 29–30
AIDS, 190
alienation, 101–2, 105, 107, 110, 122, 123, 180, 187
androgyny, 76, 141, 200

Bem Sex Role Inventory, 84

castration, 42, 43, 57, 58, 79, 88
capitalism, 7, 96, 97, 98, 99–102, 103, 104–10, 112, 113, 121, 122, 123, 125–7, 128, 129, 135, 170, 209
civilisation, 41, 43, 54, 57, 66, 150, 154, 160, 184
class, 7, 116, 128, 172: and capitalism, 102, 103, 121–3; and domestic life, 115; and marxism, 144, 145, 175; and masculinity, 104–13, 181; and patriarchy, 179, 180; as a key social division, 64, 68, 94, 96, 97, 99, 120, 129, 130, 195, 196, 208; class roles, 91; middle class, 140, 148, 149, 153, 154, 155; upper class, 143, 147, 148; working class, 151, 168, 197
cognitive developmental theories, 74, 78–81, 82, 84, 87, 210
colonialism, 112
competitiveness and competition, 46, 50, 54, 88, 89, 99, 100, 101, 103, 107, 139, 151–3, 155, 161, 200
control: and capitalism, 101, 102, 122; and masculinity, 194; and patriarchy, 118, 119, 123, 127, 129, 170, 172–80, 195; and the state, 124; desire for, 40, 62, 190; lack or loss of, 63, 100, 161; of emotions, 106, 112; of meaning, 193, 208; of self,

64, 113, 137, 139, 161; over the body, 41, 189; over others, 128, 150, 154, 187, 191–2, 204
cool pose, 112, 113
cultural studies, 131, 144, 148, 164
culturalism, 164
culture, 131, 134, 141, 143, 146, 180, 186, 190, 191, 204, 211

Darwinism, 19, 25, 139, 151: theory of natural selection, 25–7, 36, 38, 84, 165
desire, 57, 63, 88, 106, 134, 141, 153, 157, 159, 186, 207, 211: in psychoanalytic theory, 42, 43, 48, 53, 56
determinism, 29, 36, 85, 87, 120, 130, 135, 141, 164
discourse and language, 5, 39, 40, 60, 61, 62, 164, 166, 174

embedded figure test, 21
emotions and feelings, 9, 12, 89, 101, 106, 107, 112, 114–15, 134, 137, 138, 141, 153, 157, 159, 160, 200, 207, 211: in psychoanalytic theory, 38, 39, 40, 47, 50, 51, 54, 59, 61–3, 68
ethology, 6, 10, 24–5
evolution, 13, 19, 24, 25–6, 36, 38, 84, 88, 143, 150

fantasy, 38, 39, 42, 44, 50, 57, 58, 64, 68, 183, 193, 194, 197, 207, 211
fascism, 63–4
fathers and fatherhood, 3, 79, 86, 94, 102, 103, 114–5, 116–7, 118, 123, 124, 171, 179, 197, 198: in psychoanalytic theory, 42, 44, 47–8, 50–1, 52–3, 55, 56–9, 67
fear, 100, 104, 187, 195, 200, 202: in psychoanalytic theory, 39, 51–3, 56, 64; of castration, 42, 57, 59; of femininity, 58, 68; of intimacy, 40, 60, 62, 101

236